Gymnastics of the Mind

*

Gymnastics of the Mind

*GREEK EDUCATION IN
HELLENISTIC AND ROMAN
EGYPT*

*

RAFFAELLA CRIBIORE

PRINCETON UNIVERSITY PRESS

PRINCETON AND OXFORD

5-7-2003
ww
+ 39.50

Library of Congress Cataloging-in-Publication Data
Cribiore, Raffaella.
Gymnastics of the mind: Greek education in Hellenistic and
Roman Egypt / Raffaella Cribiore.
p.   cm.
Includes bibliographical references (p.) and index.
ISBN 0-691-00264-9 (alk. paper)
1. Education, Greek—Egypt—History. 2. Egypt—
Civilization—To 332 B.C. I. Title
LA75.C75 2001
370'.932–dc21   2001021986

This book has been composed in Sabon

Printed on acid-free paper. ∞

www.pup.princeton.edu

Printed in the United States of America

1   3   5   7   9   10   8   6   4   2

FOR FEDERICO AND MARTINA

*

✳ *Contents* ✳

* List of Illustrations *

✳ *Preface* ✳

THIS IS the book I wanted to write when, years ago, I started to assemble educational material from Greco-Roman Egypt. I soon realized that some groundwork was needed before I could proceed to an overall evaluation of the educational system in that period. Thus in 1996, *Writing, Teachers, and Students in Graeco-Roman Egypt* appeared with a corpus of school exercises, a detailed examination of the handwriting of teachers and students, and a focus on the first stage of education and on learning to write. After that, I thought I was ready to cast my net wider by covering all three stages of a liberal education in antiquity and considering a richer sample of educational material from Egypt. This is the result; I hope that I will be able to communicate to the reader even part of the pleasure that I felt in researching and writing this book.

A book rarely represents the effort of a single person, and this is no exception. Once more, Roger Bagnall was present at every stage and provided illuminating advice. Victor Bers, Natalie Kampen, and Suzanne Said read through the whole manuscript in draft: they will know what I have learned from them. I am also grateful to Dirk Obbink, David Sider, and Rosalie Cook, who gave me precious suggestions. A special thanks to William Frosh, who read chapter by chapter with enthusiasm even though this was not his field; I certainly benefited from his wisdom. I thank all the scholars and institutions that supplied photographs, in particular Alain Blanchard, Euphrosyne Doxiadis, Marthe Bingen, and the Istituto Vitelli in Florence for their customary graciousness. To Alberto, much love and gratitude for his support.

* *A Note on References and Abbreviations* *

ABBREVIATIONS for editions of papyri, ostraca, and tablets follow J. F. Oates et al., *Checklist of Editions of Greek and Latin Papyri, Ostraca and Tablets*, 4th ed. (*BASP*, suppl. 7, 1992). The online and expanded edition is available at http://odyssey.lib.duke.edu/papyrus/texts/clist.html tmh. Journals and standard works are abbreviated as in *L' Année philologique* and the *American Journal of Archaeology*. Ancient authors and their works are abbreviated according to the third edition of the *Oxford Classical Dictionary*. Modern works cited more than once (and some cited only once) appear in the Select Bibliography and are indicated everywhere else by author's name and date of publication; those cited only once are usually given in full in the notes.

In addition, the following abbreviations are used:

P^2 = Roger A. Pack, *The Greek and Latin Literary Texts from Greco-Roman Egypt* (Ann Arbor, 1965).

PCG = R. Kassel and C. Austin, *Poetae comici Graeci* (Berlin and New York, 1983–).

PRLE = J. R. Martindale, *The Prosopography of the Later Roman Empire*, vol. 2, *A.D. 395–527* (Cambridge, 1980).

SH = Hugh Lloyd-Jones and Peter J. Parsons, *Supplementum Hellenisticum* (Berlin and New York, 1983).

TrGF = Richard Kannicht and Bruno Snell, *Tragicorum Graecorum fragmenta* (Göttingen, 1981); S. L. Radt, *Tragicorum-Graecorum fragmenta* (Göttingen, 1985).

Gymnastics of the Mind

*

* Introduction *

A<small>N IMAGE</small> that captures the substance of an education in letters in the Hellenistic and Roman worlds is found in a dialogue of the second-century satirist Lucian. Education is represented as a steep hill that students have to climb: they start in a group and proceed, "some very little, some more," but, when they get halfway and meet plenty of difficulties, many turn back "gasping for breath and dripping with sweat." The few students who endure and arrive at the top enjoy a wonderful view: common human beings appear from there as ants or pygmies crawling on the earth's surface (*Hermot.* 5). This image embraces many aspects of ancient education: the large number of students who started on the journey, the fact that some made very little progress, the challenges that secondary education offered, and the very low number of students who reached the top and could even "get above the clouds." At the same time, the utter superiority of the educated comes into sharp relief against the background of the corresponding insignificance of the uneducated, who are clinging to the earth and are unable to ascend. Lucian, moreover, emphasizes a fundamental aspect of ancient *paideia* ("education"), namely the discipline and hardship of the training. In his educational journey, a student followed a taxonomy of intellectual exercises, faced progressive challenges, built up endurance, and finally made it to the top through a strenuous gymnastics of the mind, *gymnasia tēs psychēs*, as the rhetor Isocrates called it in the fourth century B.C.E.[1] The fixed order that characterized knowledge and its inculcation from the period after Alexander the Great through the Roman period (third century B.C.E.–fourth century C.E.),[2] and the meticulous mental gymnastics required to master it, are the focus of this book. Much information survives about education and culture in classical Greece, but it is only from the Hellenistic period on that the various elements were systematized and that education assumed the basic shape that characterized it for many centuries. This book concentrates specifically on Greek education in Egypt during this long time span because of the wealth of educational material surviving from there; but, as I hope to

---

[1] The comparison of physical and mental training runs through Isocrates' *Antidosis*; see especially 178–85, 209–14, 266–67.

[2] I shall sometimes consider education in the early Byzantine period, which in Egypt extended to the Arab conquest in the seventh century C.E.

1

show, the evidence from Egypt provides a window on the vast panorama of educational practices around the Mediterranean.

I shall investigate the literate—and, with some limits, the numerate—education of a student from primary to rhetorical instruction, that is, from approximately age seven to age eighteen.[3] As we shall see, however, in antiquity these age limits could vary widely, and age did not determine precise educational thresholds. According to the ancient literary sources, whose statements have been rigidly upheld by historians of ancient education, a student built up his intellectual stamina during three well-defined stages of schooling supervised by different teachers: the elementary instructor, the grammarian, and the rhetor. Primary instruction concentrated on the teaching of literacy and numeracy, the secondary level of studies focused on the reading and interpretation of the poets, and rhetorical instruction covered prose works and the composition of discourses. This book makes apparent the tension between this traditional view of schooling and the more fluid learning situations that the sources suggest actually occurred. Evidence continues to come to light that ancient schooling did not have the rigid physiognomy painted by historians of education. Organization, structure, teachers' functions, and even contents of the curriculum at the primary level depended on situational circumstances. I have nevertheless chosen to maintain the canonical division into three separate stages of education. This model is still realistic enough to represent properly the characteristics and functions of the various levels and the tension among the different aims and audiences that each targeted. Even if the boundaries between levels were not completely impermeable, the educational contents of each appear well defined as the levels progress in difficulty, in the increasingly more targeted "gymnastics" they require, and in the new skills introduced.

In dealing with elementary education, I shall investigate the whole spectrum of the contents of instruction, that is, reading, writing, and arithmetic, all of which were taught to students by the same teacher. It is important to identify the ways in which a primary education enabled students of various social and economic backgrounds to come to grips with the demands imposed by society. At a more advanced educational level, I shall concentrate on the two stages of a liberal education about which we are most informed, those taught by the grammarian and the

[3] Since my concern is mental "gymnastics," I shall not investigate physical education. I also shall not explore vocational and professional instruction, which were not regarded as part of standard, liberal education but formed separate areas of learning.

rhetor. I shall not cover the teaching of higher mathematics, geometry, or astronomy, which was entrusted to specialized instructors. Likewise, I shall not investigate philosophical education, which, according to the ancient sources, was not part of standard education, that is, *enkyklios paideia*,[4] but occupied a separate position in the curriculum and attracted a very restricted student population.

Lucian's metaphor of the educational hill needs to be defined in order to avoid anachronism. The image of education as a summit that male and female students of every class, squeezed between family and state control, ascend from their most tender years is also part of standard descriptions of contemporary education: some teenagers join the work force and start to drop out; a smaller portion of scholastically adapted students continue on to college and beyond; and ultimately, only a small number of students reaches "the top." The differences between modern and ancient school systems, however, are conspicuous. In ancient times, the pool of starting students was incommensurably smaller, and even at a primary stage students of the elite had much greater opportunities for education. Class and status—and, to a much lesser extent, merit—determined who continued. Graduating from a secondary level of studies was often considered a sufficient mark of distinction even for privileged students: it was grammatical education that gave a youth the potential to become a person of culture. The few male students who reached the summit of rhetorical instruction were not necessarily the intellectuals, but those who craved certain positions in law and administration.

Education was fundamentally private, since parents had to shoulder its financial burdens, and teachers mostly depended on private tuition to make ends meet. Only occasionally did the state grant some immunities to teachers, and during the Roman period it gave some grammarians and rhetors a public—albeit not very conspicuous—subvention. Parents had to exercise more control than they do today over the educators because the teachers' qualifications for teaching were not regulated, nor did institutions for teachers' education exist. And yet, describing education as private can obscure some important aspects. Even though the state did not dictate a basic curriculum for each level, and once a teacher gained the trust of parents he or she was an absolute ruler in class, nevertheless,

---

[4] The expression *enkyklios paideia* ("circular, complete, general education") was often used from the first century B.C.E. on (e.g., Ps.-Plutarch *De liberis educandis* 7c). The Roman rhetor Quintilian in the first century C.E. translates the expression literally as *orbis doctrinae* ("the circle of education"), 1.10.1.

the contents of education became fixed to a degree and showed some uniformity of cultural elements and objectives among instructors.

The modern image of students of both genders ascending the hill of learning together has a pallid counterpart in the ancient world, but one that needs to be defined and investigated with care. Studies of education have fluctuated between two positions: in the past we saw unrealistic and arbitrary statements—with little accompanying evidence—that girls had regular access to education;[5] more recently, we see a skepticism that has led some scholars always to refer to students at any level as "the boys."[6] But in the field of education as much as in other fields, it is necessary to subvert and challenge rigid notions of gender relations in favor of a more fluid and dynamic view. Women in antiquity lived in a system that historically revolved around the rule of men. The fundamental asymmetry that characterized status, rank, and area of influence also affected a woman's chances of getting an education. Wealth and social status were even more determinant educational factors for females than for males. A disproportionately high percentage of girls who completed the first educational level were elite, as compared to the more varied social backgrounds of male students. As the hillside grew steeper, moreover, it started to shed girls and women in a much greater proportion than men. And yet, it is imperative to explore in detail the role that women had in both receiving and administering education.

A conspicuous part of the work of a historian is to render visible details that were hidden in the unexceptional practices of everyday life. Digging a sort of archaeological trench in the reality of ancient education by investigating a particular society gives more precise meaning to the overall picture and helps target the details. In this way, education appears a less formidable, monolithic, and perfect apparatus, and more attention is given to specifics of context, methods, or even individuals. This book focuses on education in Egypt, where Greek was the main language for administrative, official, and educational purposes during Hellenistic, Roman, and early Byzantine times. The sands of Egypt have preserved a rich collection of educational material on papyrus, on ostraca—sherds of broken vessels or slices of limestone—on tablets, and, more rarely, on parchment: exercises written by students in school or for school, teachers' models, which served as class preparation and copybooks for pupils, and

[5] See Marrou 1975, 1: 158, 2: 36 and 75; Bonner 1977: 27, 107, and 135.

[6] See Morgan 1998: 48–49. Harris (1989: 136–37 and 239–40) is more realistic but takes into account a limited amount of evidence, since he does not include the letters written by women in Egypt. Legras 1999 is mostly concerned with male education.

books and commentaries used in educational contexts.[7] This material will show the "gymnastics of the mind" that ancient students practiced in order to master the orderly body of skills and notions that confronted them. In addition, private letters on papyrus and documentary texts present people's reactions to education. Some help to identify specific teachers and sites of schools and to illuminate aspects of ancient life that are not well known. Dates and precise provenances of school exercises are often unknown, but the lack of precise context is amply compensated by the fact that the connection to the reality of ancient education is tangible and unique. Papyrologists are not only the "surgeons of old authors" whose texts they help reconstruct,[8] but also those who attempt to restore the cultural, social, and economic backgrounds of bits of information preserved from the ancient world. Studying these texts allows us to retrieve voices from the ancient past that are unmediated by the necessity of reaching a wider public and posterity and permits us literally to touch the hands of people who left traces in writing. Past historians of ancient education were not acquainted with most of this material on papyrus and relied primarily on the literary evidence.[9] It is therefore necessary to evaluate systematically all the steps taken by students in their climb to the educational summit, focusing at the same time on certain aspects that the evidence of the papyri helps put into relief.

In classical times, Egypt was a multilingual and multicultural society. Demotic, the literary form of the native Egyptian language, continued to be written by a specialized minority but disappeared during the Roman period, and around the third century C.E. the Coptic script was invented. I have chosen to focus on Greek educational practices and not on Demotic, Coptic, or the sparse evidence concerning the interaction among languages and cultures visible in Egypt. The question of the existence of schools associated with the families of priests of the Egyptian temples providing both Demotic and Greek instruction is problematic and deserves an inquiry of its own.[10] Thus, this book is Hellenocentric. It investi-

---

[7] Exercises are collected and examined with regard to their specific characteristics and palaeographical aspects in Cribiore 1996a. The word "papyri" will also refer in a generic sense to material preserved on other mediums.

[8] See Parsons (1982: 184), who reports the words used by John Earle in 1632 to describe the classical scholar.

[9] Marrou 1975; Bonner 1977. A recent book that incorporated the papyrological evidence, Morgan 1998, focused mostly on aspects of advanced education of elite boys.

[10] Cf. Chapter 1 below. The evidence, in any case, is unclear and remains mostly unpublished.

gates Greek education in Egypt not so much in its relation to other local cultures, but in conjunction with Greek education in the Eastern world, and in some respects also in Rome.

Despite the fact that Egypt had an extraordinary and highly developed civilization before its conquest by Alexander the Great, in most respects Greek culture was able to maintain its own identity. Greek and Egyptian cultures did not develop into a mixed culture, and particularly in the Ptolemaic and Roman periods, Greeks and Egyptians continued to lead parallel—not converging—cultural lives.[11] For a long time Egypt was considered a unique country in the Greco-Roman world, and scholars have questioned the legitimacy of exploiting its abundant documentation to describe conditions in the rest of the world around the Mediterranean. But recent studies that have focused on the governmental, military, and economic structure of Roman Egypt have shown that, far from being a unique country with a special status, Egypt was remarkably similar to other Eastern provinces.[12] Naturally, all provinces had some distinct socioeconomic characteristics and cultural discontinuities, but it is especially the quantity of data preserved from Egypt that makes it appear deceptively unique. Moreover, newly discovered papyrological material from the Roman Near East and Roman Britain testifies to an extensive use of letters and written documents in these areas, showing that Egypt was not isolated in its writing practices.[13]

For what concerns Greek educational practices, Egypt was in close touch with the rest of the Mediterranean. The evidence of the papyri remarkably agrees with the information transmitted by writers such as Plutarch, a Greek biographer and philosopher of the first to second century C.E. who lived in Greece, Libanius, a Greek rhetor who practiced in Syria in the fourth century C.E., and Quintilian, a Roman rhetor who had a famous school in Rome in the first century C.E. The contributions of these and other writers to our understanding of ancient education are fundamental because they describe a taxonomy of learning that was alive in their time and of which they themselves were successful products. And

[11] Bowersock 1990: 55–56.

[12] See N. Lewis, "The Romanity of Roman Egypt: A Growing Consensus," *Atti del XVII Congresso Internazionale di Papirologia* (Naples, 1984), 1077–84; D. W. Rathbone, "The Ancient Economy and Graeco-Roman Egypt," in L. Criscuolo and G. Geraci, *Egitto e storia antica: Dall' ellenismo all' etá araba* (Bologna, 1989), 159–76; R. S. Bagnall, *Reading Papyri, Writing Ancient History* (London, 1995), 11–13.

[13] See H. M. Cotton, W.E.H. Cockle, and F.G.B. Millar, "The Papyrology of the Roman Near East: A Survey," *JRS* 85 (1995): 214–35; Bowman and Thomas 1994.

yet, not only do their accounts focus primarily on the most prominent aspects of education and overlook the details, but they reflect a highly idealized view that was less concerned with reality than with improving current standards. In order to come closer to authentic educational practices and methods, it is essential to correlate the information transmitted by the literary sources and the anecdotal tradition with the wealth of educational material from Greco-Roman Egypt.

Even though Egypt will be the main space of reference in this book, it will be necessary to make a number of excursions beyond these precise geographical limits. I shall particularly draw from the work of Libanius, who discusses many topics related to education in his orations as well as in the letters he exchanged both with the families of his current pupils and with ex-students. Not only does Libanius's testimony illuminate the teaching and learning of rhetoric, which was at the top of the educational pyramid both in Egypt and elsewhere, but it also gives a deeper perspective and a validation to educational issues echoing from the papyri. When we juxtapose widely different material, such as letters on papyrus concerning education and letters written by Libanius to his students and their parents, our perspective on this rhetor's work is much fresher. The legitimacy of such a comparison is warranted not only because most educational papyri are Roman, and particularly late Roman, but also because, when dealing with people's expectations about and responses to educational questions, we may go beyond spatial and temporal limits: not only did practices and attitudes toward education remain almost unchanged despite political and social changes in this long period, but the continuity of human experience helps to validate practices located far apart in time and geography.

Exploiting educational material contained in the work of Libanius in a relatively broad context of ancient education is also timely. In his history of education, Marrou ignored Libanius, and Bonner, in the main, referred only briefly to his work on the preliminary rhetorical exercises. Other studies on Libanius and education are rather specialized and primarily involve identification of students and teachers mentioned by him and detailed examination of his extant works.[14] Yet Libanius could be consid-

---

[14] See Wolf 1952; Petit 1956; and Schouler 1984. I am currently engaged in translating the letters that deal with educational issues, which have attracted limited attention. They have never been translated into English; the French translation of a few of them in Festugière 1959 is often inaccurate. About 500 letters concern education. J. C. Wolf, *Libanii sophistae epistolae* (Amsterdam, 1738), provided a Latin translation of all the correspondence of Libanius.

ered in some respects the Quintilian of the Eastern world, and he deserves an important place in a study concerned with education in the Greek East. It is true that in his work, Quintilian dedicated some of his attention to primary and grammatical instruction, whereas Libanius refers mostly to higher education.[15] But Libanius's orations, and particularly his letters, let us glimpse the intriguing and practical questions of the organization of schooling, the role played by parents, and the problems faced by an educator much more clearly than Quintilian's rather theoretical work.

It remains to justify the temporal limitations of this study, which treats education in this long period as a continuum.[16] Scholars have long recognized that Roman rule brought significant socioeconomic changes in Egypt and that the transition from the Ptolemaic to the Roman period could hardly be characterized by continuity.[17] Educational practices and contents, however, basically continued undisturbed throughout this period—another sign that Greek education in antiquity was virtually independent of societal changes and geography. An attempt at a more defined periodization would not capture the substantially "frozen" quality of education, particularly in the provinces. Naturally, the schema of development was not always smooth, and I shall investigate the limited changes that occurred during the course of this long span of time.[18]

Education was based on the transmission of an established body of knowledge, about which there was wide consensus. Teachers were considered the custodians and interpreters of a tradition and were concerned with protecting its integrity. Education was supposed to lead to a growing understanding of an inherited doctrine. Admiration for the past gave rise to the aspiration to model oneself on one's predecessors and to maintain the system and methods that had formed them. Continuity and transmission of traditional values are not characteristics exclusive to ancient education. The tendency to communicate an unchanged, rigid, and basically theoretical knowledge likely to promote assent continued to inspire education in the Renaissance, in the Enlightenment, and in some respects also in the liberal society fostered by modern capitalism. Schooling had to

---

[15] Libanius's school, however, apparently provided instruction at all levels; see below, Chapter 1.

[16] On education as a continuum and on the similarity of contents in the East and the West, Vössing 1997: 11; and Morgan 1998: 22–25 and 44–46.

[17] See N. Lewis, " 'Greco-Roman Egypt': Fact or Fiction?" *Proceedings of the Twelfth Congress of Papyrology* (Toronto, 1970), 3–14.

[18] I have not covered Christian education, but instead focus on the "pagan" sides of ancient *paideia*.

provide a certain amount of "know-how," a set of techniques and elements of scientific and literary knowledge enmeshed in the ideology of the moment. The schooling system, in other words, has always been an agent of social, cultural, and political continuity, serving as a tool for maintaining the social order by placing people in appropriate niches in society. Learning some skills and elements of a cultural patrimony went hand in hand with assimilation of and submission to the rules of the dominant order.

In antiquity, education served well the interests of the elite and the preservation of the hierarchical status quo. Since very little attention was given to issues of pedagogy and psychology, serious motivations for change and improvement were rarely felt. Moreover, in the Eastern world, and in Greco-Roman Egypt in particular, added factors of cultural survival and preservation of identity helped to confer a remarkable stability to education, since the Greek minority felt the need to empower itself in its daily contacts with a "barbarian" majority.[19] Education became a powerful agent for preserving "Greekness" by maintaining fixed linguistic and social boundaries, excluding almost any form of Egyptian culture, and concentrating on transmitting Greek values, language, and literacy. Cultivated individuals and students considered themselves exiles of an ideal country—Greece—and yearned to belong to that distant world, of which they were citizens by virtue of the texts they read and the values they encountered through reading. Most of these Greeks in the Eastern world could not claim to be born in Greece or to be of recent Greek descent, but they could speak a common language, read and write in an artificial Greek of the past, and follow the same aesthetic and ethical ideals endorsed by education. A somewhat similar process, *mutatis mutandis*, can be observed over the last one hundred years in industrialized nations where schooling organized by the state has supported only one standardized national language, banished what were called "dialects" and the wisdom literature associated with them, and promoted a uniform standard of culture.

Much of this book is the product of patient and slow reading of the ancient sources and of careful analysis of the handwriting of teachers, students, and people who penned epistles. The minutiae of palaeography—the study of ancient writing—have allowed the identification of the models that teachers prepared as an aid for their students, resurrecting ancient pedagogical practices. Likewise, the learning process of ancient

---

[19] Marrou (1975, 1: 153) recognizes this factor but idealizes it excessively.

9

students is illuminated by the way they penned their exercises and by the mistakes they made. Close scrutiny of the handwriting of the body and salutations in epistles has facilitated the identification of writers who signed their letters or wrote them out entirely. But this book is not based only on these meticulous and painstaking observations. I have also tried to investigate some general aspects of education illuminated by both the papyri and the literary sources, such as practical problems of organization or parental concerns about specific issues. Two voices, therefore, can be distinguished in this book. I hope that their association will generate mutual confirmation and increase the validity of the whole. Though tension between description and argument is present in every chapter, I have attempted to stay close to the ancient sources and to let them speak, providing only the necessary interpretation. As a rule, I have treasured the admonition that the grammarian Theon, who lived in Alexandria in the first century C.E., addressed to his students, who were exhorted to strive for clarity and vividness in their writing (*Progymnasmata* 71.30–72.3). It was embodied in a verse from the *Odyssey* of Homer, "Easy is the word that I shall say and put in your mind" (11.146).

This study is divided into two parts. In the first four chapters, I do not argue a single thesis; rather, I try to follow several leads suggested by the broad topic of education. My overall aim is to present some aspects of the educational scenario and to introduce its protagonists, that is, the *palaistra* ("gymnasium") of education,[20] with its young athletes—girls as well as boys—trainers, and spectators. The topics I address have not previously received a comprehensive treatment, and in most cases have elicited only broad generalizations. Chapter 1 concentrates on the evidence for schools primarily—but not exclusively—in Greco-Roman Egypt. It considers not only schools existing in somewhat formal settings but also teaching and learning environments in general, and schooling structures that depended on local situations. The overall scenario is much more flexible than has been recognized previously. The subject of Chapter 2 is the teachers who led students in the educational journey: their economic and social circumstances, coupled with the frustrations of daily life, made them sometimes less-than-helpful figures. Teachers, who had the power to rule their pupils, were ruled at the same time by parents, volatile jobs, and financial problems. Ancient schooling, therefore, provided models for oppression as well as for enlightenment. I shall briefly mention in this

---

[20] The term *palaistra*, which usually indicates the wrestling school, is also employed to designate schools of education; see, e.g., Plutarch *Demetr.* 5 and Longinus 4.4 Prickard. In the *Hermeneumata* (Dionisotti 1982: 99 line 29), it indicates the school of the grammarian.

chapter the evidence concerning the few women who taught at primary and higher educational levels in Egypt to show that they were an important part of the picture, but this evidence will be examined in detail in Chapter 3. It deserves more space particularly because the more humble women teachers of literacy, as opposed to the few exceptional female teachers of higher learning, were neglected by the literary sources, and the evidence emerging from the papyri did not find a place in histories of education. The topic of female education occupies the rest of this chapter. Finally, Chapter 4 considers a fundamental component of ancient education, that is, the active presence of parents. This chapter also investigates some issues related to education that are not well known, such as the need for male students to travel when they reached the grammatical and rhetorical levels in order to find suitable teachers, and problems of lodging and daily living for students away from home.

Chapter 5 concentrates on the instruments of learning: the models prepared by the teachers, the books used particularly at high stages of education, and the various writing materials and implements handled by students in their exercises. It investigates fundamental aspects of education that have been neglected in the past and that increased the inevitable dependence of students upon their teachers. This chapter serves as a transition to the remaining chapters, which cover the various stages through which a student built up his intellectual stamina. It is in this part of the book that the extreme order both of the elements of knowledge and of its inculcation will be investigated. Knowledge was governed by an inner order and was structured like the links of a chain, connected in the form of a graded scale of proximity and similarity. Skills and contents were organized according to resemblance. Each link resembled the one that preceded and the one that followed. Education consisted of mastering all the links in a progressive process of accumulation. I follow students' maturation from the time they were endlessly drilled on the alphabet and learned the elements of copying and reading (Chapter 6), to when their reading skills became more secure and they started to concentrate in increasing detail on a canonical list of authors and on the "technical" side of grammar (Chapter 7), to the time when rhetorical instruction strengthened the verbal ability of a male student and started to grant him some independence from the texts that were his initial models (Chapter 8).

At each educational step it will be appropriate to ask, like a certain student of Libanius, *ti kerdos*, "What is the gain?" That dissatisfied student had questioned "the aim of all the sweat" and the results he had achieved after "countless efforts" (*Or.* 62.12). But in spite of objective

11

deficiencies, each educational hurdle had some rewards, and even some practical benefits. Viewing education through the experience of real people who lived in the Greco-Roman East, and who sometimes approached limited portions of it without completing a specific course of study, will show that although the contents of education appear rigid and unchanged, its practical effect was varied.

PART ONE

*

* CHAPTER ONE *

Models of Schooling

I go to school. I enter and I say, "Good morning, teacher." He gives me a kiss and says hello to me. My slave gives me the tablets, the case; I take out the stylus and sit down at my place: I erase and copy according to the model. Afterwards, I show my writing to the teacher, who makes every kind of correction. He asks me to read and then I give [the text] to another pupil; I learn the colloquia and I recite them. "Give me a dictation," I ask. Another student dictates to me. . . . When the teacher bids them, the little ones engage in letters and syllables, and one of the older students pronounces them aloud for them. Others recite in order the words to the assistant teacher and write verses. Being in the first group, I take a dictation. Then, after sitting down, I study commentaries, glosses, and the handbook of grammar.

IN THIS VERSION of the *Hermeneumata*, grammar occupies the rest of the pupil's morning; he is asked to identify parts of speech, conjugate and decline words, and scan verses.[1]

The *Hermeneumata* (also called *Colloquia*), school handbooks in Greek and Latin that most likely derived from third-century Gaul, describe, among other things, a day in the life of a student in antiquity and were studied in schools, as the text quoted above says explicitly.[2] They are preserved in medieval manuscripts in eight different versions: the Eastern Greek teachers who composed them drew from a "deeply rooted school tradition, with which they themselves grew up."[3] These schoolbooks are composed of one or more of four parts: a general glossary, a glossary divided by topic, vignettes of everyday life, and short texts, such as fables of Aesop. School exercises analogous to all the elements but the vignettes

[1] See Goetz 1892 (*Hermeneumata Einsidlensia*, pp. 225–26). Goetz published various versions of what are known as *Hermeneumata Ps. Dositheana*. See also Dionisotti 1982. I did not translate the text where it is obscure and incoherent.

[2] The original language probably was Greek, which was translated into Latin: simultaneous teaching in both languages was a common feature of Western schools. The content of the texts reveals that these books were meant for different age groups: students of elementary, grammatical, and even rhetorical schools.

[3] Dionisotti 1982: 90.

have been preserved by the sands of Egypt, but the vignettes are the most seductive part of the *Hermeneumata*: their vivid picture of the day-to-day routine of a student in antiquity seems largely plausible. They continued to exercise a fundamental influence on students learning Latin up to the first part of this century: the *Colloquia* composed on the model of the ancient ones by the French schoolmaster Mathurin Cordier in the sixteenth century enjoyed a long-lasting popularity.[4]

In evaluating the characteristics of ancient schooling that emerge from the *Hermeneumata*, the papyri, and the literary sources, it is important to bear in mind that what now seem integral aspects of modern education are relatively recent developments. It was only in the nineteenth century that mass schooling, institutions for teachers' education, and a discipline of psychology emerged, and only at the beginning of the twentieth century that the responsibility for institutionalized education was assumed by the state. The modern institution of schooling—particularly in urban environments—is permeated by an utter verticality: students are ranked within classes, classes are ranked according to levels, and separate schools are ranked as conveying a primary, secondary, and tertiary—or higher—education. Even though schools may differ qualitatively, they are invariably characterized by some idea of permanence and possess an existence somewhat independent from that of those who organize them and administer the teaching. Traditionally, historians of education have maintained that students pursued a full course of literary instruction in antiquity in a somewhat similar system, passing through three successive stages supervised by separate teachers: they learned reading and writing in elementary school, grammar and poetry at the school of the grammarian, and the art of speaking in the school of rhetoric.[5]

The *Hermeneumata*, however, evoke a considerably different paradigm of schooling. In the version quoted above, primary and secondary students are together in one room, while instruction is imparted by a teacher, an assistant teacher, and older students: altogether, by our standards, a chaotic environment in which concentration would have been challenged and the rumble of intellection must have been boisterous. But in order to evaluate the picture realistically, two points must be borne in mind. First, this environment, which appears quaint and unconventional, continued long beyond ancient times. It is remarkably similar to that of the one-

---

[4] Cordier's *Colloquiorum scholasticorum libri quatuor* passed through innumerable editions; cf., e.g., J. Clarke, *Corderii colloquiorum centuria selecta* (New York, 1809), with an English translation. I owe this information to Whitney Bagnall.

[5] On teachers at the various levels, see below, Chapter 2.

room schoolhouse of the nineteenth-century American frontier, where the curriculum from first to eighth grade was covered by a single teacher, some teachers were hardly qualified to teach, and "education ranged from the sublime to the ridiculous."[6] Second, we need to consider how prevalent the model of schooling offered by the *Hermeneumata* was in antiquity; its vignettes suggest some stability, a specific building where instruction is imparted, and teachers with distinct identities.

The evidence of attested schools in the Greco-Roman world is admittedly thin: texts and archaeological excavations have revealed only isolated instances of schools that can be identified as such with assurance. But is this due to an actual shortage of schools, or to the fact that schools were physically makeshift affairs that did not leave many traces, and that teaching and learning often went on in various ways and in different environments, without much advertising? Recently it has been argued that an extensive network of schools was indispensable in antiquity for the diffusion of literacy beyond a privileged minority.[7] Clearly mass education and majority literacy did not exist in antiquity. But if one wants to gain a balanced view of the ancient educational scenario, it is essential to be alert to all the possible, and often unfamiliar, ways in which education may have been structured. It is thus preferable to adopt a broad definition of "school" based on the educational activities of teaching and learning rather than on the identity of the person imparting the instruction, the teacher-student relationship, and the premises in which teaching took place.[8]

In what follows, I primarily focus on schooling in Egypt in the Greek and Roman period by evaluating not only the few explicit references to existing schools in papyri but also various learning environments suggested by excavations and finds of school exercises. In light of the frequent complaints about the lack of evidence for schools,[9] an inquiry of this kind deserves much attention. Literary sources will also illuminate various school structures in the Greek East, particularly at high educational levels. The extant evidence challenges not only the rigid and uniform organization of ancient schooling that past historians of education have pronounced the norm, but also the recently proposed, more realistic model of

---

[6] J. M. Campbell, *The Prairie Schoolhouse* (Albuquerque, N.M., 1996), 13–20; quotation from p. 20.

[7] Harris 1989: 16 and passim. Harris alludes occasionally to alternative systems of teaching and learning but does not explore this possibility.

[8] Cf. Frasca 1996a: 256.

[9] Vössing 1997: 49–50 and 356; Morgan 1998: 28–29.

a two-track system, which had some validity only in certain geographical environments.[10] The picture that emerges is one of great variety. Its outlines depended on several factors: not only educational stages, but also urban education versus education in the country, economic and social status of the pupil, and purely situational circumstances. One unifying aspect was the fact that schools did not usually have an existence separate from individual teachers,[11] and even at high stages of education a teacher was responsible for finding suitable accommodations: if he decided to move somewhere else, a school ceased to exist. This increased the power that a teacher in antiquity exercised over his pupils. There was no external structure on which a student could rely, no authority higher than that of the teacher, and no external control besides that of parents. Since a school *was* a teacher, logical corollaries were the impermanence of the institution and the vulnerability of students to lack of stability and to change. One aspect that needs to be noted, moreover, is that the sources do not transmit examples of schools named after women teachers.[12] This is not too surprising, considering that the evidence of schools named after male teachers is rather meager anyway. But it is difficult to know whether this fact has a meaning beyond the chance of the finds, and whether the few women teachers mentioned in the papyri[13] taught groups of students from different environments who were unrelated to each other, or were in charge of the children of a single family.

References to Schools in Greco-Roman Egypt

The few extant direct references to schools in Greco-Roman Egypt occur in letters and documents on papyrus; at no point do school exercises mention the specific localities where they were written. In the papyri, schools are usually called *didaskaleia*, "teaching places"—occasionally *grammatodidaskaleia* when primary instruction was imparted—the same term that designates schools in the literary sources. Most of the time schools were identified by the teacher who provided the instruction. In the second century B.C.E. a school named after the teacher Tothes was located in Memphis, according to a papyrus found among the papers of Ptolemaios,

---

[10] See Booth 1979a and b.

[11] Of course, there were exceptions. In a monastery one surmises that some instruction was continued after the death of the monk who was in charge of it.

[12] But see the exceptional case of Hypatia, who assembled around herself a number of students; cf. below, Chapter 3, note 16.

[13] Cf. below, Chapter 3.

who lived as a recluse in the temple of Sarapis, where he protected twin girls who had found refuge there.[14] The school of Tothes appears in a confused dream that Ptolemaios narrates to a friend in a letter: the twin sisters had called him from there as he was passing by; after he told them not to become discouraged, Tothes himself brought the girls out to him.[15] It is likely that this school, which apparently was housed in some kind of building, was an elementary school. Another school that surely provided instruction in elementary letters was located somewhere in the Fayum in the first century C.E.: named for the teacher Melankomas, it is in fact designated in a letter with the unambiguous term *grammatodidaskaleion* ("elementary school").[16] Two more intriguing references to primary schools involve the metropolis of Oxyrhynchos in the fourth and the seventh centuries. A papyrus that contains reports to an official lists repairs to several buildings and mentions the school of the *grammatodidaskalos* ("elementary teacher") Dionysios, which was situated under the western colonnade with other buildings, such as the temple of Fortune, the temple of Achilles, and the office of a surgeon.[17] The teacher Dionysios, who appears to be responsible for the repairs to the building, which had become run down, must have rented the school space from the city. Another papyrus, dated to C.E. 610, mentions an elementary teacher as a guarantor of a steward's work contract and calls the school where he tendered his instruction "the Southern School."[18] This unusual designation is tantalizing: not only does it indicate that there were at least two elementary schools in Oxyrhynchos at the time, but it also suggests that perhaps this school, which was named not after a certain person but according to its location, was not organized by a specific teacher and sponsored privately but was a public institution.[19]

Schools of advanced education were also called *didaskaleia*. A papyrus found in Oxyrhynchos that is part of the *Acta Maximi* alludes to their existence in this city.[20] In this speech, an important personage—perhaps the prefect Gaius Vibius Maximus—is denounced on account of his rela-

---

[14] See *UPZ* I.78.9–14. On Ptolemaios and the twins, see below, pp. 87 and 188–89.

[15] Not only do Ptolemaios's dreams heavily reflect reality, but the very fact that he mentions a school named after a certain teacher vouches for the credibility of this allusion.

[16] *SB* III.7268. On this school, see also below.

[17] *P.Oxy.* LXIV.4441, col. IV.18–20, dated to C.E. 315–316.

[18] *P.Oxy.* LVIII.3952; the term used, *scholeion*, does not occur anywhere else in papyri.

[19] On the existence of a "public grammarian" in Oxyrhynchos in the third century C.E., see below, pp. 54–55.

[20] See *P.Oxy.* III.471, which belongs to the *Acta Alexandrinorum*; H. A. Musurillo, *The Acts of the Pagan Martyrs: Acta Alexandrinorum* (Oxford, 1954), no. VII. Cf. Legras 1999: 33–34, 58–63.

tionship with a certain seventeen-year-old boy who was constantly in his company and followed him in his travels so that he no longer attended "the schools (*didaskaleia*) and the exercises proper for the young." Thus in the papyrus, *didaskaleia* are considered as localities set aside for education, where a young man ought to spend his day. Schools that imparted some kind of professional education, about which not much is known, were also designated as such. The only reference comes from a Ptolemaic papyrus, which preserves on the back official instructions and letters copied for practice and alludes to students of a school again named after a teacher, Leptines.[21] That these were adult students is disclosed not only by the fact that they are addressed as *andres*, "men," instead of *paides*, "boys," but also by the verb used to exhort them to work hard, which is the more dignified *ponein*, "work," instead of the usual *philoponein*, "pay attention." It is likely that these "pupils" were officials who received some kind of literary instruction.

While surveying references to teaching and learning situations, mention should be made of the term *scholē*, which occurs both in the *Hermeneumata* and in the papyri, but with a different connotation in each. In the *Hermeneumata*, this word is always applied to a place where instruction is given: the pupil is described as entering specific premises, which in one case are located on the second floor of a building: "I went straight along the arcade that leads to the school (*scholē*) . . . when I reached the stairways, I climbed the steps."[22] The word *scholē*, which in Greek originally meant "leisure," was then applied to that for which leisure was employed, especially learned discussions and lectures, and was also used for a group to whom lectures were given.[23] In the papyri this term indicates both the activity of learning and a group of students who congregated to receive instruction. In the second century C.E. in Hermopolis, Heraidous, the daughter of the local governor, needed "material suitable for *scholē* such as a reading book."[24] For Heraidous, going to school meant learning at home with a private tutor—an arrangement that must have been popular among children of the elite, both male and female. Groups of advanced

[21] *P.Paris* 63 of the second century B.C.E. On this papyrus, see below, pp. 189 and 216.

[22] See Stephanus, Paris Lat. 6503; Dionisotti 1982: 111. In the *Hermeneumata Celtes*, the word *scholē* is used interchangeably with *akroatērion*, "room for lectures," which is glossed as "auditorium."

[23] In the fourth century C.E., the poet Ausonius mentioned the original etymology of this word in an epistle written to encourage his grandson, who had reached school age, *Ep*. 22.6–7.

[24] See *P.Giss*. 85. On Heraidous, see below.

male students, called *scholai*, followed the classes of teachers of rhetoric in Alexandria. In the second century the private teacher Didymos was heading a *scholē* that the student Neilos had decided to attend for lack of a more prestigious one.[25] Later, in the fifth century, the grammarian Flavius Horapollon is described in a papyrus as having a *scholē* in the capital, where he taught grammar and philosophy.[26]

The relative infrequency of the references to schools in papyri is at first surprising when they are compared with the numerous references to teachers.[27] This seeming paradox is partly offset by the fact that the papyri gloss teachers with a professional title only in order to distinguish them from other community members with the same name; they do not describe the professional activities of these individuals. There is no doubt, however, that this paucity of references is also a reflection of the fact that schools were not always present institutionally in specific buildings designed for educational purposes. Particularly at the lower levels, ancient schools may often have lacked formal settings.

School Accommodations

In exploring school accommodations in antiquity, it is necessary to be alert to a vast spectrum of situations: besides occupying a private or public building, a school could have been located within the perimeter of an ancient temple, in the cell of a monastery, in a private house, or even in the open air, at a street corner or under a tree. Teachers took advantage of the various opportunities offered by the place where they lived to set up a "school" whose characteristics varied according to their personal circumstances. Particularly at high educational levels, as a teacher moved up the ladder of recognition, the location and arrangement of his school often changed for the better. I shall identify various school accommodations on the basis of archaeological remains and finds of exercises. I intend only to suggest a range of possible situations rather than to give a complete and detailed account.[28]

---

[25] On Didymos and Neilos, see below, Chapters 2 and 4.

[26] See Cribiore 1996a: 19 and 169 n. 22.

[27] Cf. below, p. 46.

[28] In this area it is important to use some caution. Attempts to identify the archaeological contexts of exercises are sometimes unconvincing because the provenance of many exercises is uncertain.

In the Egyptian language, the term used for school is the equivalent of "a room for education." This expression, which came into existence in the Middle Kingdom, had a long life and passed into Coptic.[29] Even though this term clearly alludes to specific and confined premises in which education was imparted, nevertheless it is difficult to identify such places. Demotic[30] education was centered on the temples, but information concerning the exact localities used for this purpose is scarce. Scholars have attempted to visualize which parts of a temple would be more suitable to gather and instruct a group of students effectively. The temple of the goddess Hathor in Dendera in Upper Egypt, for instance, seems to offer an appropriate place: the square vestibule is a large, cool room surrounded by columns and provided with enough light.[31] On the walls are inscribed names of festive days and lists of various parts of the country that brought offerings to the goddess, which could have been used as teaching material. It is impossible, however, to go beyond the domain of speculation.

Finds of Demotic school exercises point to the presence of schools for Egyptian scribes in various parts of Egypt. Sometimes the context suggests a bilingual education. A large number of Demotic school ostraca, together with some Greek ones, were discovered in the village of Narmouthis in the second century C.E. in a building inside the *temenos* ("precinct") of a pharaonic temple, at the southeast corner.[32] A Demotic ostracon says explicitly: "Go to the southern part so that you can devote yourself to study every day."[33] Another ostracon appears to suggest some connection between the school and the temple, since it reveals that the correction of schoolwork was done in the temple itself.[34] The same school apparently also offered some instruction in Greek: the exercises that are preserved

[29] Ursula Kaplony-Heckel, "Schüler und Schulwesen in der ägyptischen Spätzeit," *Studien zur altägyptischen Kultur* 1 (1974): 238; W. E. Crum, *Coptic Dictionary* (Oxford, 1939), 12a.

[30] Demotic was the Egyptian script that was adopted starting in the Hellenistic period. It was more cursive than the older "hieroglyphic" and "hieratic" forms.

[31] See François Daumas, "Dendara et le temple d' Hathor," *Recherches d' archéologie* 29 (1969): 34.

[32] On the excavations that led to the discoveries of the Demotic and Greek ostraca, see A. Vogliano, "Papyrologica," in *Studi in onore di V. Arangio Ruiz*, vol. 2 (Naples, 1953), 509–10. See also S. Donadoni, "Il greco di un sacerdote di Narmuthis," *Acme* 8, 2–3 (1955): 73–83.

[33] Bresciani, Pernigotti, and Betrò 1983: no. 3. More than 600 of the ostraca from Narmouthis are entirely in Demotic, while 350 are Demotic-Greek and 70 are Greek-Demotic.

[34] Ibid.: no. 10: "If a boy who makes mistakes in the words does not correct them when he goes to the temple for the correction, this boy does not cultivate writing. His mind will dictate mistakes to his hand, and he will often make them." An actual connection with the temple, however, is not certain.

are written in fluent hands; they might have been practice exercises for Egyptian-speaking scribes who were learning some Greek without following a regular curriculum.[35] The bilingual program must have been unusually heavy: a Demotic ostracon with the categorical statement "I will not write Greek letters; I am stubborn" preserves the complaint of one student.[36] Evidence of Demotic educational texts in other villages of the Fayum district in central Egypt, such as Soknopaiou Nesos and Tebtynis, also shows the existence of Demotic schools associated with priests running the local temple.[37] In both places a limited number of Greek school exercises were found.[38] It is difficult to reach a clear understanding of the curriculum of these schools and to know to what extent they provided a bilingual education, since most of the evidence is unpublished.

Some connection—albeit tenuous—between school and temple can be observed in the fourth century C.E. in the village of Kellis in the Dakhleh Oasis. A mud-brick structure within the precinct of the temple of Tutu yielded fragments of several inscribed wooden boards of a scholastic nature, an ostracon with an exercise, and a number of reed pens.[39] These objects were found in the rooms of the main structure that were divided by a partition and provided with benches in the fourth century. While it is tempting—albeit too speculative—to suppose that these alterations were due to the need to adapt the rooms to school use, the atypical concentration of objects connected to learning and writing point to a place where Greek literary instruction was given.

Greek education in Egypt may have also taken advantage of the cool, private spaces provided by pharaonic tombs. In 1828, during his journey in Upper Egypt, Champollion explored a series of tombs of the Middle Kingdom built in the rocky hills in Beni-Hassan. In one of these tombs, which was covered with painted scenes, a syllabary of the Greco-Roman period written in red letters occupied an extensive space on one of the walls.[40] This syllabary included biliteral and triliteral combinations of consonants and vowels in seven long rows. Syllabaries were fundamental

[35] See R. Pintaudi and P. J. Sijpesteijn, "Ostraka di contenuto scolastico provenienti da Narmuthis," ZPE 76 (1989): 85–92; Cribiore 1996a: nos. 54, 203, 205, 285, and 286.

[36] See Bresciani, Pernigotti, and Betrò 1983: no. 5.

[37] See van Minnen 1998b.

[38] The educational material found at Soknopaiou Nesos is mostly mathematical: the well-written tables of numbers perhaps served the needs of common people.

[39] On one such board containing a Homeric exercise, see Hope and Worp 1998, with bibliography about the excavations.

[40] See J. F. Champollion, *Monuments de l' Égypte et de la Nubie*, vol. 2, ed. G. Maspero (Paris, 1889), 459–60, no. 10. It is not specified where the syllabary was found, but it probably was not very far from the entrance, which could provide light.

to teaching reading, and children trained themselves by pronouncing aloud the syllabic combinations that usually were inscribed by teachers on models.[41] This particular syllabary was like a permanent model that provided a suitable decoration to a "room for education." The voices of children learning Greek syllables—*ba-be-bi-bo-* and so on—must have echoed amid the silence of a glorious past.

Later on, in early Byzantine times, the ancient tombs with which the hills around the city of Thebes in Upper Egypt were honeycombed became homes for anchorites. When an anchorite attracted a special reputation for sanctity, and pilgrims started to visit his abode, other buildings and rooms were added, and a monastic community was formed. In these monasteries some instruction in reading and writing Coptic and Greek was necessary, because monastic centers attracted people of every age and level of literacy, among them some male children.[42] Even though in the small monasteries around Thebes schools were not organized on the grand scale of the Western monastic centers,[43] education left definite traces. Thus the excavations of the monastery of Epiphanius yielded some Greek school exercises and a notable number of Coptic exercises.[44] While there are no specific indications of the finding-places of the latter, the Greek exercises were mostly discovered in cells outside of the boundary walls. Cell A, for instance, where a teacher's model containing maxims from Menander was found,[45] was apparently the abode of a monk named Moses who copied a large number of liturgical and Biblical texts into Coptic and Greek.[46] Not far from the monastery of Epiphanius was the monastery of St. Phoebammon, which was built on the ruins of a pharaonic temple. Here, too, the excavations yielded some Greek and Coptic school exercises that testify to the existence of some kind of school.[47] It is suggestive

[41] Cf. below, Chapter 5.

[42] E. Wipzycka, "Le degré d' alphabétisation en Égypte byzantine," *REAug* 30 (1984): 279–96. See, e.g., the numerous "donations" of children to the monasteries of this region in W. E. Crum and G. Steindorff, *Koptische Rechtsurkunden des achten Jahrhunderts aus Djeme (Theben)* (Leipzig, 1971), nos. 78–103.

[43] See P. Riché, *Education and Culture in the Barbarian West*, trans. J. J. Contreni (Columbia, S.C., 1976), 109–22.

[44] I am currently working on the Coptic exercises belonging to Columbia University. On the Greek exercises, see Cribiore 1996a: nos. 66, 67, 122, 123, 168, 225, 226, 227, and 319.

[45] See ibid.: no. 319.

[46] About Moses, see *P.Mon.Epiph.* I, pp. 42–43 and note 1.

[47] See C. Bachatly, *Le monastère de Phoebammon dans la Thébaïde*, vol. 2 (Cairo, 1965); Cribiore 1996a: nos. 19, 20, 21, 22, 61, 163, and 164.

that a hexameter verse containing all the letters of the alphabet scrambled and a separate Greek alphabet were painted in red ochre in the doorway of the vestibule leading to the Southern Hall of Offering of the ancient temple. Perhaps classes were held in the vicinity.

The evidence provided by *Didaskalos—A Schoolmaster*—a mime of the third-century B.C.E. poet Herodas, who was connected with both the southeastern Aegean and Alexandria—might be useful with regard to school accommodations. Even though it is recognized that the poetry of Herodas was sophisticated and addressed a cultivated public, this poet's use of *topoi* ("commonplaces") and set characters allows one to retrieve some reality.[48] In this mime, the school of Lampriskos is situated in some kind of building: the mother of the undisciplined student Kokkalos laments that her son can hardly recognize where the classroom's door is (8–9). Lampriskos may have used his own quarters to instruct the children, or he may have rented some space in a private house. In Greco-Roman Egypt, classes at every level of education must often have been held in private houses.[49] Comparative evidence of ancient education from the third millennium B.C.E. to medieval times often points to schools situated in domestic quarters. But direct evidence of private spaces used for education is rarely found, and it is not known whether parents provided space for free or not. A Ptolemaic papyrus refers to a school of medicine that seems to have been of considerable size and that was held in the private house of a doctor, where Greek slaves followed lessons in Egyptian medicine.[50] A Greek teacher, who had learned Demotic, taught these apprentices to read and write in Egyptian and presumably to understand the doctor's treatises. In general, however, one has to resort to imagination and to comparative evidence to visualize the possible accommodations of schools situated in private quarters. In the Egyptian countryside, the houses of people of common means display narrow and badly lit rooms, which would not have been ideal for reading and writing.[51] The homes of

[48] Mastromarco 1984.

[49] On classes held in domestic quarters in Mesopotamia, see Gadd 1956: 25–26. Cf., in early medieval times, the evidence from the Jewish community in Cairo, Reif 1990: 152.

[50] *UPZ* I.148. See R. Rémondon, "Problèmes du bilinguisme dans l' Égypte Lagide," *CE* 39 (1964): 126–46.

[51] See, e.g., the tiny houses in Karanis, Elaine K. Gazda, ed., *Karanis: An Egyptian Town in Roman Times* (Ann Arbor, Mich., 1983), 19–21. These houses appear very small when compared to houses in other areas of the Mediterranean: R. Alston, "Houses and Households in Roman Egypt," in *Domestic Space in the Roman World: Pompeii and Beyond*, ed. Ray Laurence and Andrew Wallace-Hadrill, *JRA* suppl. 22 (Portsmouth, R.I., 1997), 25–39.

wealthy inhabitants, on the other hand, may have offered suitable quarters for teaching the children of the owner and perhaps some of their friends. Houses of the upper class, which appear more often in urban than in rural contexts, were of much larger proportions and possessed internal courts and towers. Great houses in Roman Africa show a variety of spaces that could be used in private and public life.[52] Thus, for instance, the House of Europa at Cuicul shows a very large vestibule, where the stairs could have served as a dais for the owner or a schoolmaster. In these houses, another room suitable to be a classroom was the exedra, the decor of which—mosaics and theatrical masks, for example—often alluded to cultural pursuits. Evidence of patrician houses used for education in the Roman world supports this assumption. Thus, in the grand house of L. Albucius Celsus in Pompeii, graffiti on the walls of an exedra painted in bright yellow show that classes attended by the children of Albucius and perhaps some of his slaves were held there. One of the graffiti says explicitly, "If you do not like Cicero, you will be whipped," testifying to less-than-gentle teaching methods.[53]

In the *Hermeneumata*, the word "step" (*bathmos*, which is glossed with the Latin *gradus*) suggests that classes could have been held outside.[54] Open-air teaching, which was more common at an elementary stage, must have been a solution frequently adopted in Egypt, with its mild climate. In the Mediterranean world, teaching outside was not unheard of. The arcades that surrounded some squares could have been used for this purpose, and in large cities such as Alexandria or Oxyrhynchos, the main streets had vaulted colonnades. Evidence from Pompeii again offers suitable comparanda: graffiti mark the sites of two elementary schools, one under the arcades of the *Forum* and the other under the colonnades of the *Campus*. The place where the first school was situated is marked by murals that depict students holding their tablets on their knees, together with passersby peeking at their work.[55] But apparently privacy was not or could not be a priority for teachers. The first-century C.E. Greek writer Dio Chrysostom, who grew up in Bithynia in Asia Minor, uses teachers

[52] See Yvon Thébert, "Private and Public Spaces: The Components of the Domus," in *A History of Private Life*, vol. 1, ed. Paul Veyne (Cambridge, Mass., 1987), 355–81.

[53] See Della Corte 1959: 626–28. On punishment, see Chapter 2.

[54] See Dionisotti 1982: 99 line 22.

[55] See Della Corte 1959: 621–24; and Bonner 1977: 118 fig. 11. Also W. Harris, "Literacy and Epigraphy, I," *ZPE* 52 (1983): 109. Cf. Augustine *Conf.* 1.13, a much commented-upon passage, where spaces used for teaching were apparently screened by some sort of awning.

and students as examples of individuals who managed to do their jobs in the midst of great turmoil. After describing flute and dance teachers who held a school in the streets, without being distracted by passersby and their noise, he goes on by saying, "But this is the most extreme case of all: the elementary teachers sit in the streets with their pupils, and nothing hinders them in this great throng from teaching and learning."[56]

In the Mediterranean world, open-air classes could also have been held in the country, without the minimal structure that a colonnade of a city street could provide. In the fourth century B.C.E., the poet Aratus composed an amusing epigram lampooning the teacher Diotimos: "I lament for Diotimos, who sits on stones teaching the children of Gargara their ABCs."[57] Since Diotimos was known as a composer of epic works and epigrams and was probably at least a grammarian, Aratus's epigram was surely a joke that made fun of elementary teachers.[58] Nevertheless, it is likely that teachers conducting school in the open air were not an unfamiliar sight. This kind of informal accommodation probably existed since time immemorial. Thus on fifth-century Attic vases, a school is often defined by the presence of a tree beside school objects.[59]

Many primary teachers in Egypt may have set up school in the open air, with a large tree providing welcome shade—a familiar scene on today's campuses in the warmest days of spring. In Egypt, moreover, students often used writing materials such as broken vessels, which could be picked up anywhere outside where people threw them away. The British papyrologist J. G. Milne, on finding a group of clay sherds that contained school exercises that were all discolored in an unusual way, imagined that a schoolmaster of Thebes "had taught his classes in the open air near a rubbish heap, on which material for writing exercises might be obtained in plenty, to be thrown away again as soon as used."[60] But of course, this rather sensational interpretation is not necessary: it is more likely that a teacher provided his class with ostraca found in one spot. In Upper Egypt students also employed flakes or slices of white limestone for writing: did they have teachers who, like Diotimos, set up school "on the rocks"? For

[56] Dio Chrysostom 20.9–10. About teaching in the streets of Rome, see S. F. Bonner, "The Street-Teacher: An Educational Scene in Horace," *AJPh* 93 (1972): 509–28.

[57] See *Anth. Pal.* 11.437 and *SH* 392–395. Gargara is a mountainous site on the gulf of Adramythium.

[58] See Alan Cameron, *Callimachus and His Critics* (Princeton, 1995), 6–7. On jokes directed at elementary teachers, see below, p. 59.

[59] See Beck 1975: pls. 22.114 and 16.84.

[60] See J. G. Milne, "Relics of Graeco-Egyptian Schools," *JHS* 28 (1908): 121.

teachers who plied their trade outside, the term *chamaididaskalos*, "a teacher sitting on the ground," was an appropriate designation. This term appears for the first time in copies of Diocletian's *Edict of Prices* in the late third century with the Latin equivalent of *magister institutor litterarum*—that is, an elementary teacher—and after that it occurs in later writers and papyri.[61] This designation, which resurfaces from the late Roman period, codified an established situation in which elementary teaching was characterized by precarious conditions: lack of proper seating meant lack of external structures.

The term *chamaididaskalos* provides graphic evidence that elementary teachers in general were not endowed with the imposing chair that usually serves to identify teachers in visual representations. But a digression is useful at this point. In school scenes depicted on fifth-century B.C.E. Athenian vases, common iconographical motifs were followed in the representation of teachers and students: teachers were portrayed sitting on chairs, and students were shown standing in front of them. The most comprehensive of these school scenes appears on a Berlin cup by Douris (Figs. 1 and 2).[62] On the exterior of the cup, a bearded teacher sits on a high-backed chair holding a roll that is inscribed with a hexameter with a Homeric flavor; a boy is standing before the teacher, probably reciting by heart. On the other side appears another teacher: he looks younger, does not have the beard that was a symbol of seniority, and is sitting on a backless stool. He is probably an assistant teacher, a *hypodidaskalos*, and he is holding an open notebook of tablets that curiously resembles a modern laptop computer. A pupil—a boy standing in front of him—is waiting for the teacher to finish writing something on the tablet, perhaps the model of a text. This school scene is completed by the presence of tutors—pedagogues—overlooking the instruction. Variations of this scene on numerous Attic vases and cups all show that a chair was an indispensable motif in portraying a teacher, even more than the rod that male teachers used as an instrument of punishment. An amusing scene on

---

[61] See *Edict.Diocl.* 7.66 (ed. K. Lauffer), pp. 124–25; anecdote 61 in the *Philogelos* (ed. Thierfelder); Macarius *Sermones* 20.3.6.1 and 23.125.29; Troilus *Prolegomena in Hermogenis Artem rhetoricam* (Walz, *Rhetores Graeci*, vol. 6, III.23); *Scholia in Ecclesiazusas* (ed. Dübner) 809.2; *Scholia in Demosthenem* (ed. M. R. Dilts) 18.228.1; *Scholia in Nubes* (ed. Koster) 770c alpha 2; *P.Sorb.* II.69 p. 63 n. 63: Cribiore 1996a: 163.

[62] See *ARV* 283, no. 47; Immerwahr 1964: 18–19 and note 3 with bibliography; Beck 1975: pl. 10, 53–54; Harris 1989: fig. 3. A. D. Booth, "Douris' Cup and the Stages of Schooling in Classical Athens," *EMC* 19 (1985): 275–80.

Figures 1–2.   School scenes on a vase from fifth-century Athens (Douris cup, 490–480 B.C.E.).

Figure 3.   Playing school: a scene on an Attic cup shows two
boys with tablets and a papyrus roll moving toward the "teacher"
(ca. 460 B.C.E.).

Figure 4.   Early Byzantine tablet with bronze handle: verses from the *Iliad*.

a cup by a follower of Douris that makes fun of a school situation, for
instance, shows on the interior a boy going to school, holding by the
handle a notebook of tablets that resembles a modern briefcase (Fig. 3;
and see Fig. 4).[63] On the exterior of the cup, two other boys are proceeding
to school: one is holding a book roll and the other tablets. These boys
move toward the sitting figure of another, who has a rod in his left hand

[63] *ARV* 524 no. 25; Immerwahr 1964: 21; Beck 1975: pl. 11, 58, 59, 60. See p. 154.

and holds on to his chair with the right: the boy is "playing teacher" and is sitting on the symbol of his power.

The same iconographical motif used to depict male teachers can sometimes be identified in scenes that show women as protagonists. A young woman, for instance, is depicted in the women's quarters: she sits on a chair holding out a book roll, while another figure—a boy reciting—stands before her (see Figs. 5 and 6).[64] This woman, who is represented as too young to be the boy's mother, looks like the female equivalent of the beardless instructor on the Douris cup. Girls playing and holding flowers and fillets appear on the other side. Another tantalizing representation that one is tempted to identify as a "school scene" located in a domestic setting appears on a vase of the Hermitage Museum (Fig. 7).[65] Whereas in the scene on the top of the vase, a child's punishment takes place at the hands of a woman who is hitting a young boy with a sandal, the learning situation depicted on the bottom shows a woman sitting on a particularly imposing chair: she is listening as a girl reads from a book roll, while another girl is perhaps reciting, and a third girl moves toward the group, holding an open notebook of tablets. The mandatory presence of a chair continued to identify male teachers in later art in scenes that appear in Roman sarcophagi of the imperial period: teachers are always portrayed as sitting, while their pupils—boys and girls—are standing.[66]

It should be noted, on the other hand, that in the visual evidence mentioned above, the educational levels of students and teachers are not always clear, and no pupil is unambiguously portrayed as receiving the rudiments. Chairs, *thronoi*, are often associated with male teachers outside primary education in the literary sources.[67] It is thus conceivable that the presence of chairs was mostly associated with the more stable conditions of schooling beyond the elementary level. As a rule, in fact, open-air accommodations did not apply to advanced education, which needed less precarious and distracting settings and happily did without the company of dogs and goats that roamed freely outside. Grammarians and rhetors used the accommodations that their personal circumstances afforded them. The teacher Didymos mentioned above probably gathered his pu-

[64] See Immerwahr 1973: 144–45, fig. 1, plates 31.4 and 32.

[65] Beck 1975: pl. 51, 268, and pl. 75, 372. Cf. also Beck 1975: pl. 74, 366, and pl. 69, 351.

[66] See Marrou 1937: 27–45.

[67] See in Plato *Prt.* 315c, Hippias sitting on an imposing chair as he gives a lecture surrounded by his pupils sitting on benches, and the formidable portrait of a teacher of rhetoric in Libanius *Chria* 3 (Foerster vol. 8).

Figures 5–6.   Athenian cup: sitting woman with a book roll listens to a boy
reciting; girls are playing on the other side (ca. 460 B.C.E.).

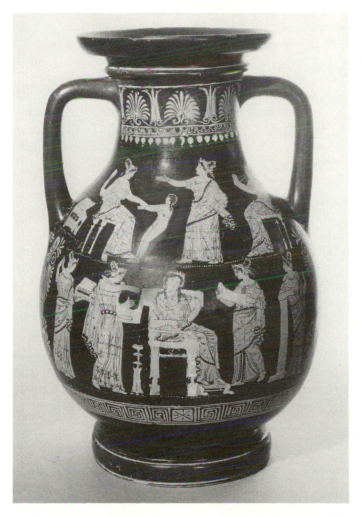

Figure 7.   Athenian vase: on top, a woman punishes a child
with a sandal; on the bottom, women with rolls and tablets move
toward a sitting woman who is listening.

pils in a rented room or even in his own residence, since he had just arrived
in Alexandria from the country. Much later, the grammarian Horapollon,
who was a distinguished teacher and also taught at levels more advanced
than grammar school, may have rented a private room or may have even
used a public space.[68] In a papyrus, the school of Horapollon is said to

[68] See above, and below, Chapter 2.

have met "by the academies," an uncertain location, apparently in a prominent place in the city. In Alexandria the remains of a limestone building dating from the time of Horapollon and located next to the theater and the baths have been identified as perhaps being the site of a school.[69] A central auditorium with the dais for the teacher (or speaker) and seats all around is flanked by two sets of smaller rooms provided with seats. The design of this building is unique and suggestive, but it may not have catered exclusively to educational needs; it may also have served as a lecture hall. In any case, a range of possible scenarios is suggested by the literary evidence. Thus, the disparate accommodations used by Libanius in his career were apparently correlated to his success. When he was a young and popular teacher of rhetoric in Nicomedia, Libanius was entitled to hold classes anywhere, even in the baths (*Or.* 1.55). But his position became less secure when he moved to Antioch, and at first he had to use his own house to teach the fifteen students whom he had brought with him. Even though moving to another room on the fringe of the square immediately brought him more students, he was not satisfied, since the other sophists who kept classes in the temple of the Muses were far more successful.[70] But, in his own account, his earnest address to the Muse Calliope was conclusive: in a matter of a few days he was able to establish a school in the City Hall and became the official sophist of Antioch.[71] Libanius's vicissitudes show that teachers of advanced education were at the mercy of the available accommodations and had to provide for themselves almost as much as the humble primary teachers.

THE GYMNASIUM

The question of where education took place brings us to the delicate problem of the role of the gymnasium as an academic institution in Egypt. Starting from the fourth century B.C.E. in Athens, gymnasia were not only places of athletic activity but also centers of intellectual pursuits. In Athens, philosophers brought their followers together in the Academy and the Lyceum. Isocrates mentions with indignation that other teachers of lower standing gathered their pupils there "discussing the poets, espe-

---

[69] B. Tkaczow, *Topography of Ancient Alexandria* (Warsaw, 1993), 99; Bowman 1990: 223 fig. 141; J. McKenzie, *Roman Alexandria*, forthcoming.

[70] Though this was an actual location, Libanius often calls his own school *Mouseia*, e.g., *Ep.* 37.5.4 and *Or.* 11.139.7.

[71] See *Or.* 1.101–4 and *Ep.* 88.

cially Hesiod and Homer, saying nothing original about them, but merely reciting their verses and repeating from memory the cleverest things that others had said about them in the past."[72] But it is particularly from the third century B.C.E. on that inscriptions testify that gymnasia were centers of intellectual and educational activity in Attica and in several parts of the Greek world. Numerous inscriptions in Hellenistic gymnasia preserve lists of victors in *agones*—contests not only in gymnastics but also in poetry or other academic subjects—and occasionally the inscriptions themselves testify that teachers tested students by examination in the gymnasia.[73] Moreover, gymnasia hosted conferences and displays by local or itinerant scholars and poets. Nevertheless, it is not entirely certain that regular educational instruction went on in the gymnasia,[74] and it is particularly doubtful that they were centers for advanced education, the equivalent of modern universities.[75]

In the Ptolemaic period, gymnasia existed in Egypt not only in large centers but also in the most hellenized villages, wherever Greeks established communities of sufficient size. In the Roman period, on the other hand, they appear to be present mostly in the nome capitals—*metropoleis*. In the gymnasium, local male youths received athletic and military training, and the Greek members of the elite gathered to socialize and to pursue intellectual activities.[76] Festivals with gymnastics displays and celebrations of every sort were held around gymnasia.[77] Membership in the "metropolitan class" was granted to individuals who could show Greek ancestry on both maternal and paternal sides, and parents belonging to this class registered their children with the gymnasium officials as soon as they reached fourteen years of age. Though most of these applications refer to boys, two, both originating from Oxyrhynchos in the third century, show families registering girls and trying to secure for them a privileged status.[78] We do not know whether this registration automatically brought these girls participation in the activities of the gymnasium as it did for boys. In the capital and in the *metropoleis*, the gymnasium was always an impos-

---

[72] See Isocrates *Panath.* 18; cf. also 33.

[73] See, e.g., *SIG* 578.34, where it is said that the elementary teachers who used to test the children in the gymnasium were to change location.

[74] Nilsson (1955: 1–29) considers gymnasia academic institutions.

[75] Delorme (1960: 316–24) is in favor of the idea that gymnasia were the equivalent of modern universities. Contra, Harris 1989: 134–35.

[76] See Legras 1999: 208–17.

[77] See Perpillou-Thomas 1986.

[78] *P.Corn.* I.18 and *P.Oxy.* XLIII.3136. Cf. *P.Ups.Frid.* 6 introduction and *P.Petaus* 1–2 introduction.

ing building with lecture halls, baths, and ball-courts, on which considerable sums of money were expended for works of maintenance and improvement. In the third century C.E. in Antinoe, for instance, where excavations unearthed the magnificent remains of a gymnasium, the roofs of the colonnades and entrances were decorated with gold leaf.[79] In the first century C.E., repairs were done to "the great exedra" of the gymnasium of the large village of Aphroditopolis, which had more than one of these large halls that were used for conferences.[80] Everywhere the gymnasium existed, it was the focus of the cultural life of a community. But were the Egyptian gymnasia real academic institutions? No evidence supports such an assumption: no libraries or areas that could be identified as classrooms have been found in their perimeters.[81] Moreover, there are no documents that disclose how the gymnasia functioned, even though gymnasiarchs, their leaders, are often mentioned: their title, however, is used as a status designation, and nothing is known of the specific duties they performed. It should be noted that women also may have served in this office: two examples—though not completely unambiguous—are known for Egypt, and women gymnasiarchs (*gymnasiarchis*) are present in Cyrene and particularly in various localities of Asia Minor.[82] At any rate, the location of a gymnasium in a particular place may serve as a hint that a school was situated in its vicinity. The school of the grammarian Horapollon, for instance, which was located "by the academies," may have taken advantage of a well-frequented neighborhood.

THE STRUCTURE AND ORGANIZATION OF SCHOOLS

Lack of uniformity characterized not only the ways in which schools in antiquity were set up and the more or less informal places where they were situated, but also the way teaching was structured from bottom to top, the identities of the teachers offering various layers of instruction, and the internal organization of the class. Ancient schools were knowledge-oriented and provided a rather uniform instruction, which was distinguished in recognizable intellectual steps. Though the content of the primary level of education might have depended to a certain extent on

[79] See Bowman 1990: 143–44; and *P.Köln.* I.52.

[80] See *Mél. Masp.* II, p. 33, line 24.

[81] See Cribiore 1996a: 19–20.

[82] *P.Amh.* II.64 and *SB* XVI.12235. L. Casarico, "Donne ginnasiarco," *ZPE* 48 (1982): 117–23; van Bremen 1996.

local circumstances, knowledge provided at higher levels was unfailingly consistent: students at the grammatical or rhetorical stage anywhere in the East would have been easily able to compare their work. It was probably the homogeneity of the intellectual contents that brought about attempts in the past to resolve a conflicting evidence of schooling by imposing a single organizational model with a strict distinction between primary, secondary, and rhetorical schools, headed by their respective instructors. The fact that the literary sources seem to endorse such a division is not particularly binding: the ancient writers allude more to the contents than to the actual organization of teaching, and they did not have any interest in nuances of schooling and in arrangements that concerned the lower classes and the periphery versus the great centers of learning. Only recently has the traditional scheme been challenged. It has been successfully argued that in Rome during the first century C.E., a two-track system prevailed that served different segments of the population: while schools of elementary letters provided a basic literacy to slaves and freeborn individuals of the lower classes, schools of liberal studies offered a more refined education to children of the upper classes who either received the first elements at home or entered right away into a grammarian's school that also tendered instruction in basic letters.[83] The presence of this socially segmented arrangement of schools can be verified in the great cities of the Roman Empire, from which most of our literary sources derive.[84] But we should beware of regularly replacing one inflexible model of the educational system with another that is only apparently less rigid. This new interpretation of some of the literary sources is particularly valid insofar as it shows that the organization of schooling was not monolithic. On the other hand, both in large centers and primarily in the periphery, there must have been situations that did not follow the two principal models of schooling. The literary sources and the papyri, in fact, testify to much variety in school structure in accordance with situational circumstances, convenience to parents, and availability of teachers.

The school of Libanius in Antioch, for instance, exemplifies a schooling system that corresponds even less to the traditional scheme and that perhaps existed in some large cities, such as Alexandria, where successful instructors acted as powerful magnets. This school, which provided instruction only to male students and primarily at the rhetorical level, sometimes seems to have addressed the needs of boys at the primary and gram-

[83] Booth 1979a: 1–14; and 1979b: 11–19.

[84] Kaster 1983: 323–46. The existence of this arrangement appears in sources from the first to the sixth century C.E.; Kaster 1988: 24–25.

matical stage. Libanius's own son learned the rudiments at the hands of teachers who worked as grammarians in the school, and other students in their early teens engaged in grammatical studies with the same instructors, who prepared them to enter the rhetorical course proper.[85] Thus, a student such as Bassianos studied grammar and the poets with the Egyptian grammarian Kleobulos, who, in the words of Libanius, taught him to "move his wings" (*Ep.* 155). An organization with all three levels of schooling combined must have been atypical, however. The *Hermeneumata*, which sometimes show incongruities and conflations of various scenes that are useful in suggesting different arrangements, present three models of a school: a primary school where initial notions of grammar were also given; a school that imparted full elementary and grammatical instruction; and a grammar school that also catered to some elementary students and to older pupils who started rhetoric.[86] This last type is only apparently similar to Libanius's school: whereas in Libanius's school, the first two levels were preliminary to learning advanced rhetorical skills, the third model described in the *Hermeneumata* is essentially a grammar school where some older male students started to read the works of orators such as Demosthenes and wrote preliminary rhetorical exercises. It is in a school of this type that Augustine received a smattering of rhetorical instruction.[87]

Though the school exercises of Greco-Roman Egypt are in general devoid of any frame concerning their creation, occasionally they offer some information through their content, showing that the boundaries between the functions of the elementary schoolmaster and the grammarian were porous and sometimes nonexistent, and one single school imparted instruction to students of different levels. An Egyptian papyrus roll of the third century B.C.E., which is usually called *Livre d' écolier,* "a student's book," from the title of the edition, offers the clearest example that grammarians sometimes also imparted instruction in primary letters.[88] The first exercises on the roll, which address students at primary levels who did

[85] See Wolf 1952: 69–70; Petit 1956: 84–88, 139–40. Cf. Libanius *Ep.* 625 and 678. That Libanius calls grammarians *grammatistai* instead of the usual *grammatikoi* is indicative of the lack of precise boundaries between different levels of teaching.

[86] See Dionisotti 1982: 98–99, ll. 18–29; Goetz 1892: 225–26; Dionisotti 1982: 100–101, ll. 30–39.

[87] Vössing (1992), who also shows Augustine providing instruction to children at lower levels of education in his initial career.

[88] See Cribiore 1996a: no. 379: it probably served a teacher's need rather than a student's. The provenance of this papyrus is unknown, but the level of instruction implied probably refers to a city school.

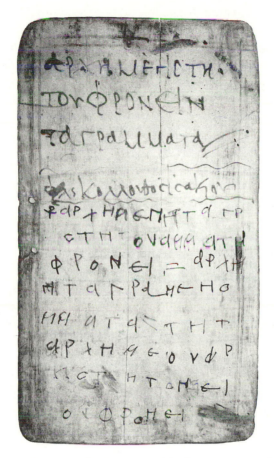

Figure 8.   An early Byzantine tablet from Antinoopolis:
a teacher's model with a maxim and the copy of the
student underneath.

not know how to read and write, are followed in regular progression by
more advanced ones. The roll ends with a series of passages that are hard
to understand, full of abstruse and difficult words and constructions—
exercises that were good stepping-stones for children of the elite, whose
language was shaped by the grammarian.

An early Byzantine tablet shows that the situation was unchanged many
centuries later, and that grammarians did not shrink from offering primary education (Fig. 8). This tablet, which was found in Antinoopolis,
contains a maxim written as a model by the teacher Flavius Kollouthos:

"Letters are the greatest beginning of understanding."[89] The teacher's own letters stand out: they are very large, graceful, and easy to read. This teacher then signed his model, perhaps in order to show the student that an exercise needed to be identified.[90] The rest of the tablet's surface is occupied by the wavering letters of a pupil who appears to be far from "understanding" and only able to copy characters that did not yet make much sense: he painfully reproduces the maxim several times in two distinct columns—perhaps imitating the *mise en page* of a papyrus book— and brutally truncates the words, without showing any knowledge of syllabic division. The honorific title Flavius, which distinguishes the teacher who wrote the model, shows that he was at least a grammarian, imparting the first rudiments of learning to a child of privilege.[91]

At a later time, in the sixth century, the teaching activity of the lawyer and poet Dioskoros of Aphroditopolis is again evidence that education primarily responded to need. Among his documents and poems, several papyri were found that testify that Dioskoros fulfilled a teaching role at various levels. These texts include metrological tables (sometimes associated with primary education); conjugations, the *Iliad*, and elementary Homeric exegesis at the grammatical level; and preliminary rhetorical exercises and Isocrates at the rhetorical level.[92] It is impossible to know— and not very important to a degree—whether Dioskoros was the teacher of his own children when he resided in Antinoe or whether, on his return to his hometown, he taught some children of the elite of Aphroditopolis: as a man of culture he might have naturally fulfilled that role.[93]

It is not easy to know in every case whether the evidence considered above presupposes the existence of a real two-track system in which education was neatly diversified on a social basis, or whether these—as in the case of Dioskoros—were all situations dictated by special circumstances. All these exercises, at any rate, probably originated in large centers, which could provide and support a variety of specialized teachers. In Egypt, *metropoleis* such as Alexandria, Oxyrhynchos, Hermopolis, Antinoopolis, and Herakleopolis, and exceptionally large villages such as Aphroditopolis, offered secondary instruction. As a rule, only one grammarian

[89] See Cribiore 1996a: no. 160.

[90] Many exercises, in fact, display the signature of the student who wrote them. On names of students appearing in exercises, see Cribiore 1996a: Appendix 2.

[91] On the title Flavius, see below, p. 61.

[92] See Fournet 1999: 688–90, and passim. A Greek-Coptic glossary also addressed learners.

[93] Cf. below, p. 106.

could be found in these centers at a time: only Alexandria, and Hermopolis in the fifth century, where two grammarians are known, are the exceptions. Teachers of rhetoric were even more confined to large centers: small towns could not supply a steady stream of pupils and could not fund a chair.

It is in the villages and towns of the Egyptian countryside that we should expect to find a variety of informal schooling, since local teaching was a function of need, expectations, resources, and teachers' inclinations. Far from the large educational centers, a fluid understanding of literacy and letters would sometimes raise the substance of elementary teaching to approach the instruction normally given in secondary schools. Thus, in two Egyptian towns, Karanis and Theadelphia, which would not support a grammarian, some students wrote exercises that traditionally belonged in a grammar school: copies of grammatical treatises and lists of difficult Homeric words, which were rendered into a more current form of Greek.[94] Two different scenarios are equally plausible—both strategies devised to avoid sending one's male children away to study too soon: either itinerant teachers were hired by upper-class families to impart some sophisticated skills to their offspring, or local elementary teachers were able to stretch their teaching functions to serve the needs of privileged students.

The latter seems to be the case of the primary teacher Melankomas mentioned above, who appears in a private letter sent by Sarapion to his friend Ptolemaios (*SB* 111.7268):

> Sarapion greets his dearest Ptolemaios. Since you are my friend in the Arsinoite and I rely on you alone because of the affection that you have felt toward me for a long time, I have to ask you something in this letter. I am thoroughly in anguish because of some problems of geometry that I was given and, with your help, I would like not to be ignorant in this matter. Therefore, as I asked you in person, now I also beg you to give the man who brings you this letter that very papyrus about which you talked to me, out of your friendly feelings. Feel assured that this favor will not be in vain, but I will hold it in due account for when you will need me. Do then what you think is right. I hope you are well.

This letter was sent from the Herakleopolite nome, where Sarapion lived, to a village or town in the Arsinoite, and precisely—as the address specifies—to the school of the elementary teacher Melankomas, which Ptole-

---

[94] See Cribiore 1996a: nos. 330, 345, 359, 362.

maios apparently was still attending. The two lads were friends from school times: they were—to use an expression coined centuries before by the Greek writer Lysias—"friends by education."[95] Apparently Sarapion had moved, perhaps to pursue a more advanced education in a larger center: he was in fact studying geometry, a discipline traditionally associated with secondary schooling and distinguished from arithmetic, which was the province of the elementary teacher.[96] Sarapion's handwriting, visible in the final greeting, is minute and fast, and reveals a considerable familiarity with the pen.[97] The exact circumstances are unknown, but for some reason Sarapion, who was oppressed by the typical anguish of the conscientious student, urgently needed a certain book of geometry. It seems likely that Melankomas, the primary teacher who kept this book in his school, was an elementary teacher whose functions were somewhat fluid.

The relatively low number of students at the same level in a given school and the lack of sharp distinctions between educational levels call for further reflections on the organization of classes. When schools included students of different levels and abilities, it seems unlikely that they occupied separate rooms. In the version of the *Hermeneumata* quoted at the beginning of this chapter, elementary and secondary students are shown as working together in one room. Even though the principal instructors are the teacher and an assistant teacher, the *hypodidaskalos*, older and more able students also discharge some teaching functions by dictating a text and helping the primary students learn their syllables. Other versions of these schoolbooks that present novices together with advanced students who were learning rhetoric point to common spaces used in education. Since in antiquity the concept of *paradeigma*, "example," governed family life and intellectual pursuits, this school structure, where more capable students contributed to the success of the enterprise, was partly dictated by the desire to exploit competition among the students, as well as their imitative skills. In antiquity, age differences were not emphasized as they are today.[98] An indistinct period of immaturity led to the time when a youth was finally accepted as a full member of society. It is also possible, moreover, that the ages of some of the students at different levels who worked together in the same environment were not sharply differentiated, since there were not definite age limits for admittance to a certain level.

[95] Lysias (ca. 459–380 B.C.E.) 20.11 (*For Polystratus*), *ek paideias philos*.
[96] Cf. Petron. *Sat.* 58.7; Marrou 1975, 2: 84–85; Clarke 1971: 45–52.
[97] The rest of the letter was penned by a professional scribe according to a common usage.
[98] Kleijwegt 1991: 88–123.

The school of Libanius, which was divided into five classes, called *symmoriai*, accommodated students in an open space, one large lecture hall.[99] This was also the arrangement in the school of Ulpianus of Ascalon, the old teacher of Libanius, and in the school of Zenobius, Libanius's predecessor in Antioch (*Or.* 36.10–11). To serve the needs of his crowd— "herd" (*agelē*) or "flock" (*poimnion*)—Libanius also employed assistant teachers who prepared students to enter the top class, which was taught personally by him. Information about the size of this school is especially welcome because no other such evidence exists in the Greek world. Apparently the number of Libanius's students oscillated at the different moments of his career: though he had eighty pupils in Constantinople, the number went down to fifteen when he had just arrived in Antioch (*Or.* 1.37 and 101; *Ep.* 405) but rose again to about eighty per year when he became public teacher of rhetoric.[100] Repeatedly Libanius calls his school *choros* and dubs as *koryphaios*, "chorus leader," the older student who represented his classmates and could even do some teaching when the teacher was sick.[101]

A confirmation that ancient schools of any level were not usually divided into separate classes comes from the school exercises of Greco-Roman Egypt. Even though, as a rule, students did their work on individual material such as a piece of papyrus, an ostracon, or a tablet, occasionally pupils of various levels of ability shared some writing materials. In the first or second centuries B.C.E., for instance, when the student Maron wrote and signed a passage from a lost tragedy of Aeschylus, on the left side of the same papyrus one of his schoolmates, who had just learned to wield a pen, copied a few verses from Homer.[102] Both students studied together in Oxyrhynchos or in its vicinity, in a school where learning the poets was a priority from the start. Students, moreover, often shared notebooks made of several tablets bound together, which did not belong to them but were the common property of a school.[103] A late Roman or early Byzantine notebook of five waxed tablets, for instance, displays the work of novices writing alphabets and practicing their names, and the writing exercises of students of superior ability—perhaps apprentice

---

[99] See F. Schemmel, "Die Hochschule von Konstantinopel im IV-ten Jahrh.," *NJBB* 22 (1908): 147–68. See also Petit 1956: 93–94.

[100] See Petit 1956: 84.

[101] See ibid.: 21–22; cf., e.g., Libanius *Ep.* 1408: the student Basilides is "leader."

[102] See Cribiore 1996a: no. 250.

[103] On this, see below, p. 157.

scribes—who copied in fluent letters parts of documents.[104] All these students worked together in a school that offered diversified instruction that depended on the local notion of what constituted literacy.

Uniformity and consistency did not characterize the organization of ancient schools even in large urban environments. But particularly in towns and villages that were away from the main centers of education, teachers did not follow fixed schemes; rather, they catered to the population according to its needs and their own capabilities. Far from conforming to prearranged educational models, teachers aimed at leading each student up to the level of literacy demanded by that pupil's place in the social and economic pyramid and his or her future role in the community.

[104] See Cribiore 1996a: no. 400, of unknown provenance.

The Teachers and Their Burden

Hermotimos, in the dialogue of Lucian mentioned in the Introduction, is an advanced student struggling to climb the steep hill of education. By his own disconsolate admission, he is in need of help: he is still down in the foothills, because the road is hard and slippery. His friend Lycinos has the solution: he should not worry, because Hermotimos's teacher can give him a hand, or, even better, "he can let down his own teaching from the top like Zeus's golden rope in Homer, and can indeed pull and lift you up to himself and excellence. He made the climb long ago."[1] In every age and at every level of instruction, teachers have had a principal role in guiding students up the hill of learning. But were they always the helpful figures who had reached a secure position of power and generously shared with students the secrets of knowledge? The image of the golden rope in Homer is far from comforting; indeed, it is fraught with danger. In the passage from the *Iliad*, Zeus is menacing the gods: if they disobey him, he will hurl them down to the Underworld; if they attempt to reach Olympus by climbing on a golden rope, he will pull on the rope and shake them, together with earth and sea, and let everything dangle in space. Lucian must have been aware that the world of education had its undertones of struggle.

The most obvious aim of most of this chapter is to investigate the evidence concerning teachers and their social and economic positions, trying to incorporate the documentation from Greco-Roman Egypt into a coherent picture. A student in antiquity met a number of teachers along the path of education. While the academic and moral instruction of tutors—pedagogues—extended from the early years through adolescence for both girls and boys, a course of education in letters was supervised by the primary teacher, the grammarian, and the rhetor. Throughout the Greco-Roman world, education—and a teacher's social standing—was structured according to a basic pyramidal scheme, but, as was shown in the previous chapter, the terms designating the instructors overseeing each stage were not always the same, the division into three neatly distinguished levels was not always so rigid, and the same teacher might be in

---

[1] Lucian *Hermot.* 3. Cf. *Iliad* 8.19–26.

charge of more than one level. Teachers of every level are mentioned in the papyri, and some of them are identified by name. Not all of them were male: eight out of eighty-seven references concern women teachers.[2] Unfortunately, though, most of these references say little or nothing about the teaching activities of these individuals: they may appear in tax registers, in accounts of payments whose purpose is not specified, in contracts of sale, or in receipts that provide some information about them as functioning members of a community. More helpful in delineating the role of a teacher in a society where many people did not have direct access to literacy are those documents where some teachers acted as notaries and signers for people who could not write.[3] But it is particularly when teachers appear in private letters, or, more rarely, in petitions, that their identity as teachers and their social circumstances are illuminated.

This chapter also implicitly addresses another set of questions that will be dealt with directly in the last part but that should be kept in mind from the beginning: the relative position of power of ancient teachers, the limitations of that power, the ways in which it affected the student-teacher relationship, and the nature of the final message that education communicated to the student. Power relations have always been central to educational processes, which are tied to a project of transformation of an individual and have generated an apparent continuity in pedagogical practices over time and across places.[4] The authority of teachers naturally resides in the fact that they are keepers of knowledge, and their right to monitor students, evaluate them, or exclude them has usually been recognized in educational settings. After the attacks on teachers' rule in post-1960s educational politics, today there are attempts to revive a traditional image of the Teacher and to restore pedagogical authority, together with a heightened emphasis on teacher accountability and control of teachers' work. Moral fervor and nostalgia would like to resurrect times when learning meant doing exactly what the Teacher said, and when children were silent and listened to the Teacher dispense knowledge.[5] Ancient education, which consisted of an accumulation of systematic rules administered in order, identified a teacher as the individual who had the key to interpret some or all of those rules. As always, moreover, a teacher manifested

[2] Cf. Cribiore 1996a: 161–70, with a list of references.

[3] See below, pp. 60–61.

[4] See J. M. Gore, "Disciplining Bodies: On the Continuity of Power Relations in Pedagogy," in Popkewitz and Brennan 1998: 231–51.

[5] See B. Green, "Born-Again Teaching? Governmentality, 'Grammar,' and Public Schooling," in Popkewitz and Brennan 1998: 173–204.

his or her authority not only through grading, evaluating, inspecting, or disciplining, but also in subtler ways, through praising and rewarding. Squeezed between teachers' and parents' overbearing control, ancient students were in some respects the casualties of this system. And yet, the picture is one of nuances. Students were not only inert targets: through education they assimilated mechanisms of authority and learned to become elements of its articulation. They learned to monitor each other, inevitably mimicking the power relations that were in play. At the same time, teachers who exercised control from the top of the hill experienced the effects of parental authority, unstable jobs, and uncertain economic circumstances.

THE PEDAGOGUE: TUTORING IN AND OUTSIDE THE FAMILY

Pedagogues were first entrusted with children's upbringing within the family when the children left the arms of their nurses. The authority these figures exercised over young children of both sexes and over male adolescents who studied away from home was an extension of that of parents, but when pedagogues were not under families' direct control, their sphere of influence became wider and their authority more independent. They were most often employed by upper-class families, but at least in Rome, the practice of using pedagogues was sometimes extended to other social levels.[6] Ancient representations on vases and terracottas of the classical and Hellenistic periods often portray a pedagogue as an old, bearded man who takes a young boy to school or reads a book with him.[7] The epigraphic evidence in the Roman world indicates that it was not unusual for pedagogues to supervise girls as well as boys, but that it was invariably men who discharged this function. The papyri, on the other hand, preserve a single reference to a female pedagogue.[8] From Roman Oxyrhynchos comes a petition from a woman who cared for a young slave, Peina, as a daughter and provided her with some education. But while this girl was on her way to a lesson in singing and other skills (*mathēmata*) accompanied by a freedwoman, her pedagogue, she was knocked down by a donkey driver, and her hand was hopelessly crushed.

[6] On the inscriptional evidence concerning pedagogues in Rome, see Bradley 1991: 37–75.
[7] See Beck 1975: e.g., pl. 12, 65, 66, 67; pl. 13, 71, 73, 74; pl. 15, 81, 82, 83.
[8] See *P.Oxy.* L.3555, first to second century C.E. Cf. below, p. 87.

Though historians of education most often associate pedagogues with the care they gave to young children,[9] their role extended beyond that: they functioned as links between students and families, supervised the process of learning, and provided a sense of balance and continuity as male youths progressed in their education. Most of the references to pedagogues in the papyri lack context but are useful testimonies that these tutors often served the needs of families in Greco-Roman Egypt. Some of the papyri, however, do illuminate the role that pedagogues exercised on upper-class male adolescents.

In the third century B.C.E., Zenon, who was the agent of Apollonios, the treasury minister of the king Ptolemy Philadelphos, provided for the education of his younger brother, Epharmostos. This young man, who had acquired a sophisticated education in Alexandria,[10] was assisted by a pedagogue, Styrax, who acted as a surrogate parent and followed Epharmostos when he moved to Philadelphia in his adult years.[11] Another pedagogue of servile background is praised in a papyrus letter written in the Roman period by a mother to her son Ptolemaios:[12]

> Do not hesitate to write to me about anything you might need. It grieved me to learn from the daughter of our *kathēgētēs* Diogenes that he sailed down, for I had no anxiety about him, knowing that he was going to take care of you to the best of his ability. I took care to send him a letter and ask about your health and learn what you are reading: he said that it was the sixth book. He also testified at length concerning your pedagogue. So, my son, now it is up to you and your pedagogue to take care that you go to a suitable teacher. . . . Salute your esteemed pedagogue Eros.

In Oxyrhynchos Ptolemaios was pursuing a secondary education. He was reading Book 6 of the *Iliad*[13] when his instructor, an itinerant tutor,[14] decided to depart, probably in search of more lucrative employment in Alexandria. Eros must have been in the service of Ptolemaios's family for a long time and may have taught him the rudiments. But what exactly were his functions now that Ptolemaios was not a child any more?

[9] Cf. Marrou 1975, 1: 217–18, and 2: 65–66.

[10] See *P.Col.Zen.* II.60. Cf. below, p. 188.

[11] See *P.Lond.* VII.2017.

[12] *P.Oxy.* VI.930. Cf. below, pp. 54 and 195.

[13] The reference to Homer's Book 6 is certainly to the *Iliad* rather than to the *Odyssey*, which was less read. Cf. below, pp. 194–97.

[14] On *kathēgētai*, see below.

The literary and epigraphic sources help reconstruct the background of this letter by showing that pedagogues, far from fading away during the education of an adolescent, were very much at center stage. In the fourth century, the Roman emperor Julian left an eloquent portrait of his pedagogue Mardonius in *Misopogon* (351a). Not only did Mardonius teach Julian such points of etiquette and decorum as walking in the street with head bent down—a cliché of a child's modest demeanor[15]—but he also had an academic role. Whenever he tried to dissuade his ward from the theater shows and spectacles that his friends loved, it was by way of examples taken from Homer: "Do you have a passion for horse races? There is one in Homer, very cleverly described. Take the book and study it. Do you hear your friends talking about dancers in pantomime? Leave them alone! Among the Phaeacians the youth dance in more manly fashion," and so on. He was also versed in philosophy and taught Julian to appreciate Plato, Socrates, Aristotle, and Theophrastus.

But it is primarily Libanius who shows how much influence pedagogues had on some of his students who came from abroad to attend his classes.[16] His feelings toward them are usually, but not always, positive. In a long letter to a father about the progress of his son Titianos, Libanius praises Marcellus, the boy's pedagogue, who followed his charge like a shadow and stimulated his love of learning (*Ep.* 44).[17] Oration 58, moreover, was composed to reproach some students who had treated a pedagogue roughly, tossing him up and down on a rug: the ideal pedagogue was a "guardian of youth in flower" who protected young men from lovers and immorality, "barking like a dog against wolves" (7). But the function of pedagogues extended beyond moral protection. When classes were over at noon, they were in charge of assisting their pupils with homework, helping them memorize, giving them more exercises (9). Not only were they instrumental in the academic success of their wards, but, when teachers changed towns, or students were not satisfied with the quality of the instruction, one of their tasks was to help their charges choose a new teacher. But this was a sensitive issue that brought to the fore Libanius's occasional ambivalent feelings toward tutors. He thought that some of them abused their influential positions: they demanded to be invited to

[15] Cf. Xenophon *Lac.* 3.4; a comic fragment Kock 366; Plutarch *Mor.* 439f; Lucian *Amores* 44.

[16] Two, for instance, came from Egypt; about countries of provenance of students of Libanius, see Petit 1956: 114.

[17] On Titianos, cf. below, pp. 102–3 and 121.

dinner, to have their own benches in class,[18] and even asked teachers for money, threatening to withdraw their wards (*Or.* 34.30).

In Oxyrhynchos, therefore, the pedagogue Eros was in a powerful position. In her village, Ptolemaios's mother could rely only on letters to make her voice heard. When young men left home to pursue a secondary education, parents were at the mercy of the news that their children chose to send them and had to safeguard themselves. A parent appearing in another letter, Theon, "high priest of the Nile," Neilos's father, sent Neilos and one of his brothers to study in Alexandria in the company of two slaves: one was a pedagogue named Isidoros; the other was supposed to work in order to cover the expenses of the boys with his salary.[19] When the latter started to cause trouble, Isidoros shackled him and helped the young men get through the crisis. For families of high social status who could afford to send sons away to obtain a better education, pedagogues were some guarantee that the needs of their loved ones were attended to. But this was not always the case: without direct control, abuses of power and tyrannical behavior were always possible.

TEACHERS OF THE FIRST EDUCATIONAL CIRCLE

Though pedagogues could leave an indelible mark on the character and intellectual growth of the children and adolescents they supervised, they still represented an extension of the family. The first teacher a student met who did not have a direct link with the family circle was an elementary teacher—or, in any case, a teacher who fulfilled this role.[20] The goals of education at this level, and pupils' attainments, were modest,[21] but in a society where most people could not read and write, the teacher of elementary letters had an important role, since he or she equipped students with skills that already formed some base of distinction and had some practical value. Many of the references to teachers (*didaskaloi*) found in the papyri must be to elementary instructors, but judging the significance of the evidence is not always easy. A prerequisite is a proper evaluation

---

[18] Libanius *Or.* 43.9: *bathrou tychein* (342.21). The *bathron* was the chair reserved to students. Originally pedagogues stayed outside of the class and waited in a room called the *paidagogeion*; see, e.g., Demosthenes 18.258.

[19] See *P.Oxy.* XVIII.2190; Rea 1993. See below, pp. 57–58 and 121–23.

[20] Grammarians sometimes taught elementary letters.

[21] Cf. below, Chapter 6.

of the terminology used to designate primary teachers within and outside Egypt. In the Greek-speaking world, several terms distinguished an elementary teacher: *grammatistēs*, *grammatodidaskalos*, and *didaskalos*. The first term was not in use in Egypt, perhaps because of its ambiguity, and the significance of the other two designations is also not clear in every instance.[22] Thus in two Ptolemaic papyri of the second century B.C.E., the word *grammatodidaskalos*, which apparently exactly defined the functions of a teacher of elementary letters, refers to Egyptian scribes of Demotic documents, who did not belong to the world of Greek education but may have fulfilled some teaching role in a scribal school.[23] The general designation *didaskalos*, "teacher," is particularly vague, since it also applied to those individuals who took young apprentices into their service and taught them different skills; such "teachers" did not receive any pay because they could take advantage of the apprentice's work.[24] Through apprenticeship, young people of a social status lower than that of those who obtained a liberal education learned the role they would have in the working world. It should be noted, in any case, that when the term *didaskalos* refers to apprenticeship, it is defined by a word that specifies the area of instruction, such as "weaver" or "hairdresser." A few women are also identified in the papyri as "teachers," either by the term *didaskalos* with a feminine article (*hē didaskalos*, "lady teacher") or by abbreviated forms of it with the same meaning, such as *deskalē* or *hē deskalos*. These references deserve close attention, and I shall examine them in the following chapter. For now it suffices to say that, though they usually appear without much context, it is reasonable to suppose that these women imparted elementary and not more advanced instruction. But the bare term *didaskalos* applied to a male teacher is ambiguous: since it can refer to teachers at various stages, each occurrence needs to be evaluated carefully.

---

[22] At least from the second century C.E., *grammatistēs* sometimes also designated the grammarian. See Aelius Aristides *Or.* 28.26, p. 150.8 Keil; and Libanius, who always avoided calling the grammarian *grammatikos*. Wolf (1952: 34–35) mentions a few examples in authors earlier than or contemporary with Libanius. Kaster (1988: 447–50) collects the evidence for late antiquity. Festugière (1959: 105 and n. 6) believes that also in ancient times the *grammatistēs* was the exegete of the poets and, in support of this, cites Plato *Laws* 7.809e–812b.

[23] *See P.Ryl.* IV.572 and *BGU* VI.1214; cf. Maehler 1983: 196–97; S. P. Vleeming, "Some Notes on Demotic Scribal Training in the Ptolemaic Period," *Proceedings of the Twentieth International Congress of Papyrology* (Copenhagen, 1994), 185–87.

[24] See Bergamasco 1995; Bradley 1991: 106–12. On apprenticeship, see below, Chapter 3.

Letters found among the papers of the businessman Zenon provide suitable examples.[25] In the period to which the letters refer, 257–256 B.C.E., Zenon resided in Alexandria but often traveled around the country. One of his Alexandrian friends, Hierokles, kept Zenon informed about his business in the metropolis. It is Hierokles who writes Zenon a partly preserved letter whose subject is the education of Pyrrhos, a boy who was to be sent to another *didaskalos*.[26] This letter also mentions ambiguously a payment in drachmai to a certain grammarian. Three more letters of Hierokles concern this protégé of Zenon, who apparently received athletic training in addition to a regular education:[27]

> You wrote to me about Pyrrhos, to train him if we know for certain that he will win, but if not, that it should not happen both that he is distracted from his studies and that useless expense is incurred. Well, far from being distracted from his lessons, he is making good progress in them, and in his other studies as well. As for *knowing for certain*, only the gods would know; but Ptolemaios says that he will be far superior to the existing competitors, despite the fact that at the moment he lags behind them, because they have got a long start and we have only just begun training. You should also know that Ptolemaios does not charge any fees, as do the other trainers, but simply hopes to win you the crown in return for the kindnesses that you, when a complete stranger, volunteered to him and are continuing concerning the palaestra.

The educational ideals that this letter reveals are far from those praised by "Just Argument" in the *Clouds* (961–83), which the comic poet Aristophanes composed in 423 B.C.E.; there, training in the gymnasium was represented as the principal foundation of the old educational system.[28] Not only was Pyrrhos trained to win glory for his patron rather than for personal excellence, but Zenon worried that physical training might distract the boy from mental gymnastics. While Pyrrhos lived in a circle of educated people—Hierokles, for instance, was a cultivated Alexandrian who wrote this letter using choice words and a balanced clause structure—it is not easy to be sure about the identity of his *didaskalos*.

---

[25] *P.Cair.Zen.* 59098, 59060, 59061; *P.Lond.* VII.1941. On Zenon, see above, p. 48, and below, p. 188.

[26] See *P.Cair.Zen.* 59098, very fragmentary.

[27] I will give below part of the letter *P.Lond.* VII.1941, which was written first. Where something is missing, it can usually be restored from the other two letters, *P.Cair.Zen.* 59060 and 59061, which are almost identical.

[28] Cf. Morgan 1999.

Even though in the papyrus the lessons from which the lad risked being distracted are called *grammata*, that is, "letters," in this case the word may have meant something more than the ability to read and write.[29] It is likely that Pyrrhos was a teenager, like that fourteen-year-old whose application for membership in the gymnasium in the second century C.E. mentioned that "he was learning letters," that is, literature, the province of the grammarian.[30] But even an educated guess of the age of Zenon's protégé is no guarantee of the level of studies he was pursuing with his teacher. This boy may have blossomed physically and intellectually with age, thus acquiring the patronage of Zenon, who opened for him the doors of athletic prowess and literacy. It is also possible that Zenon, who acted as a surrogate father in providing generously for Pyrrhos's education at the hands of a *didaskalos*, was sexually attracted to him and had other interests at stake.

SECONDARY TEACHERS

After primary instruction, children of the elite learned grammar and studied literature.[31] The vast majority were boys, but, as we shall see, some girls also had access to this level of education, and a few exceptional cases are known of women teachers able to offer secondary instruction.[32] Throughout the Greco-Roman world, instruction at this level was much more uniform than it was during primary schooling, the characteristics of which might vary depending on local need. Secondary teachers provided students with an education that gave them a distinct identity as members of a privileged class. Even though in theory education at this level was always supervised by the grammarian (*grammatikos*), in practice instructors designated with different names could impart the same traditional knowledge: secondary teachers might be called simply *didaskaloi*—as perhaps in the letter cited above—or the same level of instruction could be offered by private tutors, called *kathēgētai*. The latter were itinerant teachers who moved from town to town offering their services and always looking for better employment. It is not always clear at which level *ka-*

[29] See Cribiore 1996a: 20 n. 60.

[30] See *P.Oxy.* XXII.2345, in which the age of the boy and the fact that this achievement is not mentioned in other documents of this type suggests that he was at a level higher than elementary education.

[31] Cf. Chapter 7.

[32] See below, Chapter 3.

thēgētai taught, but it is likely that they were especially needed in advanced education to cater to male and female students who lived in the country, away from the large educational centers.

A letter cited above vividly shows how a teacher of secondary education had some power to control his clientele. In this letter, Ptolemaios's mother manifests her preoccupation with the sudden departure from Oxyrhynchos of the *kathēgētēs* Diogenes, who sailed downstream to Alexandria. In the second and third centuries C.E., Oxyrhynchos was a prosperous city with imposing baths, gymnasia, vaulted colonnades, magnificent temples, and a grand theater.[33] It is actually a mathematical school exercise of a student at a secondary level of education that permits us to have an idea of the number of spectators that this theater could hold.[34] In Oxyrhynchos there were artistic contests in the classes of trumpeters, heralds, and poets, gymnastic displays by the local youths, and recitations of the Homeric poems by professionals.[35] It is likely that Ptolemaios was able to find there another private instructor to teach him Homer, since there was a continuous cultural exchange between this city and Alexandria, and people flocked to Oxyrhynchos from other parts of the country in search of employment. Nevertheless, the anxiety of this student's mother seems justified: capable teachers were hard to find, and the unexpected departure of a tutor deprived a student of continuity. The unreliability of teachers was one of the factors that characterized the ancient educational scenario. Since competition was limited to a degree, a teacher of secondary education was in the position of controlling his clients. Naturally, the consequences were particularly disastrous in the country, where a departing *kathēgētēs* was likely to leave a student in the lurch, with his journey up the hill of learning suddenly cut off. At the same time, though, it is important to realize that a teacher's lack of dependability was often due to his usually precarious financial and social position.

Ptolemaios, however, may have been lucky enough to have the option of following the lessons of the public grammarian of Oxyrhynchos. Lollianos was appointed "public grammarian" by the town council in the third century. Although no other holders of such an office are known in Egypt, this is probably due to the accidents of survival for texts, since an imperial

---

[33] See E. G. Turner, "Roman Oxyrhynchus," *JEA* 38 (1952): 78–93, and "Scribes and Scholars of Oxyrhynchus," *Akten des VIII Internationalen Kongresses für Papyrologie* (Vienna, 1956), 141–46.

[34] See *PSI* III.186, which preserves a geometrical problem about a theater, together with a sketch. The number of seats given as a solution in the exercise is 8,400.

[35] See *P.Oxy.* XXII.2338, I.42, and VII.1050. Cf. below, p. 241.

policy in favor of higher education is well attested in other parts of the Roman Empire. A papyrus roll preserves two drafts of a petition and a letter of Lollianos, who complained about the salary that he received.[36] These texts, with choice verbal forms and elaborate vocabulary and syntax, amply testify to the education of the grammarian. It is enough to consider the beginning of the petition to the emperors:

> Your heavenly magnanimity, which has irradiated your domain, the whole civilized world, and your fellowship with the Muses—for *Paideia* sits beside you on the throne—has given me confidence to offer you a just and lawful petition.

Grammarians were not always the pedantic teachers who scrutinized a text in search of particular linguistic usages. Occasionally they had a deeper understanding of the works of the poets and composed poetry themselves. Some grammarians who worked in the school of Libanius, preparing the younger students for higher education, also wrote poetry and prose.[37] One of them was Kleobulos, who came to Antioch from Egypt: Libanius, who had been a student of his, called him a good poet, a *didaskalos*, and a *paideutēs* ("educator"), and offered him a post as grammarian in his school in a moment of need.[38] In the fourth century, the grammarian Palladas, who taught in Alexandria and considered his profession a burden, was a poet.[39] Somewhat later, Horapollon was grammarian in Alexandria and Constantinople. He was a brilliant teacher and composed works of poetry and commentaries on the poets.[40] A few papyri concern his son and his grandson, Asklepiades and Flavius Horapollon, grammarians in the fifth century—an example of the profession passing through three generations of the same family.[41] Asklepiades is said to have cultivated the Muse of philosophy and to "have dedicated all his life to the Muses, teaching young men the old *paideia*." His son Horapollon, who became a distinguished grammarian in Alexandria, was said to have been a philosopher. Father and son, therefore, though they supported themselves by teaching, had much broader interests. The same can be said

---

[36] See *P.Oxy.* XLVII.3366; cf. below, p. 64.

[37] See Wolf 1952: 39–41.

[38] See ibid.: 71–73; see especially *Ep.* 361. Cf. above, Chapter 1.

[39] Over a hundred epigrams attributed to Palladas are preserved in the *Greek Anthology*. See A. Cameron, *The Greek Anthology from Meleager to Planudes* (Oxford, 1993). On Palladas's discontent, see below.

[40] See Kaster 1988: 294 no. 77.

[41] See Cribiore 1996a: 168–69; cf. above, Chapter 1.

of the grammarian Aurelius Kyros, who is mentioned in a series of receipts on papyrus and should probably be identified with the homonymous poet from Antaeopolis.[42] Grammarians such as these are likely to have been influential teachers who left permanent marks in the cultural development of their pupils. In general, however, this profession was characterized by mediocrity and engaged a student in mental acrobatics of limited value. Moreover, as usual, the merit of a teacher depended on individual qualities, and, as the fourth-century rhetor Themistius recognized, there were people who were authentic teachers and others who only liked to believe they were.[43]

TEACHERS OF RHETORIC

Problems with the quality of instruction and the reliability of teachers did not cease to plague male students who aimed at competitive professions and public careers and thus continued their educations to the rhetorical level.[44] As a rule, women did not have access to this educational level. Even though it was the secondary level of instruction that fundamentally shaped an adolescent's mind, a rhetorical education provided an entrée to positions of power. Since in the Greco-Roman world there was no uniformity to the length of studies or age required for admittance to this level, and much is left in the dark, the details provided by Libanius are valuable. A youth began to study rhetoric at about age fourteen or fifteen: in the first year he learned theory, in the second he studied prose works with Libanius's assistants, and in the third year he entered the class taught by Libanius himself and started with the "preliminary exercises," *progymnasmata*.[45] The fourth and fifth years were used to reinforce a student's ability to compose discourses (*meletai*) until, in the sixth year, the pupil might be promoted in rank, becoming an assistant teacher himself.[46] The proportion of students who actually completed the whole course, however, was not very high. The papyri occasionally mention *rhētores* and *sophistai* as teachers at this level. The writings of Libanius clarify the differences between their responsibilities, at least in a formal school set-

---

[42] Cf. Kaster 1988: 265 no. 41.

[43] *Or.* 11, p. 220 Schenkl, ll. 18–19.

[44] On the curriculum in rhetorical schools, see below, Chapter 8.

[45] See Petit 1956: 88 and 90–91.

[46] Some students were engaged in these studies for a longer time, such as the youth who studied with Libanius for eight years; see Festugière 1959: 179.

ting: *rhētores* taught the theory but did not expose students to the exercises, which were the province of the *sophistēs*. Thus *rhētores* were not really professors of eloquence but were at an inferior level: they occupied a chair, a *thronos*, but one of second rank.[47] Much teaching, moreover, was left in the hands of private tutors, *kathēgētai*, who frequently moved from place to place. The letter that the student Neilos wrote to his father Theon in the first to second century C.E., with its spontaneous outpouring of unedited feelings, gives a vivid idea of the problems that a student might encounter:[48]

I had hoped to win splendid advantages by sailing down quickly, and what return have I got for my eagerness? Now in my search for a tutor I find that both Chairemon the *kathēgētēs* and Didymos the son of Aristokles, in whose hands there was hope that I, too, might have some success, are no longer in town, but only trash,[49] in whose hands most pupils have taken the straight road to having their talents spoiled. I wrote to you before, just as I wrote to Philoxenos and his friends, to consider the matter, and was introduced by them to the man they favor, whom, although he "begged the indulgence of Theon," you immediately rejected, for you condemn him as possessing a completely inadequate training. When I informed Philoxenos of your view, he began to be of the same opinion, declaring that it was on account of this shortage of *sophistai* alone that he felt compassion for the city. He said that Didymos has sailed down [the Nile to Alexandria], as it seems, who is a friend of his and keeps a school, and he will look after the others, and especially he began to urge the sons of Apollonios, the son of Herodes, to attend Didymos's classes. For they, too, along with Philoxenos, have been searching till now for a better *kathēgētēs*, since the tutor whose classes they used to attend has died. I, for my part, since I would vow never to see Didymos even from afar, if I found *kathēgētai* worthy of the name, am depressed by the very fact that this person, who used to be a teacher in the country, has made up his mind to enter into competition with the others. So, bearing this in mind—I mean that there is no good to be gotten out of a teacher, unless it is paying exorbitant fees to no purpose—I am depending

[47] See Pinto 1974: 157; Wolf 1952: 9–24; A. Boulanger, *Aelius Aristide et la sophistique dans la province d' Asie au II*[e] *siècle de notre ère* (Paris, 1923), 76. Even though we may call Libanius a rhetor, he was not a *rhētōr* according to Greek terminology; he was, however, a *sophistēs*.

[48] *P.Oxy.* XVIII.2190, cf. above, and below, pp. 121–23.

[49] On this interesting word, *katharmata*, "trash," see below, pp. 110–11.

on my own efforts. Write to me quickly what you think. I have Didymos, as Philoxenos, too, says, always at my disposal and providing all the help that he can. By listening still to the rhetoricians declaiming, including Poseidonius, perhaps, with the help of the gods, I shall do well.

This letter portrays a number of students as desperately looking for good teachers. The sons of Apollonios remind one of young Libanius, who was following the lessons of a fine rhetorician, Ulpianus of Ascalon, when the latter suddenly died. Longing for his dead teacher, Libanius "began to attend the lessons of the living, mere shadows of teachers, as men eat loaves of bread for want of anything better."[50] Apparently unable to find satisfying professors, Libanius adopted an unusual solution: he abandoned the study of rhetoric and returned to the works of the classical authors with a grammarian. But this was a resolve of desperation: Neilos and his friends kept looking for suitable teachers. Neilos had moved to Alexandria in the hope of attending the classes of two instructors who had left the city by the time he arrived. Since his father did not approve of another professor, whom he judged inadequate, Neilos was left with Didymos, who, in his opinion, was better suited to the "country bumpkins." A partial solution, to get some exposure to rhetoric, was to attend the public displays of some rhetoricians.[51] These declamations, which rhetors used as self-promotion, gave students models of speaking and a way to evaluate and choose new teachers.

One should not forget, in any case, that Neilos's defensive letter reflects not only his point of view but also the reality that he wanted to present to his father. In that period, Alexandria was not so lacking in rhetorical instructors as this lad claimed.[52] It is useful to consider a very different perspective: how a professor such as Libanius regarded the teaching situation and his students' behavior in fourth-century Antioch. Over and over Libanius complains of the fact that pupils were in a perennial state of discontent and looked around for different teachers. Changing from school to school, they ended up "touring all the schools, until they went back to the teacher whom they left in the first place" (*Or.* 43.8). When one of his pupils defected and joined the class of another instructor, the

[50] Libanius *Or.* 1.8. On Ulpianus, see Libanius *Or.* 36.10.

[51] On auditing rhetorical displays, cf. below, p. 239.

[52] Schubert (1995), who discusses Philostratus's silence in this respect. On Theon of Alexandria, who composed a handbook of preliminary rhetorical exercises, see below, Chapter 8 and passim.

professor was dejected, hated his school, and viewed his remaining students with suspicion (*Or.* 43.6). But of course Libanius's complaints should also be taken with a grain of salt.

THE SOCIAL AND ECONOMIC STANDING OF TEACHERS

Like their duties and abilities, the social and economic status of teachers varied greatly. The evidence suggests that individuals' standings might vary, according to personal circumstances and family fortunes and connections, even within a particular educational level. In general, as today, the higher a teacher stood on the educational pyramid, the more credibility and respect he was accorded and the more secure his economic situation. Though the social distance between a teacher of higher learning in a great educational center and a village teacher of primary letters was about the same as the corresponding difference between their pupils, one should be wary of accepting without reserve the uniform image that the ancient literary tradition imposes, especially with regard to primary teachers.

It is well known that many ancient authors, from the orator Demosthenes in the fourth century B.C.E. to Libanius in the fourth century C.E., express utter contempt for the elementary teacher, who sold his humble knowledge for money and could not claim any status. Accusing someone of being a schoolteacher, or of having a schoolteacher as a father, was a common insult.[53] In the third century B.C.E., the poet Callimachus was derided for being a primary teacher himself. The tenth-century lexicon known as *Suda* says that he taught elementary letters in Eleusis, a village close to Alexandria, before being introduced to court. But this was certainly a lampoon or derived from a joke in contemporary comedy. Far from being an elementary teacher, Callimachus himself displays contempt for the humble schoolteacher; in his fifth *Iamb*, he ridiculed one and warned him not to molest his students.[54]

Even though the cliché probably reflects reality to a certain degree, it is likely that the profession of teaching elementary letters earned some respect, especially in small communities where even the children of families of high social standing usually depended upon local teachers for a while. A Roman terracotta represents one of these elementary teachers sur-

[53] A. D. Booth, "Some Suspect Schoolmasters," *Florilegium* 3 (1981): 1–20, collects all the evidence. See, e.g., Dem. *De cor.* 129 and 258.

[54] See Cameron 1995: 3–7.

Figure 9. Roman terracotta: a teacher with children.

rounded by a flock of children (Fig. 9).[55] The images, practically fused together, indicate an extremely close bond. In some cases, the papyri reveal that an amicable relationship was possible between teachers and their past students. An inscription found in the temple of Isis in the Egyptian island of Philae preserves a dedication to the goddess made by a man, Korax, not only for his son but also for an individual who had been his own teacher and for the latter's son.[56] In doing so, Korax wished health and wealth to be showered upon his schoolmaster of old. A papyrus letter, moreover, reveals that when students left town to continue their education, they remembered with longing the teachers who remained behind.[57] In Greco-Roman Egypt, moreover, elementary teachers often offered their services as scribes and notaries.[58] In a society where most people were not literate, helping out when a letter had to be written or a signature was

[55] Cf. Besques 1992: plate 39, D 4384, where the central figure is described as a pedagogue. But this is unlikely, because pedagogues are usually represented with only one child.

[56] *SB* I.4099.5, second to first century B.C.E.

[57] Cf. the nostalgia of the student Thonis in *SB* III.6262; see below, pp. 112 and 217.

[58] See Cribiore 1996a: 22 n. 82.

needed on a document was an activity that was probably rewarded with gratitude. On the other side of the Mediterranean, an inscription on the funeral monument of Philocalus, who was primary teacher at Capua in the first century C.E., offers a seemingly close parallel, showing that he supplemented his income with this secondary activity and "faithfully wrote out wills."[59] It is nowhere stated, however, that in Egypt teachers received money for their activity as scribes: it cannot be ruled out that they performed this service in their communities for free or in exchange for gifts in kind. Succoring illiterates in moments of need was a natural extension of a teacher's role: even in the modern world, it is not unheard for teachers to perform such a service.[60]

Undoubtedly grammarians and rhetors had claims to a higher status than that of teachers of mere letters.[61] The evidence suggests that at least in late antiquity, starting in the fifth century, they enjoyed high rank and possessed the title Flavius, which distinguished those who had served in the imperial, military, and civil service from the masses, who retained the name Aurelius.[62] It is difficult to evaluate correctly the significance of this title when it distinguished a teacher of advanced education, since it is unclear how the title was bestowed on those outside the imperial bureaucracy. Thus it cannot be ruled out that some advanced teachers gained the Flaviate not through their teaching but because of their service as imperial functionaries. Even harder to evaluate is the evidence that some grammarians, such as Flavius Horapollon, who taught in Alexandria, possessed the more prestigious title *lamprotatos* ("most illustrious"), since there is no evidence indicating whether they had inherited the title or acquired it as a special distinction.[63] In spite of much uncertainty, however, the general scenario suggests that teachers of higher education were surrounded by an air of respectability.

A number of inconsistencies appearing in the sources prevent us from forming a single, coherent picture of the economic situation of teachers. The papyrological evidence is in this respect uneven and incomplete. In

[59] See Bonner 1977: 150.

[60] Cf. the protagonist of a modern Brazilian movie by Walter Salles, *Central Station*, a retired teacher who wrote epistles for illiterates for a fee.

[61] Their social and economic position is treated in detail by Kaster 1988: 99–134.

[62] See J. G. Keenan, "The Names Flavius and Aurelius as Status Designations in Later Roman Egypt," ZPE 11 (1973): 33–63 and 13 (1974): 283–304; "An Afterthought on the Names Flavius and Aurelius," ZPE 53 (1983): 245–50. About a grammarian with this title who taught elementary letters, see above, pp. 39–40, and below, p. 170.

[63] It was the equivalent of the Latin *clarissimus*. Horapollon calls himself *lamprotatos*.

the third century B.C.E., a royal benefaction enhanced the social and economic status of primary teachers. An edict of king Ptolemy Philadelphos exempted from the salt tax Greek elementary teachers, teachers of gymnastics, priests of Dionysos, and victors in the public contests.[64] All the people in their households—that is, their wives, children, and slaves—were also exempted from the tax. Through this edict the king manifested his philhellenism, and in particular promoted Greek education. Primary teachers, in any case, belonged to a lower socioeconomic category than grammarians. Many centuries later, in C.E. 301, the *Edict on Prices* of the emperor Diocletian underscored this hierarchy by fixing a grammarian's fee at four times that of a teacher of letters, while a rhetor's fee was only a little higher than a grammarian's.[65] In C.E. 376, however, the superiority of a teacher of rhetoric was recognized, and Gratian decreed that a rhetor should be paid twice the salary of a grammarian.[66]

The papyri occasionally show *didaskaloi* who possess a slave, a house, and land: these were probably—but not certainly—teachers of mere letters. Documents that show that some elementary teachers received payments in kind such as wheat, barley, grapes, oil, and wine are only partly informative: it is impossible to know for which services these were paid and the length of employment for these individuals, since it was common for workers in many fields to receive part of their compensation in kind. In a letter of the second century C.E., a person in the circle of the governor Apollonios asks the letter's recipient to send pigeons and other birds to the teacher of the girl Heraidous—probably a secondary teacher—and the leftovers from his table to the teacher of his own daughter "so that he pays attention to her."[67] It is difficult to know whether these were mere gifts or part of the salary. Libanius, using the contempt of the highly educated, speaks of an elementary teacher, Optatos, who was paid with two loaves and other foodstuffs.[68] But he himself received gifts such as valuable garments, gold, and pigeons: since these gifts were usually given the first day of the year, they should be considered compensation for his services.[69] Though the economic status of an elementary teacher usually did not allow luxuries, sometimes a surprise is in store, such as the fact

[64] See *P.Hal.* 1.260–65; Cribiore 1996a: 21.

[65] *Edictum de Pretiis* 7.66 (ed. Lauffer), pp. 124–25: 50 *denarii* per month were decreed for elementary teachers and pedagogues, 200 *denarii* for grammarians, and 250 for rhetors.

[66] *Cod. Theod.* 13.3.11.

[67] *P.Giss.* 80; on Heraidous, cf. below, Chapter 3. Cf. also *P.Oslo* III.156, and below, p. 87.

[68] Libanius *Or.* 42.26.4–7.

[69] See Petit 1956: 145 n. 40.

that an elementary teacher reconstructed at his own expense a wall in the temple of the goddess Leto in C.E. 108.[70] Usually it was grammarians and rhetors who were able to afford occasional public dedications;[71] for example, the rhetor Didymos son of Theon made a similar dedication to Isis in C.E. 103.[72]

It is likely that many grammarians and rhetors enjoyed a comfortable standard of living. In addition to receiving a public salary—when that applied—and students' fees, during the Roman Empire, under Vespasian, Hadrian, Antoninus Pius, and Commodus, they benefited from considerable immunities, being exempt from levies, municipal liturgies, guardianship, and service as jurymen, ambassadors, or soldiers.[73] But a good lifestyle must have depended heavily on family wealth. The family of Flavius Horapollon, for instance, had landholdings in Egypt for at least three generations, and the grammarian Didymos, who had been Libanius's own teacher and was a native of Egypt, had maintained a parcel of land in Egypt while teaching in Antioch and Constantinople.[74] Libanius himself belonged to a family of high social and economic status. His standard of living was well above that of most of the other rhetors of his time: he had money, land, a house, horses, slaves, and books.[75] After teaching for less than eight years in Nicomedia, he was robbed of an enormous sum of money, 1,500 *solidi* in cash, but he kept his composure (*Or.* 1.61). Admiring his indifference to money, the citizens tried to reimburse him, but he refused their offer.

When the income of a grammarian or rhetorician depended exclusively on salary and students' fees, and, in the worst case, when a teacher with no public subsidy taught only a few fee-evading students, economic problems and bitterness were in store. The Alexandrian grammarian Palladas often cursed his profession. In an epigram he described the methods used by his students to cheat him of his fee: some gave him copper or lead instead of silver, others changed schools after eleven months, before paying the gold *solidus*, which was the yearly fee.[76] Even though Palladas revealed in another poem that he could afford to have "children, a wife,

---

[70] *SB* I.680.

[71] On impressive public dedications by grammarians and rhetors, see Kaster 1988: 111–12.

[72] *SB* V.8815.

[73] See P. J. Parsons, "Petitions and a Letter: The Grammarian's Complaint," *P.Coll.Youtie* (Bonn, 1976), Appendix II, pp. 441–46.

[74] See Kaster 1988: 112–13 and 269–70.

[75] See L. Petit, *Essai sur la vie et la correspondance du sophiste Libanius* (Paris, 1866), 62–63.

[76] See *Anth. Pal.* 9.174; Cameron 1965a. In all times, people attempted to lower school fees. In the third century B.C.E., the philosopher Theophrastus (*Char.* 30.14) describes par-

a slave, birds, and a dog" (*Anth. Pal.* 10.86), he usually complained of an oppressive poverty. His profession, which was based on the study of the poets, and especially of Homer's *Iliad*, was in his view the cause of all his evils:

> The wrath of Achilles was the cause of pernicious poverty to me, since I became a grammarian. Would that that wrath had killed me with the Greeks before the harsh hunger of grammar is the end of me. But all to let Agamemnon run away with Briseis, and Paris with Helen, I have become poor. (*Anth. Pal.* 9.169)

Another grammarian who lamented his insufficient means was the Egyptian Lollianos.[77] It is a paradox that this grammarian, who could approach the Roman emperors in his petition with the awareness of the prestige of his profession and education, claimed to be a starving man who had trouble sustaining a family. The post of "public grammarian" that he held in Oxyrhynchos entitled him to a salary that in theory was substantial but in practice was rarely paid, and then only with sour wine and worm-eaten grain. Since his teaching duties left him no time to continue pestering the authorities, Lollianos proposed that the city assign to him one of the public orchards, which he could lease out, using the rent as his own salary. At the end of his petition, and showing a touch of a teacher's dignity, Lollianos claimed that the grant of the orchard would allow him to have "ample time for teaching the children."[78]

The request was probably not so unusual. A century later Libanius appealed to the Council of Antioch: the four rhetors who were his assistants were in dire financial straits because their civic salaries were paid irregularly (*Or.* 31). Libanius proposed that they be able to enjoy the income of a municipal property that had been assigned previously to his predecessor, Zenobius. In Libanius's words, his assistants were even in debt to the bakers, whom "they tried to avoid, since they owed them, and at the same time pursued, since they were in need" (*Or.* 31.12.15–16). When the debt was too large, a rhetor might grab the last necklace from the neck of his wife and give it to the baker in pledge. We should not lose sight of the fact that these pitiful details, which were supposed to melt the heart of the council members whom Libanius was addressing, stand alongside the statement that these teachers had only two or three slaves.[79]

---

ents who did not send children to class for the whole month of Anthesterion to avoid paying the fee, since this month had many holidays.

[77] Cf. above, pp. 54–55.

[78] *P.Oxy.* XLVII.3366.C68.

[79] But it is true that slaves were quite inexpensive.

Teachers were often in financial straits, complained bitterly, and thought of changing profession—says Libanius (*Or.* 43.19). One teacher said, "I should be a farmer," and another, "Better to enter in the public service." Libanius himself, who had a comfortable way of life, often rants about not receiving his fees. Even though, when a student was poor, he was ready to grant his pardon, as a rule he was infuriated, because apparently his pupils spent the money received from their parents for the tuition in other ways, such as drinking, playing dice, and pursuing sexual escapades.[80] Students, moreover, complained of the high tuition, especially when they were not satisfied with the teaching and planned to look for a different teacher. They lamented that they had spent their time in vain and thought that they should not have to pay the tuition for the months in which they had not learned (*Or.* 43.6). In spite of some rhetorical exaggerations, not only are the parallels with the complaints of the student Neilos in the letter quoted above striking, but the outlines of the battleground of education are emerging more clearly.

WHIP-WIELDING MASTERS

Far from standing comfortably on top of the hill of learning and helpfully monitoring a student's climb from the heights of their excellence, teachers stood on shaky ground, often battling against economic hardship and insecurity. Even at advanced levels of education, when their position of dominance seemed a bit more secure, they were subjected to the control of powerful families who could threaten to withdraw a son suddenly, particularly in large educational centers such as Alexandria or Antioch, where there was a certain amount of competition. Teacher-student relationships occasioned bitterness, grudges, complaints of selfishness, and incorrect behavior on both sides. It is not surprising that instructors, like Zeus, could succumb to the temptation of violently shaking the rope they had lowered, on which students were making the climb. Inevitably the skills of schoolmasters in planning, scheduling, and grading have always being viewed as instruments of intimidation. Throughout antiquity, moreover, physical punishment was the standard method used to correct a child who misbehaved or did not want to learn. A schoolmaster wielded a stick to make pupils love him—or, at least, love his doctrine. Through a rigorous mental gymnastics, students were supposed to acquire good

---

[80] See Libanius *Or.* 3.6. Libanius is not very specific and only says that the sexual revels of students "were sometimes more daring than custom permitted."

Figure 10.   A street scene: an Egyptian primary school
before 1870. The children are sitting on the ground, the
teacher on a chair.

habits; lapses into the old habits were corrected with a beating. Rough, coercive methods continued to embitter teachers' relations with students beyond ancient times. A poem from about 1500, for instance, represents the rough treatment of a schoolboy at the hands of his master; after the beating, the boy visualizes his teacher as a hare and all his books as hounds that are joyfully released to kill the hare-teacher.[81] In Arab schools in Egypt at the end of the nineteenth century, a chair and a stick were still symbols of a teacher's power (Fig. 10).

[81] See F. J. Furnivall, ed., *Early English Meals and Manners: John Russel's Boke of Nurture* (London, 1868; Detroit, 1969), 385–86; Hanawalt 1993: 84. In England, brutal flogging started to decline in public grammar schools in the late seventeenth century (Stone 1977: 439–44). Some forms of physical punishment still exist today in rural areas of the United States.

References to coercive methods in Greek and Roman literature are legion.[82] In the vast majority of cases, it is boys who are subjected to violence at the hands of schoolmasters. It is difficult to be sure whether the paucity of examples showing girls struck in school[83] indicates that there was a more indulgent attitude toward them or that the *topos* of the punishing schoolmaster somehow missed them, or whether it merely reflects the fact that girls appear more rarely as the subjects of education. Although the literary sources have not handed down examples of fathers punishing freeborn daughters, it was not unusual for women to be subjected to domestic violence at the hands of their husbands.[84] It is likely that girls were physically punished by mothers and older female slaves of the household, that some abusive fathers did not refrain from disciplining them, and that they did not escape violence at the hands of male and female teachers, even though the extent of such violence is unknown.

It is sometimes said that severe methods were used less often in classical Greece than in the Roman period and later, but copious references to punishment appear very early.[85] Representations in vase paintings and terracottas often allude to coercive discipline. The visual evidence shows that the typical instrument of punishment in the home was the sandal, which was used by both parents.[86] Mothers, both goddesses (such as Aphrodite chastising Eros) and common mortals, seem to have found the sandal very practical. On an Athenian vase, for instance, a woman in the women's quarters holds a little boy still as she hits him: in vain he struggles to escape (see Fig. 7). Hitting students with a sandal was not unknown in schools: even though only Phanias, the epigrammatist of the first century B.C.E. mentioned below, writes of a teacher using this method, it is suggestive that in vase representations that portray schools, a sandal often hangs on the wall among other educational objects. School representations, moreover, clearly underline that severe methods were used not only to chastise misbehavior but also to punish failure to learn and to perform adequately, or even to win at a competition.[87]

---

[82] Some references to punishment are collected by Booth (1973: 107–14); I shall mostly concentrate on different examples.

[83] See Bonner 1977: 135–36; Martial 9.68.1–2; Ausonius 22.33–34.

[84] See P. Clark, "Women, Slaves, and the Hierarchies of Domestic Violence," in Joshel and Murnaghan 1998: 109–29.

[85] Müller (1910: 292–317) argues that in the fourth century, coercive methods became more common.

[86] See, e.g., an Attic vase, Beck 1975: pl. 53, 274: a child shows five sandal marks on his body.

[87] See, e.g., Beck 1975: pl. 52, 273: a music school.

One of the classic references to punishment comes from the *Didaskalos* of Herodas, where Metrotime takes her rebellious son, Kokkalos, to the schoolmaster to be punished. In vain the boy repeatedly invokes the "dear Muses" whom he failed. In fact, even though Kokkalos is reproached for running away and playing dice, he is mostly punished for his failure to learn. After an outraged Metrotime dwells at length on Kokkalos's faults, the schoolmaster flogs him with his "biting strap, the bull's tail," declining to use the less harsh whip that Kokkalos would prefer (68–73). Schoolmasters had at their disposal a variety of educational instruments, as the epigram of Phanias about the teacher Kallon shows:

> Kallon, his limbs fettered by senile fatigue, dedicates to Hermes the Lord these tokens of his career as a schoolmaster: the staff that guided his feet, his strap, the fennel-rod that lay ever ready to his hand to hit little boys on their heads, his lithe whistling bull-tail, his one-soled slipper, and the skull-cap of his hairless head. (*Anth. Pal.* 6.294)

The walking stick mentioned by Phanias was also used to punish students in school, but in vase paintings it is usually associated with pedagogues.[88] The fennel-rod, which often appears on fifth-century vases, was called *narthex* and *ferula* in Latin and was also used as a chastising cane in the schools of the West.[89]

Educational methods did not change in the Roman period. In the second century, Lucian's parasite compares education unfavorably with his own art: "Who ever went home from a dinner in tears, as we see some going home from their schools? Who ever set out for a dinner looking gloomy, like children who go to school?" (*De parasito* 13). And a Christian writer such as Augustine in the fourth century recalls with some emotion the corporal punishment administered in school: "Racks, claws, and such varieties of torments . . . we schoolboys suffered from our masters" (*Conf.* 1.9). It is somewhat ironic that the same Augustine who complained about the harsh treatment he had received in childhood applauded in the *Letters* the practice of beating children.[90] The advent of Christianity did not bring a change in educational methods.

Harsh discipline ruled education in Greco-Roman Egypt as much as anywhere. Drastic punishment already characterized the educational system of pharaonic Egypt: a maxim on a papyrus read, "The ears of a youth

[88] See Beck 1975: 46, 276a.
[89] See Martial 10.62.10; J. D. Beazley, "Narthex," *AJA*, 2d ser., 37 (1933): 400–403.
[90] See Wiedemann 1989: 105–6.

are on his back: he listens when he is beaten."[91] These methods persisted into later times, as two school exercises testify. On a waxed tablet of the Roman period, a student who was learning to write copied four times a maxim that had been inscribed by the teacher on the first line: "Work hard, boy, lest you be thrashed."[92] And another student at a higher level, who shared a piece of papyrus with a different pupil, wrote a maxim from the fourth-century B.C.E. poet Menander: "He who is not thrashed cannot be educated."[93] It is symptomatic that in the fourth-century *Canons* of the famous grammarian Theodosius—a collection of rules about declensions of nouns and adjectives and conjugations of verbs—the verb adopted as the model is *typtein* ("to beat"), which is also conjugated in many school exercises.[94] This verb already appears in some of the examples cited by Apollonius Dyscolus, the Alexandrian grammarian of the second century C.E.: thus, a model sentence used in the *Syntax* is "Let us beat the child who misbehaves" (1.111 Uhlig). But some of the examples cited in the works of Apollonius, and of grammarians in general, have that simple and unrefined quality that makes one suspect that they derived from actual school life. In another example, Apollonius uses the same verb, *deirein*, that was used by the students of the two exercises quoted above with the meaning "to thrash."[95]

But violence in the schoolroom needs to be evaluated against the background of the universality of violence in the ancient world. Far from being the sole practitioners of this philosophy of punishment, teachers adopted corrective systems similar to those practiced in the home. Greeks and Romans considered it normal to beat children and slaves, who could not be controlled by rationality and occupied an intermediate position between human and beast.[96] Thus, for instance, the fourth-century B.C.E. philosopher Plato was of the opinion that not only teachers but all the people who participated in rearing a child—parents, nurses, and pedagogues—should discipline him strictly, since a child had to be straightened "like a bent and twisted piece of wood."[97] A papyrus letter of the Byzantine period underscores parental feelings about severity. Writing to the teacher

[91] Cf. *Papyrus Anastasi* V.3.9.

[92] See Cribiore 1996a: no. 134.

[93] See ibid.: no. 257.

[94] On the *Canons*, cf. below, p. 214.

[95] See *Syntax* 1.141. On the use of the verb *deirein* in a letter, see below, p. 219.

[96] Wiedemann (1989: 27–30) considers the beating of children to be characteristic of peasant societies.

[97] Plato *Prt.* 325d; see also *Laws* 7.808d–e.

of his own son Anastasios, who was not doing well in school, a father encourages the schoolmaster to punish him: "Chastise him, for ever since he left his father he has had no other beatings, and he wants to get a few, his back has got accustomed to them and needs its daily dose."[98] It is the same rage that is visible in the reaction of the mother of Kokkalos: not only is Metrotime witnessing her son's cruel flogging unflinchingly, but she beseeches the schoolmaster to "flay him until the sun sets" (*Didaskalos* 88). Parents and pedagogues, who practiced corrective methods from a child's early years, sometimes continued their harsh treatment even when that child became an adolescent and moved to advanced education. Libanius describes eloquently "the battle" at home, where tutors and fathers were the protagonists. His ambivalent presentation of pedagogues must have some grounds in reality. In a rhetorical exercise, he depicts the type of the harsh tutor, glued to his victim all day long, nagging, scolding, and following the student with his instruments of intimidation, the strap and the stick.[99] This tutor acquires a face in a letter in which Libanius warns a father that his son's pedagogue kept on beating him, as if he were a sailor beating the sea with his oar (*Ep.* 1188.3–4).

But although they beat their children, most elite parents seem to have been conscious to some degree that they should not be humiliated like slaves and repressed to the point of servility.[100] The beating of children by parents, moreover, never became a cliché and was not frequently mentioned by the literary sources. But both the beating of slaves at the hands of their masters and the beating of schoolchildren at the hands of teachers became *topoi*: though in the first case this cliché responded to a daily reality, it is difficult to assess the actual incidence of physical punishment in school.

Occasionally in the Greek and Roman world a few voices rose against corporal punishment at school. Thus Plutarch and Quintilian protested against the harsh methods that were prevalent in education on the grounds that they were fitting only for slaves and were counterproductive.[101] These, however, were the isolated cries of enlightened theorists that did not affect the general violence that ruled early education. It should be noted, in fact, that there was a perceptible difference in the way teachers treated children and adolescents: coercive methods were especially di-

---

[98] See *SB* V.7655. Cf. below, pp. 218–19.

[99] *Chria* 3, Foerster vol. 8, pp. 84–85.

[100] See Saller 1994: 133–53. Discussion about physical punishment in the home in the Roman sources is limited to male children of the elite. The extent to which children of lower status were beaten is unknown.

[101] Plutarch *De liberis educandis* 8f; Quintilian 1.3.14.

rected at the youngest and supposedly more "irrational" pupils. Intimidating methods were also prevalent in higher education, but teachers refrained from the most violent manifestations of their anger.[102]

There are many reasons for this differential treatment. A fundamental one resides in the nature of the social conditioning that education intended to impart. In the same way that a teacher's position was one of dominance, yet also one of subjugation to others and to life circumstances, a student's role was not only that of a recipient of violence. Examples in late antiquity of students viciously turning against a teacher's authority are symptomatic of the tension that characterized the schoolroom and of the sources' awareness of it; nonetheless, these stories are highly exceptional.[103] Power and violence permeated education in many other insidious ways. As students received or saw others receive chastisement, they started to rehearse their own future roles in society. While free women, and particularly those of the upper class, had to negotiate in their household subservience and dominance at the same time, being recipients of violence but also dispensing it to their subordinates, the role of elite men was simpler: they were in many respects vehicles of power. Already at the primary stages of education, pupils started to identify with power and to become accomplices to violence. On a vase described above, the student who plays "teacher" holds on to his chair and to the chastising rod (Fig. 3). In the *Didaskalos*, classmates hold Kokkalos tight as the teacher whips him (59–62), and similar scenes appear on a mural at Pompeii and on a gem of the Greco-Roman period.[104] But the elite male who had access to high levels of education became ever more aware of his future role as an agent of power. Since one of the purposes of advanced education was to prepare students for positions of dominance, teachers at higher levels tempered violent methods. Through rhetorical exercises of impersonation and declamation, a boy learned to command and rehearsed his future roles as head of his household, slave owner, advocate, and holder of influential positions.[105]

Other, more practical reasons, such as the larger "size" of students at this level and their invariably upper-class origin (versus the mixed pool served by primary instruction), must have played a role in the milder treatment reserved for older students. Wealthy parents were probably more capable of protecting their sons, particularly because they were often

[102] I disagree with Booth (1973: 109), who maintains that punishment was enforced with brutality at every level.

[103] Cf. below, pp. 156–58.

[104] See Beck 1975: 275, pl. 53.

[105] See Bloomer 1997.

themselves bound to an influential teacher by intense personal loyalties, as the correspondence of Libanius shows repeatedly. Moreover, the studies in which these young men were involved must have represented a sort of protection against ill treatment. Rhetoric was a training in order and self-control: physical violence did not suit this suave world, governed by the harmony of well-balanced phrases and the dignity of controlled voices. Thus Libanius maintained that he preferred to inspire in his students a sense of reverence rather than fear (*Or.* 58.1 and 38). On defending himself from criticism leveled against his teaching methods, he proudly affirmed, "I impart into the subject an element of genteel pleasantry; that is the reason why I do not need to beat my students, for they do everything willingly" (*Or.* 2.20). Only occasionally were harsher methods needed, as when a student devoted his energy to physical training rather than to mental gymnastics. Thus Libanius responded to an influential parent who had inquired why the teacher had beaten his son by saying that he had caught the lad in a moment of laziness, when he was "showing the speed of his legs: therefore it was on the legs that he has been punished, so that he would be concerned in the future with another race, that of the tongue" (*Ep.* 1330.3).[106]

Sheer convenience must have also advised teachers of higher education against excessive maltreatment of students: unhappy adolescents, who were learning to become articulate, could convince pedagogues and parents to let them change schools. The fear of losing pupils was a constant factor in a teacher's professional life in ancient times. As he grew older and saw the prestige of his rhetorical school diminish somewhat, Libanius, who still had a very solid position and no financial preoccupations, nevertheless grew ever more insecure. In a discourse composed to denounce students' defections, he maintained that, even though discipline had become lax, teachers were impotent: "When students are lazy, teachers do not dare to scold them; when they sleep, teachers do not dare to wake them up; when they misbehave, teachers are silent; they are aware that they do not act well, but they know from experience that it is not without danger for themselves that they will chastise" (*Or.* 43.10). As usual, it is advisable not to take at face value what Libanius says in the heat of declamation. Nevertheless, it seems that it was education itself that gave students the power to defend themselves from the excesses of their educators.

---

[106] Cf. Norman 1992: no. 139.

The tension that characterized the functioning of classrooms in ancient times, which was partly a reflection of the unequal relationship existing between students and teachers, also depended on the precariousness of the teachers' position. In Greco-Roman Egypt as everywhere else, the lack of security and the reality of economic situations that could vary widely according to circumstance added to the everyday frustrations of class-room life. Libanius was not too unrealistic when he proclaimed that a teacher had to account to everybody—students, parents, pedagogues, even grandparents—and that, if an instructor did not triumph over stu-dents' dull natures, making them appear, "even if they were of stone, sons of the gods," he became a target of everybody's accusations (*Or.* 25.46). This was surely the plight of many teachers in antiquity, at the mercy of a volatile demand for their services and parents' willingness—or unwill-ingness—to pay. In the midst of many pressing necessities—says this rhe-tor—teachers invoked the Erinyes against students who did not under-stand their predicament (*Or.* 43.17). Was it a teacher expressing his rage who wrote such an invocation to the Erinyes on a Roman ostracon found in Egypt?[107] Though pupils were slaves of their teachers—says Libanius— a teacher was a slave of many masters. Students had their share of diffi-culties as they climbed up the hill of education, but a teacher was like "that Sisyphus who in Homer struggles with his rock," rolling it up a hill, only to see it perpetually roll down (*Or.* 25.46).

---

[107] See *O.Edfou* II.308, which only preserves the scanty beginning of such an invocation. Since the whereabouts of the ostraca found at Edfou are unknown, it is impossible to check on the hand in search of some clues about its origin.

Women and Education

Tʜᴇ ᴀɴᴄɪᴇɴᴛs showed an active interest in women's education well
before the Hellenistic period. Plato wondered whether women should aspire to something more than wool-work and "weave" themselves a life
more useful and less insignificant (*Laws* 7.806a). He and Aristotle were
both committed to quasi-universal, mandatory elementary education for
all children. This was no extreme ideological position.[1] These theories
were able to gain some acceptance outside philosophical circles only because they were to a certain degree symptomatic of changing attitudes
and evolving expectations. Specific evidence for the education of girls in
classical Greece is scanty, but the period under consideration in this book
offers a much richer textual and visual documentation.

From the discussion of the role and status of teachers in the previous
chapter emerged a picture in which the subjects were almost exclusively
male. This chapter covers women and education from two perspectives:
women appear as providers of education at various levels and as recipients of primary and grammatical instruction. In a world where male
teachers and students were the norm, women attempted to negotiate new
spaces for themselves, but were sometimes forced into the corners. Men
and women need to be defined in terms of one another, and separate areas
of participation and influence existed in education only to the extent that
they did in other areas of society. This will be evident in the chapter in
many respects. And yet, I chose to focus primarily on women here—instead of incorporating this material into other chapters—because the
question of their contributions to and participation in a world of literates
demands attention at length and in detail. The study of women's education has been discontinuous and has rested on the consideration of fragments of evidence, focusing primarily on isolated examples of women
of outstanding culture and status whose achievements hardly reflect the
opportunities offered to girls of unexceptional backgrounds.[2] But a collec-

---

[1] See especially Plato *Resp.* 5.452a and 456b–c; *Laws* 7.804d. The education that was
reserved to the women guardians in the *Republic* was extended to all girls in the *Laws*. See
also Aristotle *Pol.* 1260b.

[2] Handbooks on ancient education contain vague generalizations. This topic is absent
from the numerous books concerning women's and gender issues, such as Gardner 1986 or
Joshel and Murnaghan 1998, with a few exceptions: Cole 1981, primarily focused on classi-

tion of exempla, which would have pleased an ancient grammarian, is hardly satisfying for a historian: such an approach either has the limited impact of those case studies that do not offer a synthesizing perspective or gives rise to vague generalizations camouflaged as objectivity and producing false effects of homogeneity and coherence. It is essential to consider other layers of evidence. In this respect, the papyri provide some welcome links with the rest of the textual and visual documentation, even though their contribution is uneven and they do not offer a smooth schema of the development of female education. But a rigorous focus on them will make visible previously unseen aspects of women's participation in the culture of literates.

A crucial question to keep in mind is the bearing of economic and social stratification on the educational upbringing of women. While the acquisition of some literacy helped men cope with the realities of daily life, the principal aim of a liberal education was to reinforce the position of privilege for those men who could afford it, readying them for the responsibilities of power. Women's role in society was generally more private and less exposed to the demands of the outside world. More than for men, their education was a function of their social status. The evidence concerning women teachers of primary education is not always clear in this respect, but one suspects that it was primarily women of relatively low social background and freedwomen who filled these positions. In urban environments, elementary education was probably offered to some female students of the low-middle class, but information is scattered and largely incomplete. Even though access to education was smoother for girls of the upper class, it is likely that not many of them went beyond the primary level. It is useful to keep in mind the words of the mother of the Christian preacher John Chrysostom (ca. C.E. 354–407), who observed that there was a fundamental difference between raising a daughter and raising a son: a daughter was a cause of anxiety but not of great expenses, whereas bringing up a son involved great sums of money for a liberal education (*De Sacerd.* 1.2.50–56, fourth century C.E.). Even upper-class parents did not always find it imperative to provide daughters with an education, particularly beyond the acquisition of the rudiments. The evidence of women's correspondence on papyrus, in any case, shows that the women who had attained some degree of education belonged to the upper strata of society and came from propertied environments.

---

cal Greece; Pomeroy 1977 and 1984, heavily centered on exceptional women; Pomeroy 1981, in need of qualifications. A more realistic but limited assessment of the situation is in Harris 1989: 136–37 and 239–40.

A saying of the Cynic philosopher Diogenes (ca. 400–325 B.C.E.) that captured only a fragment of reality described education as an ornament to the rich.[3] For males, education had a much wider meaning and provided effective ways to gain access to power and to maintain fixed hierarchies. The meaning that it had for women was not immutable and unified, and the power education conferred on them through concrete social interactions did not operate in linear ways. Education was not an ornamental attribute that only served to increase the *value* of a woman. In what follows, one should be alert to the many and often subtle ways in which education gave women a degree of control over their lives. The evidence from Greco-Roman Egypt indicates that the possession of some instruction was protection against deceit and augmented women's control over their property and their ability to conduct business. But this reduction of the significance of literacy solely to protection and promotion of a woman's material interests[4]—undoubtedly a crucial function—is too limiting. The prestige that even minimal educational attainment carried for men and the pride that they derived from such accomplishments as the ability to sign is undeniable.[5] Some women also chose to perform as "slow-writers" or to be described as "knowing letters," even in situations where that achievement did not bring any material advantage.[6] Letters that they sent to relatives and friends concerning family or other matters confirm the impression that literacy had a deeper function for women and allowed them to be an integral part of a society that was fundamentally literate in the sense that many people were familiar with literate modes, if not themselves literate. Moreover, archives[7] containing letters of particularly distinguished women, such as those in the family circle of the governor Apollonios—examined below—show that education left permanent traces in them and to some degree shaped their thinking.

But the exciting reality that resurfaces throughout the papyri concerning some women and education should not obscure the fact that illiterate women were the norm; further, their role in family and society revolved around domestic matters and was far more passive than that of their male partners. Though some women were able to gain a relative command over

---

[3] Diogenes Laertius 6.68.

[4] See Sheridan 1998.

[5] Cf. below, Chapter 6.

[6] See, e.g., the pride of Aurelia Thaisous, also called Lolliane, in *P.Oxy.* XII.1467 and 1475. She may have come from the family of the grammarian Lollianus.

[7] I use here the term "archives" in the sense of troves of personal and/or official papers concerning one individual or family.

their lives, for others it was natural or inevitable to accept a subordinate role. Power operates in subtle ways: one should keep in mind concepts of complicity and approval of traditional standards that made many women unwilling to change. Some school exercises, for instance, have a clear misogynistic tone.[8] Menander's maxims disparaging many aspects of women's lives, including education, were favorites in schools up to the Byzantine age. It is reasonable to assume that female students swallowed them without much resistance.

Concerns with periodization will apply more to this than to other chapters, even though I will not always follow a chronological approach. The evidence relative to women teachers is much richer in the Roman than in the Hellenistic period, but it does not offer per se sufficient clues indicating a degree of change: as always, one has to take into account that chance determines which papyri survive, and that there is a marked imbalance in the preservation of documents.[9] Women's correspondence, on the other hand, seems to yield some clearer indications in this respect, even though the same caveat is valid. Few Ptolemaic letters are preserved—and much caution is needed in venturing conclusions—but the early ones in particular are relatively long and well written: they appear to be superior to Roman letters, which are generally shorter and more often display limited linguistic and syntactical capability. One has the impression that it was the general attitude toward letter-writing that changed, and that Roman women perhaps received a less sophisticated educational training but were less intimidated by written correspondence. The presence of women teachers at primary levels in the Roman period might be tentatively connected to the exposure of more women to basic literacy. This issue, at any rate, is part of a larger and still-debated question concerning general levels of literacy among the population as a whole.[10] In this respect, the evidence of the school exercises brings an important contribution insofar as it converges with the evidence of letters. Ptolemaic exercises, which do not yet include grammar and line-by-line commentaries to Homer,[11] nevertheless cover a range of authors who disappear from later education. This would

[8] Morgan 1998: 135–38.

[9] The ratio of preserved Ptolemaic to Roman documents and letters is approximately one to five or six.

[10] See lately Harris 1989, in favor of higher literacy in Hellenistic times; Morgan 1998: 58 and 63, for lower levels in the Ptolemaic period. Pomeroy (1981) favors higher women's literacy rates in Hellenistic Egypt but mainly considers a few exceptional women—royal women and grammarians.

[11] Cf. below, Chapter 7.

suggest that in the Roman period, education lost some degree of sophistication. Finally, a thornier problem is represented by the meager evidence of women's correspondence during the early Byzantine period. The very few letters preserved were in general elaborately penned by professional scribes, even when a woman was literate,[12] and show a higher degree of formality than Roman letters. Formulating an opinion on women's education on the basis of these letters is impossible, but it seems that letter-writing in Greek had reverted to an artificial and less spontaneous production. The transition to writing practices of the early medieval period can perhaps be perceived.[13] But the question is further complicated by the presence of a notable number of Coptic letters sent by women between the sixth and eighth centuries that include short and simple letters next to longer and more formal ones.[14] Were women in late antique Egypt expressing themselves in writing mostly through Coptic? This intriguing question is beyond the scope of this book.

WOMEN TEACHERS

The literary sources do not disclose much about women teachers in antiquity, just as they overlook other aspects of women's experience. This is hardly surprising, since the reality of the ancient world is viewed through male and upper-class sources, who were interested in the achievements of adult male citizens. Moreover, the class bias of the sources is such that it allows us still less knowledge of the activities of women of the lower classes. The scant literary evidence on women who fulfilled some kind of teaching role in higher education in the Greek world concerns some grammarians and philosophers who lived in Alexandria in the Hellenistic times and in late antiquity and owed their scholarly achievements to the presence of a father or other male relatives, who introduced them to a world of "male" cultural pursuits. The accomplishments of grammarians such as Agallias, Hestiaea, and Demo in the Hellenistic period,[15] and of

---

[12] See, e.g., *SB* XVIII.13762, in which the woman who dictated the letter added some remarks in her own hand.

[13] See Clanchy 1993.

[14] There are about sixty Coptic letters, mostly on ostraca.

[15] See Athenaeus 1.14d; Pomeroy 1984: 61; Strabo 13.599; Eustathius on B 538, 280, 19; Pomeroy 1977: 60 and nn. 78 and 79. Further bibliography in F. De Martino, *Rose di Pieria* (Bari, 1991), 59–60 n. 40.

philosophers and scholars such as Hypatia or Aedesia in the fifth century C.E.,[16] are brilliant testimonies that some exceptionally gifted women privileged by birth and social status were able to enter male-dominated fields. The visual evidence offers another attestation of a woman who might have been a grammarian in Egypt in the first century C.E.: a mummy portrait-head displays the fine features and inquisitive eyes of Hermione (Fig. 11).[17] Wrapped in hundreds of yards of very expensive linen, Hermione certainly came from a wealthy family. Though it is not completely clear whether in this case the term *grammatikē* referred to this woman's profession or to her culture, it is suggestive that an inscription from the second to third century found in North Africa reveals that another woman was perhaps engaged in that profession. The fact that the term *grammatica* probably alluded to more than the personal erudition of Volusia Tertullina finds supports in a second inscription concerning a member of the *gens* Volusia, a Volusius, who is defined as *grammaticus latinus*.[18]

The achievements of these women were extraordinary enough to be considered worthy to be handed down to posterity. It was less noteworthy, in the eyes of the male literary sources, to be an elementary teacher. Only one testimony of women's presence in this profession emerges from the visual evidence. A Hellenistic funerary monument found in Cyrene, close to Egypt, called *The Tomb of the Swing* displays metopes that show different moments in the life of the deceased female whose body is contained in the cell.[19] In one, a female teacher is portrayed in an open-air setting: she holds a rod and is pointing to something as the woman "pupil" sitting in front of her counts on her fingers.[20]

[16] See M. Dzielska, *Hypatia of Alexandria* (Cambridge, Mass., 1995). See also the tenth-century lexicon known as *Suda* under this entry; A. Cameron, "Isidore of Miletus and Hypatia: On the Editing of Mathematical Texts," *GRBS* 31 (1990): 103–27. G. Clark, *Women in Late Antiquity* (Oxford, 1993), 130–38. For Aedesia, *PRLE* 2: 10–11; *Suda* s.v. Aidesia 2.

[17] See *SB* I.5753.3; Doxiadis 1995: 50–51, no. 33; Walker and Bierbrier 1997: 37–38, no. 11, dating this portrait to about C.E. 40–50; and D. Montserrat, "Heron 'Bearer of *philosophia*' and Hermione *grammatike*," *JEA* 83 (1997): 223–26.

[18] See S. Agusta-Boularot and M. Bousbaa, "Une inscription inédite de Cherchell (Algérie): *Volusia Tertullina grammat(ica)*," *L' Africa Romana* 11 (1994): 163–73.

[19] See L. Bacchielli, "Le pitture della 'Tomba dell' Altalena' di Cirene nel Museo del Louvre," *Quaderni di archeologia della Libia: Cirene e la Grecia* 8 (1976): 355–83.

[20] In funerary art, the deceased is usually portrayed as seated. The objections of Harris (1989: 136) against recognizing education in this scene are easily overcome: an open-air setting for school was quite common, the age of the pupil is unimportant, and in the other metopes the figures also have bare chests.

Figure 11.   Mummy portrait of Hermione *grammatikē,*
about C.E. 40–50.

But in the papyri, more women teachers resurface. Not unlike their
male counterparts, they appear by their titles in letters and documents
that do not disclose anything about their teaching positions or activities.
The papyrus evidence, moreover, needs to be assessed with caution: some
of it is fragmentary or presents a complex background. A proper evaluation of these documents, which date from the first to the sixth century
C.E., should start from a fragmentary letter from the fourth century addressed to a teacher (*didaskalos*) that twice mentions a woman, Kyria,
who is designated by the same title preceded by the feminine article (*hē
didaskalos,* "lady teacher.")[21] The situation is complicated by the text's

[21] See *SB* XIV.11532; M. Nagel, "Lettre Chrétienne sur papyrus," *ZPE* 18 (1975): 317–
23. It is not certain that Kyria was a personal name; it might have meant "lady."

background. The letter is of Christian provenance, as the final salutation testifies, but since the Church did not allow women to teach, Kyria was not entrusted with the teaching of the religious doctrine in a Christian milieu. The Church of Egypt admitted a school (*didaskaleion*) that was directed by several teachers who imparted instruction in theology, but not only were these teachers usually part of the clergy, but they were always males, and women were categorically excluded from teaching. Women, however, were not excluded from teaching in gnostic milieus, where they held positions of power,[22] and therefore the papyrus's editor concluded that Kyria was a teacher of religion in a gnostic milieu, even though he had to admit that there are no texts of gnostic provenance in the fourth century where women with the title *didaskalos* appear. But could Kyria be a woman in charge of teaching something other than religious material, an elementary teacher perhaps? The editor discarded a priori this possibility, on the presupposition that there was no evidence of women teachers at low levels and "the profession was not open to women." In the papyri, however, women with the title "teacher" occasionally appear: they are not designated with the full title *hē didaskalos* ("lady teacher") but with a shortened form of this word, *deskalē* or *deskalos*, which had the same meaning.[23]

A survey of the evidence includes first a letter from C.E. 99 that Apollonous writes to her husband, who is away in military service.[24] In his absence she oversaw the land that the family possessed. Among other things, she tells him that he should not be concerned about affairs at home: "And do not worry about the children; they are in good health and attend classes with a lady didaskalos (*deskalē*)."[25] In another papyrus of the first century, a teacher makes a quick appearance: in this case, only the title, *deskalos*, reveals that Sarapias was engaged in the teaching profession.[26] Not much more is known about a woman teacher mentioned by an energetic businesswoman in a second-century letter found in the village of Tebtunis: in writing to the manager of her property, Diogenis adds some remarks in her own hand telling him to go see the son of the "woman teacher."[27] A further letter is only slightly more revealing of the back-

---

[22] See E. Pagels, *The Gnostic Gospels* (New York, 1979), 60–61.

[23] See Cribiore 1996a: 23–24. These terms always refer to women.

[24] See *P.Mich.* VIII.464.

[25] Cf., for the expression "attend classes," *PSI* I.94.

[26] See *P.Mich.* II.123 recto col. 21.9.

[27] *P.Mil.Vogl.* II.76; cf. *P.Kron.* 16, p. 36. The editor, however, did not recognize the fragmentary word. I owe this information to R. S. Bagnall.

ground of the teacher mentioned, the *deskalos* Athenais.[28] A mother writes from Alexandria to her children Ptolemaios and Apollinaria a letter full of longing and affection: at the end she lists people who send their greetings, among whom is their nurse (*trophos*) and their teacher. A *deskalos* also appears among the relatives and friends that a man greets as he writes to another man to invite him to visit for a few days.[29] A much later letter, from the fifth or sixth century, is unfortunately in a very fragmentary state.[30] The background is the same as in the Christian letter mentioned above, but in this case the letter was addressed to a woman teacher, who is greeted by the sender with words of affection such as, "You are my joy."

Among the low-status jobs that a woman could hold in Greco-Roman Egypt was teaching manual skills to young people, who were apprenticed for one or more years. In Egypt, children younger than fourteen years old, and from families of comparatively low social status, entered into apprenticeships to learn a skill, such as shorthand-writing or weaving.[31] Apprentices were mostly boys, freeborn or slaves: only a handful of girls occur in these contracts, usually but not always slaves.[32] In contracts of apprenticeship, the individuals with the title *didaskalos* ("teacher") appear to have been men, with one exception. In a contract from the third century, a woman, Aurelia Libouke, appears as a *deskalos* ("lady teacher") in the art of weaving: she was supposed to teach for a year in her house a young girl of a different town, giving her an allowance.[33]

In the papyri considered above, one cannot in every case be sure of the subject of instruction imparted by a *deskalos* ("lady teacher"), particularly when mention occurs out of context. On the analogy of documents where male teachers of letters appear, one might conclude that a woman mentioned with the title *deskalos*, without the indication that she also possessed special manual skills, was a teacher of letters, and probably of elementary letters. But even more suggestive of a literary education versus apprenticeship is the background of these letters. The children of Apollonous or Serapias, for instance, were certainly not placed into apprenticeship, because they came from fairly wealthy families. In Alexandria, Ptolemaios and Apollinaria in their early years were attended by a nurse but

---

[28] See *BGU* I.332, second to third century C.E.

[29] See *P.Oxy.* XXXI.2595, third century C.E.

[30] *P.Iand.* VI.101.

[31] About the prestige carried by apprenticeship in the Middle Ages, Hanawalt 1993: 129–53.

[32] Van Minnen 1998a.

[33] *SB* XVIII.13305.

later passed into the care of the teacher Athenais, who probably taught them the rudiments of education. It is likely that Athenais was a freed-woman who still lived in the family household, had some knowledge of reading and writing, and was thus employed as teacher.

The few names of women who taught in and partook of the "male" world of higher education do not fully reflect the extent of female teaching. Women teachers of primary letters—and most male primary teachers—were disregarded by the literary sources because they did not hold prominent jobs: women, moreover, might have brought to their profession "feminine" qualities, such as patience, that might not have been particularly appreciated. The important role that women of low social groups and of limited literacy played in primary education in the seventeenth century and later, when women were rarely educated themselves, is a suitable comparandum.[34] One is also reminded of the feminization of teaching on the American frontier, which resulted from a combination of low salaries, minimal literacy requirements, and concepts of womanhood and domesticity that justified the employment of women as teachers.[35]

WOMEN'S EDUCATION IN THE GREEK EAST

Important evidence concerning the availability of education to girls in the Hellenistic and Roman periods is found in epigraphical sources, terracottas, and sarcophagi. This evidence, which is scattered in the eastern part of the Mediterranean and concerns only specific geographical settings, is not always easy to interpret in isolation. Its value is greatly increased, however, by the fact that these sources and the papyri agree in suggesting an authentic growth in female literacy starting from the Hellenistic period. A brief summary of this well-known evidence, therefore, provides an essential background to the information emerging from Egypt. The novelties of Hellenistic education were the endowments for the primary instruction of male children found in some Greek cities of the Mediterranean.[36] In the city of Teos, the privileges were extended to all children, boys and girls. Even though, curiously, girls did not receive musical and physical education, and not all of them appear to have had access to an

[34] Spufford 1981. Cf. Stone 1969: 94–95, for the nineteenth century.

[35] See M. Hurlbut Cordier, *Schoolwomen of the Prairies and Plains* (Albuquerque, N.M., 1992).

[36] Teos, Miletus, Delphi, and Rhodes. See *SIG*[3] 577, 578, 672, and Polybius 31.31.1. It is not unlikely that other school endowments occurred.

Figure 12.   Roman terracotta of a schoolgirl with tablets.

education in letters,[37] this benefaction represented a fundamental victory for female literacy. Another inscription found in the gymnasium of Pergamon, which shows that some girls had won prizes in contests for epic, elegiac, and lyric poetry, reading, and calligraphy, is at least as suggestive, even though prizes might have been awarded for feats of memorization.[38] The visual evidence of Hellenistic terracottas that were produced all over the Mediterranean, including Egypt, while not free of problems of interpretation, seems to point in the same direction. The typical representation portrays a schoolgirl looking at a diptych of tablets placed on her lap, but even more suggestive are the few Alexandrian images of girls on their way to school (Fig. 12).[39] It is true that since fashion played some role in the

[37] Pomeroy (1977: 52 and 1981: 320 n. 32) argues, wrongly in my view, that throughout the inscription, the term *paides* ("children") refers to both boys and girls.

[38] *MDAI* 35 (1910), 436, no. 20; 37 (1912), 277–78, no. 1; M. Fraenkel, ed., *Die Juschiften von Pergamon* (Berlin, 1890–95), 463; L. Robert, *Études anatoliennes* (Paris, 1937), 58–59; cf. *CIG* 3185.

[39] Cf. bibliography in Pomeroy 1977: 64 n. 9; M. Chehab, *Les terres cuites de Kharayeb, Bulletin du Musée de Beyrout* 10 (1951–52): 55 pl. LXV 2–4; Besques 1992: 64, pl. 31e–f; J. Fischer, *Griechisch-Römische Terrakotten aus Äegypten* (Tübingen, 1994), 130, 52 pl. 8.

choice of the iconographical motifs, and molds and artists traveled far, it is difficult to see what the real connection was between representation and local reality. Yet the proliferation of terracottas representing girls in connection with education is significant, even though it cannot be taken as proof—or even as an indication—that elementary female instruction became the norm.[40]

The Hellenistic endowments for elementary education have in the Roman period only one counterpart, but other school endowments may have existed. An inscription shows a benefaction in favor of the children of Xanthus in Lycia, which offered free education to girls and boys alike: all citizen girls benefited, with none of the restrictions valid in Teos.[41] Funeral monuments, moreover, occasionally allude to the literacy of girls, who are shown with reading and writing implements, and once in a while in the company of teachers.[42] Sometimes on the sarcophagi, girls appear to receive instruction from female figures, who are always interpreted as mothers.[43] Scenes on sarcophagi associating girls and education are rare, but it should be taken into account that girls are not often portrayed on sarcophagi in general: a boy's death had a stronger significance for the family's future and was commemorated more publicly.

The literary evidence of female literacy confirms that in the Hellenistic period, female education was present in urban environments and in reasonably comfortable circles. In Herodas's *Didaskalos*—strongly connected with Alexandria—the grandmother of Kokkalos, significantly, was represented as illiterate, "widowed of letters," but she was at least able to recite speeches from tragedy. Her daughter, however, had received some instruction in reading and writing and supervised her son's homework, together with her husband (22–26).[44] The *Hermeneumata*, which are connected with the Eastern as well as the Western world in the Roman period, provide further testimony in this direction. As a rule, the various versions of these schoolbooks address and represent male students. In two cases,

---

On a girl represented with her hand raised in the act of writing, S. Mollard-Besques, *Catalogue raisonné des figurines et reliefs*, vol. 2, *Myrina* (Paris, 1963), 111, pl. 134f. Cf. also Pomeroy 1984: pl. 7; and Beck 1975: pl. 71, 358.

[40] Marrou (1975, 1: 218) is too optimistic; cf. Harris 1989: 136–37.

[41] A. Balland, *Fouilles de Xanthos*, vol. 7 (Paris, 1981), no. 67 = *SEG* 30 (1980), no. 1535, second century C.E.

[42] See, e.g., a sarcophagus from Asia Minor, Marrou 1937: 37–39, no. 11, plate I; p. 28, no. 1. See also Huskinson 1996: 6.30, 10.14, and 10.19. Cf. the well-known grave relief of Abeita, Beck 1975: pl. 71, 359; British Museum 649.

[43] Marrou 1937: 33, no. 8, and pp. 40–42, no. 13.

[44] It should be noticed that this family could afford to pay for private education.

however, the *Hermeneumata* casually allude to female pupils: one version includes girls among the addressees in the preface, and another repeatedly mentions them in a list of words related to school.[45]

FEMALE LITERACY IN THE PAPYRI

The papyri allow us to make significant gains in ascertaining the extent of female literacy in antiquity, particularly because the information that they provide is not scattered but is securely located within a certain society. The reality of women's education and literacy in Egypt, however, is laden with the irreducible complexities inherent in the country's ethnic, linguistic, and cultural background.[46] It is practically impossible, for instance, to determine how widespread the knowledge of spoken Greek was among women, not only those who lived in villages but also those in towns. The ability to write and read Greek was limited to a minority of women living in urban environments and belonging to the upper strata of society.[47] It is essential to reiterate that the testimony of the letters sent by women applies only to this restricted pool of literates. Although the unique value of this evidence derives from the fact that it reveals significant examples of women who used literate modes of expression, one should not be blinded to another reality: the vast majority of women of the lower classes never learned to wield a pen. It is likely, in any case, that the educational opportunities offered to elite girls who spoke Greek in cities such as Alexandria or Hermopolis were not very different from those available in other cities of the Eastern empire. They usually consisted of primary education, and occasionally of some secondary instruction, but female students did not have access to advanced, rhetorical education.

Besides the more continuous testimony offered by private letters, the evidence concerning women's education is suggestive but uneven and needs to be closely investigated to ascertain its background. In the third century B.C.E., a petition that is usually taken as an indication that a father thought it part of his duty to give a daughter an education raises some

[45] See Dionisotti 1982: 97 line 1. See also Goetz 1892: 352, *Hermeneumata Stephani*. Bloomer (1997: 75) wrongly asserts that only boys are mentioned.

[46] For an assessment of languages, literacy, and ethnicity in Egypt that is valid for the Roman period as well as for late antiquity, see Bagnall 1993: 230–60.

[47] Cf. the modern scenario: nowadays the literacy rate for women in the poor southern Egyptian town of Mallawi—a stronghold of Islamist radicals—is only 10%: "School's Out," *The Economist* (January 25, 1997).

questions.[48] The text shows an old man enraged at his daughter Nike because, "corrupted" by a professional dancer, she has stopped paying her father a generous monthly contribution: he feels entitled to her support because he had raised her and "had given her an education." But a more careful investigation of the content provides some surprises. Even though the Greek expression that Nike "worked with her body" is far from clear,[49] the whole picture—her relative freedom and high pay, and the people with whom she consorted—makes one suspect that at least some of the education she had received consisted of instruction in dancing and playing music, and that she worked as some kind of entertainer.[50] Another testimony that education—probably Egyptian education—was sometimes available to girls of various social backgrounds comes from the city of Memphis in the second century B.C.E., where two young girls lived in the temple of Serapis under the protection of Ptolemaios son of Glaukias.[51] These girls, who were once chosen to impersonate two sister-goddesses in a solemn religious ceremony, continued to perform cult duties and apparently attended the school of the teacher Tothes.

In the papyri of the Roman period, direct allusions to girls in the process of obtaining an education are rare. It is likely that most of the *paideia* ("education") that the young slave Peina was receiving consisted of the acquisition of musical skills.[52] But a short private letter definitely refers to literate education: writing to the private teacher (*kathēgētēs*) about Tatoes, a girl who may have been the writer's daughter, a certain Ammonios asks the instructor to tell him how he wants to be compensated and announces that he is presently going to send him a jar of wine (or oil) and a basket of grapes.[53] Unfortunately, the lack of context makes it impossible to know whether this *kathēgētēs*—usually a teacher of secondary education—was instructing Tatoes beyond the primary level. However, it is very likely that the *kathēgētēs* of Heraidous mentioned below was not a primary teacher.

Legal documents may also supply information about female education: a woman may subscribe in her hand or may be described as "know-

---

[48] *P.Enteux.* 26, dated to 220 B.C.E.; Harris (1989: 137 n. 108) includes it among testimonies of education in letters.

[49] This is its only occurrence in papyri. Similar, but not identical, expressions usually refer to manual workers; see, e.g., *PSI* VI.554 and *P.Lond.* IV.1433.

[50] We do not know whether Nike also provided erotic entertainment. About the sexual availability of women dancers and musicians, see Montserrat 1996: 117–19.

[51] See Thompson 1988: 232–45. Cf. above, p. 19.

[52] Cf. *P.Oxy.* L.3555; see above, p. 47.

[53] *P.Oslo* III.156.

ing letters" because she was a party to a contract.[54] Occasionally, more details emerge to define the contours of the picture: an Aurelia Ptolemais, who belonged to a well-to-do family of Oxyrhynchos and signed with rapid characters, was also the owner of papyri from the *Iliad* and of more recherché works, such as the history of Sikyon and Africanus's *Kestoi*, that she probably inherited.[55] But the infrequency of female signatures and descriptions of women as literate is not in strict correlation with a corresponding rate of female literacy, since women had fewer occasions than men to be parties to contracts. The example of a woman such as Aurelia Charite in the fourth century C.E. shows that wealth, the capability and desire to manage one's property, a relative independence or the lack of a male partner, and even family models were powerful determinants of a woman's performance, in addition to her command of reading and writing.[56]

THE WOMEN'S LETTERS

More information about women's access to literacy can be derived from the private and business letters that they sent.[57] This aspect of personal correspondence was not exploited in the past: scholars have been skeptical about the possibility of extracting information about education from letters on the grounds that one was unable to distinguish whether the sender or a scribe had penned a letter.[58] The situation, however, is not so hopeless. More importantly, it involves a variety of aspects and offers indications in many directions: a close examination of the text of a letter and of the characteristics of the handwriting may yield unexpected evidence about a woman's education and language.

When a woman—or a man—needed to make use of written communication, various scenarios were possible.[59] If she was literate and thought

[54] Sheridan 1998; J. Sheridan, "Women without Guardians: An Updated List," *BASP* 33 (1996): 117–31.

[55] P^2 2181 and P^2 53: cf. Bagnall 1992. We do not know, however, whether or not this woman actually read these books.

[56] See *P.Charite* 8, 27, 33, 36, and 37; 38 was penned by her mother.

[57] I am currently engaged, together with R. S. Bagnall, in a larger project of collecting women's letters on papyrus. There are about 230 extant Greek letters sent by women from the Hellenistic to the early Byzantine period.

[58] Cf. Cole 1981: 234–35; and Harris 1989: 143.

[59] On private letters both dictated and handwritten by elite Romans, see McDonnell 1996: 474–76.

the circumstance required it, she might write the whole letter herself. In this case, body and salutations are in the same hand: the attribution of the letter to the woman writer is easier when there are several texts that concern her. But when a scribe or a secretary was available, that same woman might choose to dictate her letter, and only add final salutations and sometimes a date at the bottom. From the available evidence, there does not appear to be a correlation between dictation and the nature of the letter; that is, both formal and informal letters might be either dictated or self-written. Dictated letters do not speak against the literacy of the writer. Women of the upper class might have had a certain volume of correspondence to discharge when they wanted to maintain close contacts with family members or had to take care of their businesses and property. But it is also likely that some literate people who could easily rely on a scribe found it distasteful to write a letter in their own hand, since letter-writing required the employment of large, comprehensible characters, the production of which took a certain amount of time and effort.[60] Countless examples on papyrus show that, for the sake of legibility, when people wrote letters, their characters were always more slowly and carefully written and of larger size than those employed for documents.[61] The salutations penned by a woman at the bottom of the letter may disclose a lot about her familiarity with writing. If she was frequently engaged in correspondence—even simply by subscribing her letters—her hand may be rapid, fluent, and perceptibly different from that of a whole text that she penned. But the same unevenness is not noticeable in the handwriting of a woman who sporadically sent and subscribed letters. We also have to make allowance for the possibility that a literate woman could have dictated a letter without subscribing: in this case, detecting clues about her literacy may be very hard in the absence of other indications.

At the other end of the spectrum, a woman who could not write but needed to use written communication had to rely on the service of someone else, a professional scribe, a relative, or a friend. But even in this circumstance, a letter may reveal something about a woman's upbringing, particularly when the text exhibits signs that a scribe did not entirely transform it, and the seams of the fabric are evident. An uneven text does not inevitably point to the limited literacy of a woman who spoke in chopped, harsh sentences without articulation and connectives. Even when a woman was educated, lack of smoothness in a dictated letter may

---

[60] Cf. *P.Oxy.* LVI.3860, written by a man, Alexandros, on behalf of the woman who was his host: he declares that he wore himself out writing the letter.

[61] On distinctions of handwriting, cf. Cribiore 1996a: 4–7.

reflect her train of thought emerging among conventional expressions and may disclose her emotions and her distinctive vocabulary. It may be even easier to detect a woman's speech when she was educated and used scribes at her service who did not attempt to standardize her language.

Is it possible to capture a woman's *voice* through the papyri? It depends on the connotations one gives to this slightly abused word. The answer is positive if "voice" refers to a specific woman's way of expressing herself and to her conversational language. Several letters—both dictated and written by the sender—reveal idioms and locutions that are likely to have been part of a particular woman's personal lexicon. But if by "voice" one intends something more objective and universal that denotes the language of a woman seen as a representative of her gender, much caution is required. Although conversational language reflects social structure to a much greater extent than does literary language,[62] gendered speech, that is, a woman's voice as opposed to a man's voice, is elusive, especially when one tries to identify it in the written word. Should a woman's "voice" be envisaged as a reflection of her "feminine" concerns, style, experience, dependence on male figures, and relative lack of involvement with power? This notion does not seem to hold entirely true in the papyri. Even though a comprehensive study of men's letters is still a desideratum, and many more men were involved in correspondence,[63] it does not appear that the concerns of propertied men were much different from those of women of the same class, or conversely that men were less sensitive to family matters. From archives that include male and female letters, it appears that the topic of a private letter was a function of situational circumstances and cultural and social environments rather than of "typically" male and female concerns. Looking specifically at language is not particularly illuminating: no distinctive locution encapsulates Woman's speech.[64] Forms of address do not seem to be gender-specific: most letters were dictated so that addresses reflected formulaic expressions of male scribes, but gender differences do not emerge from letters penned by the sender, either. From archives that contain a variety of letters, it appears that no different epistolary conventions applied to letters written by women to men or to other women: the gender of the person addressed did not reflect

[62] See Dickey 1996: 32–33.

[63] Preserved letters by women are roughly one-fourteenth as numerous as letters sent by men.

[64] The fact that an expression may be more common in a woman's than in a man's letter is significant, but not a decisive argument. Cf. the phrase *mneian poieisthai* ("to remember") in some women's letters (e.g., *P.Lond.* I.42).

to a great extent how a letter was formulated. The variations are again mostly due to the cultural background of the writer and the difference in the social and economic standings of writer and addressee.

A striking type of woman emerges from some of the most eloquent letters, and particularly from those written or subscribed by the sender herself: a relatively independent person, who sometimes traveled to pursue her business interests or to maintain family relationships, took care of financial matters, often sent and received goods of some value, and did not shrink from occasionally addressing male relatives and dependents in a sharp, peremptory tone. Many of the isolated letters—those not part of archives—are not very informative about the writer as an individual: their content is often brief and allusive and takes for granted previous correspondence and situations obscure to us. Sometimes, however, a single letter brings to light fascinating aspects of a woman's world. Two Ptolemaic texts, for instance, are illuminating. The urgent appeal of Isias to her husband Hephaestion to return home shows not only anxiety and irritation at his behavior but also a juxtaposition of well-balanced phrases that appear to be a trademark of a woman who, in her own words, had learned to "steer herself and her child through crisis."[65] It is likely that Isias penned the salutation at the bottom of her letter in minute characters that reveal a good familiarity with writing.[66] Another letter evokes effectively the outlines of the life of a girl in antiquity, which, not surprisingly, consisted of playing, staying inside, helping out with housework, and studying, probably with private instructors.[67] The older sister, who advised two younger sisters who were away from home to "devote yourself to learning" (philomathein), probably penned the letter in its entirety.

But it is especially women's letters that are part of archives that illuminate a woman's place in family and society, her relationships with other women and with male relatives and subordinates, her upbringing, the level of education she had attained, and her familiarity with writing. In what follows, I shall consider three archives of the Roman period: those of Asklepiades in the Augustan age, of Pompeius in the second half of the first century C.E., and of Apollonios at the beginning of the second century. They all contain letters sent by women, particularly—but not exclusively—to male correspondents.

[65] P.Lond I.42, Atlas I plate 17 (UPZ I.59); Select Papyri 97.

[66] This was not noticed by Harris (1989: 143). Hephaestion's brother, who wrote another letter urging Hephaestion to return (UPZ I.60), probably wrote the body of Isias's long letter.

[67] P.Athen. 60.

ISIDORA TO ASKLEPIADES: ACT LIKE A MAN

In the four letters that Isidora sent to Asklepiades, she calls him "brother," but their actual kinship—if any—is unclear.[68] Her letters can be divided into two groups: two are written in a capable and fluent scribal handwriting, and the other two are in an uneven hand with characters that are well formed at the beginning but that degenerate as the letter proceeds. The latter was very likely Isidora's hand. But this distinction carries further. The letters that are proficiently penned are written in competent business Greek and address Asklepiades by his full name. In the other letters, Isidora addresses him with the nickname Asklas and writes her own name with a superfluous character, Isidoira. The command of the language exhibited by the letters of the second group corresponds to their less-polished appearance. Besides a rich vocabulary and a rather complex sentence structure, they show an oral style, some mistakes due to phonetic spelling, and occasional uncertainty in case forms. The education of the writer was not faultless, but it allowed her to manipulate the written word efficiently.

Isidora is unmistakably the same in all the letters. She does not lose much time in salutations, but goes directly to the point and gives orders concerning selling produce from her land, transferring money, or providing someone with boats for a trip. She requests that Asklepiades send a variety of specific items, such as red, sky-blue, and mulberry-colored bedspreads and an incredibly expensive sleeping rug for a child.[69] She shows much impatience: her imperative and condescending tone (take care "that you do not fall into difficulties"), her reproaches ("you are not even consistent with yourselves"), and her injunctions ("send me a reply to everything quickly") betray a woman used to command. In every letter she urges Asklepiades to "behave in a manly fashion" (*diandragathein*), a very rare word that was part of her personal lexicon and was preserved by the scribe who took down her dictation.[70] While it is not sure what male qualities she was invoking, the whole scenario conjures up the image of a woman for whom education was far from being an ornament.

[68] As usual, appellatives indicating degrees of family relationship in letters are not to be taken literally. *BGU* IV.1204 and 1207 were penned by a scribe, and 1205 and 1206 were probably written by Isidora herself between October 2 and November 5, 28 B.C.E. The archive of Asklepiades includes *BGU* IV.1204–1209; on p. 347, two more women's fragmentary letters are mentioned. See also *BGU* XVI.2665.

[69] *Egkoimētron* ("sleeping rug," *BGU* IV.1204.10), a rare word that may have indicated a piece of furniture.

[70] *Andragathein* ("behave in a manly fashion or honorably") was a later form for *andragathizesthai*. The compound verb appears only one other time in papyri.

HERENNIA TO POMPEIUS: DO NOT FORGET US

Herennia was the daughter of Pompeius, whose archive includes five letters sent to him individually by four women belonging to his family.[71] It is unclear how exactly the other women were related to him. Herennia lived with her own family in the country—"little" Pompeius might have been her son—probably not very far from her father, who resided in the metropolis of Arsinoe.[72] Since the other female relatives dictated their letters and did not subscribe them, their literacy is questionable.[73] But Herennia wrote one of her letters and subscribed another. Writing for her was not a daily occupation. In the first letter, the characters are large, stilted, and all separated, and they become perceptibly more ill-formed toward the end, as the writer was forced to reduce their size. Herennia's hand has an unmistakable Ptolemaic flavor. The handwriting taught in school, in fact, always clung to past and more formal forms, and this woman did not practice enough to develop a personal hand. An attempt at such a personal hand can be seen in her subscription, where her satisfaction at writing characters that are a bit more elaborate is palpable (Fig. 13).[74] Herennia's capability in drafting a letter is consonant with her command of the pen. She is able to string together simple sentences in a paratactic style, but is not able to go much beyond that. When she attempts to express to her father a more intricate situation—he is supposed to pay a certain levy for an Egyptian temple, and she is unsure whether she should pay for him—her stilted Greek is unmasked. Undoubtedly her education was more superficial than that of Isidora.

Herennia's preoccupations are mostly domestic. Even when her main concern is the temple's dues, she starts her letter by saying, "I have bought you the olives." She is close to her parents and appears to have been to some degree in charge of their well-being. Apparently her father resided with her for a period.[75] She asks her mother not to forget to tell her father to buy "a colored himation suitable for a gentleman" and not "to forget"

---

[71] The letters were sent between C.E. 57 and 64. *P.Mert* II.63 and *SB* VI.9122 were written by Herennia; three other female relatives sent *SB* VI.9120 and 9121, and *P.Fouad* 75, which announced Herennia's death.

[72] Herennia, her father, and her son bear Roman names, but not the *tria nomina*, so they are unlikely to be Roman citizens. Other relatives bear Greek or Egyptian names.

[73] *SB* VI.9121, dictated by Heraklous, is broken at the bottom so that a possible subscription is not visible.

[74] *SB* VI.9122 (*P.Oslo* inv. 1444). Herennia subscribed this letter, and it is not inconceivable that she wrote it in its entirety.

[75] Cf. *SB* VI.9120.

Figure 13.   Papyrus letter of Herennia (P. Oslo inv. 1444), between
C.E. 57 and 64.

to buy something else for another person. In both letters she prays, "Do
not forget us," an expression that seems to be her own and not a conventional phrase. But in C.E. 64, it is a letter written probably by her sister that
tells Pompeius not to forget his "poor daughter" (*talaipōron*) and to come
quickly if he still wants to see her, for Herennia "gave birth to an eight-
month child, dead, and lived on for four days, and after that she died."

Heraidous: A Schoolgirl

At the beginning of the second century C.E., in the Egyptian cities of Hermopolis and Heptakomia, the lives of a circle of women revolved around
a single man, who was respectively their son, husband, father, master, or

social acquaintance. The archive of Apollonios includes twenty-five letters sent by women.[76] Apollonios's family belonged to the upper class of the Greek population of Hermopolis. When he became *stratēgos*, that is, head of the civil administration of the district of Apollonopolites Heptakomia in Upper Egypt, he transferred there with part of his family. His wife Aline followed him with the younger children but went sometimes back to Hermopolis to check on things at home. Their oldest daughter, Heraidous, remained in the metropolis with Apollonios's mother, Eudaimonis. This archive, therefore, allows us not only to appreciate the level of education of a group of women, but also to define more precisely a girl's upbringing.

Even though Heraidous is always referred to in the letters as "the little one," she was not a little girl anymore. It is unnecessary to assume that "she was her mother's favorite" and that therefore "more attention was given to her education than it was ordinarily given to daughters even in the same economic and social class."[77] The other children in fact are briefly mentioned with the collective name *tekna* ("children") only because they were younger and were staying with their parents. But Heraidous kept in touch with her family by correspondence. In a letter to an old servant (*P.Giss.* 68), Aline manifests some concern about her oldest daughter: "My little Heraidous, in writing a letter to her father, did not say hello to me, and I do not know why." Had Heraidous simply forgotten to mention her mother, or was this a symptom of mother-daughter tension and of a teenager's mood? The latter supposition is more likely, since salutations were not perfunctory additions but fundamental components of ancient letters that served to maintain family contacts.

Some letters provide specific information about Heraidous's education. In *P.Giss.* 80 she is mentioned with two other students, a girl and a boy, Hermaios, who was the son of a certain Helene and the brother of an Apollonios.[78] The unknown sender gives the addressee a few concise directives: "Send the pigeons and the other birds that I do not eat . . . to the *kathēgētēs* of Heraidous; Helene, the mother of Apollonios, is asking him

---

[76] These letters amount to twenty-five, but some are very fragmentary. See R. Cribiore, "The Women in the Apollonios' Archive and Their Use of Literacy," in H. Melaert, ed., *Le rôle et le statut de la femme en égypte Hellénistique, Romaine et Byzantine*, forthcoming, and "Windows on a Woman's World: Some Letters from Roman Egypt," in A. Lardinois and L. McClure, eds., *Making Silence Speak: Women's Voices in Greek Literature and Society* (Princeton, 2001), 223–39.

[77] Pomeroy 1981: 315.

[78] Neither this letter nor *P.Giss.* 85 was sent by Aline. Contra, Pomeroy 1981: 314.

to take under his care her own son Hermaios. Also send the leftover food
. . . to the *kathēgētēs* of my own daughter, so that he pays attention to
her."[79] The last phrase may contain a touch of irony. As a rule, it was
students who were supposed to *philoponein* in school—"pay attention,
be industrious"—but here the expression is applied to a teacher who, in
the eyes of a father, needed some encouragement. The same Hermaios,
moreover, sent a letter to his older brother Apollonios (*P.Giss.* 85) in
which he mentions Heraidous: "Heraidous and our mother Helene say
hello and I, Hermaios, also salute you. Please [ask] my guardian to get
me all the things necessary for school, and a reading book for Heraidous
as well." Apparently Hermaios's father had died some time before, and
therefore his mother and older brother were responsible for his education:
he was not yet fourteen years old and was still in the care of a guardian,
who needed a formal request from Hermaios's brother before procuring
him material suitable for school.

Hermaios and Heraidous—as well as Tatoes and the girl mentioned in
P.Giss. 80—were taking advantage of private education at home. They
were children of privilege, and their families may have thought that private instructors could give them undivided attention of better quality,
even though in Hermopolis schools of various levels certainly existed.[80] It
appears that these students were using the same tutor and may have received their instruction together: they must have been of comparable age
and very likely had progressed beyond the primary level.[81] Another point
of interest in the letter *P.Giss.* 85 is its date. It was written at the end of
August, when Heraidous and Hermaios were still on vacation. In Hermopolis, school probably had not started yet, and private instruction may
have followed the same calendar. The Egyptian summer months were too
hot to permit a profitable use of either open or enclosed spaces for education. It is likely, then, that classes were not held in summer but resumed
around October.[82] In Antioch, which had a climate comparable to Egypt's,
classes were usually suspended in the summer months, and the school
year started again at the beginning of October.[83] What is valid around the
Mediterranean for rhetorical schools surely must have applied to lower
levels of education, where academic pressure was less intense. At the end

[79] It is hard to say whether these were real compensations or gifts.
[80] Cf. Aristotle *Pol.* 8.1337a; Quintilian 1.2.1–10.
[81] On coeducation, cf. Philostratus *Imag.* 1.12.3; Bonner 1977: 135–36.
[82] On the meager evidence for summer vacations, see Bonner 1977: 139; Augustine *Conf.* 9.2.
[83] See Libanius *Ep.* 894 and 419; cf. Festugière 1959: 135.

of the summer, Hermaios and Heraidous were starting to think of the work ahead.

In the absence of Heraidous's parents, it was her grandmother, Eudaimonis, who exercised supervision. In a letter addressed to Heraidous's mother Aline (*P.Brem.* 63), Eudaimonis reassured her, saying, "The little one sends you her greetings and is persevering with her studies." The close attention that Heraidous was dedicating to her *mathēmata* is further indication that she was beyond her ABCs. Her grandmother appears to have been perfectly capable of monitoring her behavior as well as the progress of her education. In all her letters, Eudaimonis comes across not only as a strong personality but also as an educated woman: besides adding fast greetings, she is capable of writing an entire letter in a slower hand. Even the texts of the letters that she dictated reveal her ease in dealing with written correspondence (Fig. 14).[84] Turns of phrase, abrupt interruptions and resumptions of thoughts, and some colorful expressions were not toned down by the various scribes she employed, perhaps because Eudaimonis reread her letters, like other literate women.

Not surprisingly, Heraidous's mother, Aline, was also literate. Her evident interest in the pace of her daughter's learning was in large measure a reflection of the fact that she herself had had an education. The final greetings that she added to a letter show that she was capable of writing at least as well as—perhaps even better than—her mother-in-law.[85] Moreover, the texts of all her letters reveal that she composed them personally, using choice words with some literary flavor.[86] The same is true for other women of Apollonios's family, who communicated effortlessly by letter, showing some command of the pen. When a sister of the *stratēgos* writes to him about a certain theft that had occurred in her house while she was visiting him, it is fascinating to follow the train of her thought, the personal language that she uses, and the alliterations and repetitions that bring out her indignation.[87] The handwriting of this woman, as revealed by the final greetings that she added, is noteworthy: it shows large, even,

---

[84] See, e.g., *P.Flor.* III.332, dictated but subscribed by her.

[85] See *P.Giss.* 78, which Aline subscribes with minute and even characters.

[86] See *P.Giss.* 78, 19, and 20, which may have been an autograph letter. Terms such as *phēmizein* ("to report"), *anegeirein* ("to revive"), and *ageustos* ("without eating") do not belong to the language of the papyri.

[87] See *P.Brem.* 61. In *P.Giss.* 21, Eudaimonis reveals that another of her daughters, Soeris, wrote to her.

Figure 14.   Papyrus letter of Eudaimonis (*P. Flor.* III.
332), first quarter of second century C.E.

and somewhat pretentious characters that are reminiscent of those usually employed in the writing of books.

The archive of Apollonios also includes letters by women not belonging to his family, who seem to have used the epistolary medium with ease, such as an acquaintance who describes her son as "the poet with his own lyre."[88] The fact that she makes one of the few jokes found in papyri is suggestive of the level of her education. Wishing to make fun of her son,

[88] *P.Brem.* 59.

she probably alluded to the expression *onos autolyrizōn*, "the donkey with his own lyre," which is found in Lucian as a derogatory remark and was part of a proverbial expression.[89] This letter is written in its entirety in stiff and uneven characters that suggest that this woman penned it herself.

Another woman who did not belong to the domestic circle of Apollonios was Arsis, an energetic businesswoman who worked in the weaving enterprise that the family owned. Arsis was in charge of purchasing the material, and she handled considerable amounts of money. Two letters sent by her are extant: one, which displays very large, clumsy, back-slanted characters, may have been penned by her.[90]

The scenario evoked by the letters of another woman, Teeus, may be even more intriguing. She was a servant who had been working for Apollonios's family for a long time, and she dictated two letters for Apollonios and Aline that show her special bond with the family and with Heraidous.[91] But it is a third letter, to Apollonios, that catches us unaware with its unabashed outpouring of affection and arresting expressions (Fig. 15).[92] It is not written in a scribal hand but in a clumsy and uneven handwriting that is the worst among those appearing in the archive. Did Teeus herself write it?

> Teeus to Apollonios her lord, many greetings. First of all I salute you, master, and I pray always for your health. I was in no little distress, my lord, hearing that you had been ill, but thanks be to all the gods, for they keep you safe from harm. I beg you, my lord, if you so wish, to hurry back to us, else we die because we do not see you every day. Would that we were able to fly and come to you and embrace you, for we are anxious to follow you. So change your mind for us and hasten back to us. Goodbye, my lord. . . .

It is conceivable that before taking care of his daughter, Teeus had raised Apollonios and had learned to write together with the other children of this affluent household. Now Apollonios was in danger. In her desire to be close to him, Teeus may have tried to reach him also with the traces of her hand on papyrus.

[89] Cf. Lucian *Dial. Meret.* 14.4 and *Ind.* 4.
[90] See *P.Giss.* 68, probably penned by a left-handed person. Another letter, *P.Brem.* 57, was dictated to a scribe.
[91] *P.Alex.Giss.* 50 and *P.Giss.* 77.
[92] *P.Giss.* 17.

Figure 15. Papyrus letter of Teeus (*P. Giss.* 17), early second century C.E.

SOME QUESTIONS

Some women, mostly belonging to the elite, achieved an impressive familiarity with the written word and learned to use the education attained in school for purposes ranging from attending to financial matters to common social interactions. The *realia* of their lives acquire a genuine immediacy through the fact that they were expressed not in male-authored texts but by the women themselves. Quantifying the education of these women in comparison to that of males and of other females who were silent is a formidable endeavor. We could consider letters that can be recognized as having being written or subscribed by women as the tip of the iceberg. The criteria used to identify them, in fact, inevitably miss the writing efforts of competent female writers, since in these cases the presence of a scribe is taken for granted. In any case, the relatively small pool of women who enjoyed a literacy that went beyond the technicalities of writing can be set against a larger proportion of those who confidently—but indirectly—handled written modes of expression.

How far can we go in generalizing the experiences of women in Greco-Roman Egypt against those of other women in the East and West? Two brief considerations are necessary. First, the letters of these women emanate from affluent milieus of the Greek and Roman minority. Though it is undeniable that in Egypt there were native traditions of relative female freedom, such traditions were probably less operative with respect to these social and economic groups: it is likely that this testimony of female literacy has a validity beyond Egypt. Moreover, comparable pictures of female literacy are evoked by finds in other parts of the Greek and Roman world, such as Palestine and particularly Britain, at Vindolanda. In both cases, the writing materials were crucial in preserving examples of female literacy that would have otherwise sunk into oblivion: papyrus in the Judaean desert and wooden tablets the size of modern postcards at Vindolanda. In the Judaean desert, Julia Crispina, a fully literate Roman woman who was very involved in local affairs, stands out in contrast to a few illiterate Jewish women who nevertheless handled the written word through intermediaries.[93] Even more striking is the example of some wives of equestrian officers at Vindolanda who kept up a regular correspondence. When Claudia Severa writes to her friend Lepidina to invite her for her birthday, the closure that she adds is less smooth than that of the scribe, but her language is elegant and recherché, and her education palpable and vibrant, as in the best letters written in Egypt.[94]

[93] On Julia Crispina, see *P.Babatha* 20 and 25; *P.Babatha* contains the archive of a Jewish woman, Babatha. On another woman, Salome, see H. M. Cotton, "The Archive of Salome Komaïse Daughter of Levi: Another Archive from the 'Cave of Letters,' " *ZPE* 105 (1995): 171–207.

[94] Bowman and Thomas 1994: no. 291; A. K. Bowman, *Life and Letters on the Roman Frontier* (New York, 1998), 56–57 and 93.

Parents and Students

I am glad that you are well, and that your Titianos loves to work hard rather than to be lazy, as the others do. I do not know if the teacher whose lessons he is following now is better than the teacher you were for him before. When you say that it is imperative that he surpass his father's excellence, in a little while you will require your boy to have wings. Surely it would be easier for him to grow wings like Perseus than to surpass his father in eloquence, for not even Perseus bettered Zeus. (Libanius *Ep*. 44.1–2)

To Aphrodisios, a greeting. First of all, I salute you, and so does everybody in our household. It is a big treat for those who want to be educated when they know how to carry out the tasks entrusted to them and have no desire to pursue foreign pleasures. For those who at first are initiated in the mysteries of the Muses, it happens to them later. . . .[1]

THE FIRST PASSAGE comes from a letter that Libanius wrote from Antioch to the father of one of his students, the second from a letter that someone, probably a father, wrote to his son in Egypt at about the same time. Libanius's addressee, Akakios, an eminent lawyer, was the father of Titianos.[2] Before sending him to Libanius's school, Akakios had tried to teach his son as best he could. Even afterward, he apparently never ceased to monitor his son's studies, for during the summers, when Titianos came back for vacation to his native Cilicia in Asia Minor, it was his father who, "in the oppressive heat," chose suitable readings to strengthen his son's memory and ability to compose. When Titianos returned to school after such training, Libanius remarked with surprise that he had acquired a "golden soul" (*Ep*. 121.3). The metaphor of growing wings in connection with reaching rhetorical excellence[3] is further enriched in this letter. The wings are now those of the hero Perseus: Akakios's demand that his

---

[1] See *SB* V.7567, which should be dated to the third to fourth century c.e. The provenance of this papyrus is unknown, but it was addressed to a student living in a large city. Only the beginning of the letter is preserved.

[2] See Petit 1956: 153–54. Cf. below.

[3] Cf. below, Chapter 8.

son learn to spread the wings of eloquence could be more easily fulfilled than his hope that Titianos will surpass his father's excellence.

The second letter was addressed to the student Aphrodisios, who lived in Egypt in the Roman period and was likely at the same level of studies as Titianos. The writer, who sends greetings from the rest of the family, was probably Aphrodisios's father. Like so many other students who wished to pursue advanced studies, Aphrodisios had to leave his native town or village to reach a center for higher education. From there he must have written to his father saying that, after all, school was not too hard. The letter he received perhaps quenched some of his enthusiasm. His father approved of his good start but also alluded to the possibility that a youth could be distracted by "extraneous pleasures," the dangerous temptations that haunted students living in large cities, far from the eyes of their families. Unfortunately, it is impossible to know whether the learned beginning of this letter was followed by praise or a reproach of this youth's conduct. Aphrodisios was a privileged young man who was called to share in the "mysteries of the Muses," an expression without exact parallel that conveys well the sense of being selected to partake in a world of the elect.[4] Moreover, he had a cultivated father who knew the value of culture and education for a youth's future.[5]

The interest of families in their children's learning experiences, the efforts they expended so that their education might be crowned by success, and the high expectations that these studies generated are well documented in the literary sources and in the papyri. The evidence is balanced in favor of families of students who were pursuing at least secondary studies with a grammarian. Parents of children receiving primary instruction expressed their feelings about education more infrequently, since this stage was regarded, at least in upper-class circles, merely as a step toward more rewarding instruction. Children acquired an elementary education, moreover, in the same towns where their families resided; this circumstance and the young age of the students prevented an exchange of letters, which are a good source of information about parents' hopes and students' educational struggles. The testimony of Libanius, and especially the letters that he exchanged with the parents of his students, are very useful in this respect, since he is far less guarded in the letters than he is in the orations. When Libanius's writings are juxtaposed with discussions

---

[4] Perhaps the *orgia Mousōn* ("the rites of the Muses") of Aristophanes *Frogs* 356 inspired the writer. The actual expression, however, is his own. Cf. Kaster 1988: 16 nn. 7 and 8.

[5] All the language of this letter is recherché. Some of the expressions are original. The syntax, with its balanced clauses and rhymed endings, is a mark of a rhetorical education.

of educational issues and practical matters that emerge from the papyri, we see that what Libanius offers is generally not a stylized, literary picture of education but a reflection of reality, and that the concerns of his students were those of upper-class male adolescents who pursued advanced education away from home anywhere in the ancient world.

Only male voices will be heard in this chapter. Even though some elite girls had access to grammatical education, leaving home was out of question for them: they either had to rely on the resources offered in their area or use the services provided by itinerant teachers. Even when, as in the case of Heraidous, they were separated from their parents, they remained in the care of other relatives.[6] Some elite families went to great lengths to educate both their sons and their daughters, but girls did not reach the rhetorical level, and when they acquired some education, they did so at home, so that correspondence between female students and parents does not exist as a source of information for their education.

An inquiry into parental attitudes toward education and students' reactions to the bit of freedom and independence that education away from home allowed them discloses ways of thinking, feelings, and behaviors that sound familiar. The desire to protect and control their offspring, anxiety about educational expenses, identification with the successes and failures of their children, and firm expectations that an education will buy their children a brighter future and more rewarding opportunities than those offered to themselves have been an aspect of Western culture at least from the eighteenth century on.[7] We are less prepared, however, for the astonishing similarity of the details. Thus, parental intrusion into school life, homework supervision, requests for progress reports, discussions about education at dinner time, dispatch of supplies to children away at school, and periodic visits to check on them suggest some continuity of human experience.

Yet the correspondence of external situations is in some measure deceptive, and it is essential not to be tempted to draw anachronistic conclusions. The issues discussed in this chapter are intimately connected to others considered above and cannot be investigated in isolation. An un-

---

[6] On Heraidous, cf. above, Chapter 3.

[7] These were the concerns of relatively elite groups. Interest in the children's education is not an invariable characteristic of family relationships in the past. Stone (1977), for instance, traces changes from the remote, unfriendly attitude of upper-class parents in early seventeenth-century England to affectionate involvement with education in the late eighteenth century.

derstanding of ancient families' reactions to education must take into account factors specific to Greco-Roman times: the lack of centralized education, the precarious organization of schooling, the common reliance on individuals privately hired who generally put their own interests before those of their pupils, and the absence of appropriate measures to test teachers' qualifications, so that word of mouth spread by other parents, general reputation, and recommendations that were not always disinterested dictated the hiring of an instructor. All this gives an uncommon urgency to the voice of ancient parents, those appearing in the literary sources—often well known and illustrious—and the more modest ones whom we meet in the papyri.

Ancient family members of necessity served pedagogical functions in order to remedy the deficiencies of formal schooling. Parents themselves—primarily fathers—were sometimes invested with direct pedagogical authority and provided instruction that might extend beyond the elementary level. More often, their efforts supplemented those of teachers, controlling the contents and timing of their children's learning. When sons were away to study, direct visits and letters provided an indispensable connection. Pedagogues, moreover, were an extension of parental control. Parental investment of time, energy, and money in education may appear comparable with modern cultural norms. It should not be forgotten, however, that in antiquity—more than today—children were considered a projection of their parents' ambitions, a continuation of the family's line, and a protection and support for their parents' old age. Parents were unable to see their children as persons separate from themselves, entitled to pursue their own happiness; they valued their children for what those children could give them, progressively identifying the maturing child as the care provider.[8] But even though it is important not to read into ancient parents' reactions too many analogies with our own ideals, the papyri and Libanius's correspondence nevertheless reveal the strong interest that families had in their children's education.

Though it attempts to build a picture of parental involvement in schooling, this chapter also touches on other issues that confronted elite youth studying away from home. Such matters as the need to travel for education, the organization of the students' new life, their lodging in the new residence, the support students received from friends and acquaintances of their parents, and the dispatch from home of supplies of all sorts vividly

---

[8] L. DeMause, "The Evolution of Childhood," in DeMause 1974: 17–18.

emerge from ancient letters. These are practical and significant details that help us fill in the outline of education in antiquity, details that have not so far received much attention.

TEACHING WITHIN THE FAMILY

In the Greco-Roman world, the education of a youth was strongly tied to his upbringing: education in its simplest form was a son's imitation of the excellence and conduct of his own father. The principle of imitation of *paradeigmata* ("examples"), which was originally an integral part of aristocratic ethics and education, never ceased to be a guiding force. The papyri show that a work particularly cherished in schools in Egypt was the *Ad Demonicum*, in which the fourth-century B.C.E. orator Isocrates offered advice on practical ethics to Demonikos, the son of his friend Hipponikos. But in imparting his instructions for a successful journey along the road to virtue, Isocrates did not forget whom Demonikos was to consider his first teacher: the youth was supposed to pattern his entire life after his father's, "striving to imitate and emulate his excellence" (*Ad Demonicum* 9–11). The two figures, the father and the teacher, had joined their efforts, and their images blended.

Fathers such as the lawyer Akakios in the letter quoted above, who could rival a rhetor of the stature of Libanius and had the ability to monitor his child's education up to the final stages, were exceptions. The correspondence of Libanius isolates a few more examples.[9] The papyri provide one instance of paternal teaching in higher education: the lawyer Dioskoros of Aphroditopolis may have instructed his children personally up to the rhetorical level in the sixth century.[10] Some illustrious examples also stand out in the literary tradition: Quintilian, Plutarch, and Stobaeus showed an active interest in the educations of their own sons.[11] But active parental involvement in children's education was much more common at the elementary level: it must have been an essential feature of ancient society, since it attempted to compensate for schooling deficiencies. As

---

[9] See, e.g., *Ep.* 1261.4, in which a cultivated father is called *ho eisō didaskalos* ("the teacher inside," "the domestic teacher").

[10] Cf. above, p. 40.

[11] See Plutarch *Quomodo adul.*; Quintilian and Stobaeus (fifth century C.E.) wrote their works for their sons. For other examples of parents' participation in the education of their children, see Harris 1989: 233 n. 296; for Cicero's attitude, see Wiedemann 1989: 86–87; for dedication of literary works to sons in late antiquity, Kaster 1988: 67 n. 142.

early as the turn of the fourth century B.C.E., the Greek historian Xenophon noted the spontaneous tendency of parents to rely on their own knowledge in the instruction of their offspring (*Mem.* 2.2.6). Homeschooling, however, is difficult to document: it was probably not a full-time activity, and it went on in the privacy of the family, without much fanfare. Only rarely do the literary sources hand down examples of parents taking an active part in their children's primary instruction: the concerned behavior of the elder Cato in Rome in the second century B.C.E. stands out in this respect.[12] One guesses that in Greco-Roman Egypt, homeschooling must have been a necessary component of family life when a parent possessed some literacy, when teachers were not available in the village, and when children were too young to be sent away to study. An Oxyrhynchos papyrus of the first century C.E., probably written by a housewife, contains a long account of private expenses that gives a suggestive picture of daily life.[13] Apparently the children of the household had their own needs: milk, pure bread, cakes, pigeons (to eat, or perhaps as pets), pomegranates, toys,[14] garlands for birthdays, and materials for writing, such as wax (for tablets) and a stylus. Was this mother in charge of teaching the ABCs to her children? It is more likely that this woman's involvement with her children's education consisted of buying school supplies and inspecting homework. Such were the thankless tasks of Kokkalos's parents in Herodas's *Didaskalos*, an activity that went on amid shouting and frustration and made an exasperated Metrotime wonder whether she herself was a fool, since she pretended to teach her son "to read and write instead of feeding asses, thinking to have in him a support for old age" (26–29).

Investing in children's education in order to have a return in the future and to guarantee oneself livelihood and assistance in old age is a frequent motif in the sources. Petitions on papyrus show one side of the reality: disappointed hopes. A father bitterly accused a daughter of neglecting him in spite of the fact that she had received from him an education.[15] A man named Pappos, who lived in Egypt in the same period as Metrotime,

---

[12] Plutarch *Cat. Mai.* 20.

[13] This papyrus, *P.Oxy.* IV.736, contained at least seven columns of writing, with the expenses listed according to the day of the month.

[14] On dolls found in Roman and Byzantine Egypt, see R. M. Janssen, "Soft Toys from Egypt," *Archaeological Research in Roman Egypt, JRA* suppl. 19 (Ann Arbor, 1996), 231–39; P. van Minnen, "House-to-House Enquiries: An Interdisciplinary Approach to Roman Karanis," *ZPE* 100 (1994): 233. Cf. *PSI* IX.1080, a private letter in which a woman mentions sending eight toys to a child.

[15] *P.Enteux.* 26; cf. above, pp. 86–87.

filed a petition against his son, who appears to be the grown version of Kokkalos.[16] Even though this man gave his son a complete education and taught him grammar—either directly or through a teacher—he did not receive any support from him; quite the opposite.[17] Ill and resentful, the old man disclosed in his petition to the king that his son had insulted him in the street and penetrated his house by force to take away some of his furniture. But of course, it is difficult to be sure what the reality behind these complaints truly was. One is reminded of an episode reported by Heliodorus, a later writer of prose fiction (ca. C.E. 220–250), in which a youth was unjustly accused by his father of assaulting him. What were certainly identical were the claims to merit of both fathers, since the latter one disclosed during the trial in which he tried to have his son indicted: "I did not expect this when I raised him, but hoping that he was going to be the crutch of my old age, since the day he was born, I gave him the education of a freeborn man and first of all I taught him grammar" (*Aeth.* 1.13). Providing children with education was apparently a father's duty in Roman Egypt. A marriage contract of the first century C.E., which is unfortunately fragmentary, contains a clause that specifies that a husband was responsible for giving "his children the education proper for free people."[18]

ALL EYES AND EARS

Since education was characterized by much impermanence and instability, to be "all eyes and ears"—in the words of Ps.-Plutarch—was the fundamental duty of parents, who had to safeguard their educational investments so that they would bear fruit.[19] Money in fact was often invested somewhat blindly in children's instruction, and parents hired teachers without guarantees that they could perform adequately. The situation had been virtually unchanged since classical and Hellenistic times.[20] Going to

[16] *P.Enteux.* 25; Cribiore 1996a: 15–16 and n. 26.

[17] Already the laws of Solon had codified the duty of supporting one's parents; see Plutarch *Sol.* 22. Herodotus (2.35) curiously reports that in Egypt, only daughters had the obligation of supporting their parents.

[18] *P.Oxy.* II.265. A similar clause is not appended to other marriage contracts.

[19] *De liberis educandis* 9d, *autoptai, autēkooi*: parents were even supposed to test their children on a regular basis to ensure that they were learning appropriately. Cf. also Quintilian (1.2.5), who reproached those parents who are afflicted with a "blind indifference."

[20] Cf. the vague requirements in Aristotle [*Ath. Pol.*] 42.2, and *SIG* 577, ll. 38–39.

extremes, some parents tried to fulfill the role of pedagogues, haunting their sons' teachers.[21] Libanius, for instance, talks about a father who had come from abroad to take his sons to school, but then never left; every day he sat in class with his children, catering to their educational needs and supervising their learning.[22] In the meantime, his affairs at home were not well taken care of, and he was in danger of being wronged by his worst slaves. When questioned, the man admitted that nobody knew the situation as well as he did, but he considered the damage he did to his affairs as nothing compared to what he gained. Abandoning one's business was not always an option, however: only a few could afford such detachment from worldly affairs.

When students attended school in the same town where their parents resided, it was naturally easier for the latter to keep some control over pace of learning, indolent behavior, and slackening discipline, even without attending classes. In the *Didaskalos*, a disconsolate Metrotime could not help but look every day at the waxed tablet that her son left "orphaned" in the corner of the room, with no writing on it (14–18). Other parents checked that children did their schoolwork and finished their reading assignments. An amusing vignette is represented in the *Philogelos*, a Greek collection of ancient jokes dated to the late Roman or the early Byzantine period:[23]

> A student found some gladiator's armor in the house and started to play with it. Suddenly someone announced that his father had returned. He threw down the shield and began taking off the greaves. But his father came before he finished, so he grabbed his book and began reading it, with the helmet still on his head.

This compressed anecdote presents a familiar story. A student plays happily in his father's absence, instead of doing his reading. He dresses up with a suit of armor that was probably a toy.[24] But the toy and his daydreaming betray him, and he is miserably caught.

A suitable time to talk about schoolwork—in antiquity as today—seems to have been dinner time. A student then was trapped and besieged by many questions. When Libanius, in a rhetorical exercise, paints a grim picture of the life of a student who is constrained on every side, his words

---

[21] Cf. the father of Horace *Sat.* 1.6.81–82.

[22] *Or.* 55.28. This father was perhaps Achillios of Ankyra (*Ep.* 355); see Festugière 1959: 439 n. 1.

[23] See Thierfelder 1968: no. 87; in pp. 5–27, a date to the third century or later is discussed.

[24] B. Baldwin, *The Philogelos or Laughter-Lover* (Amsterdam, 1983), 76.

ring true, even though he emphasizes only one aspect of the problem. At the end of a day, students would have to report about progress and difficulties, and critical parents would question and listen avidly:

> Instead of offering food and drinks, "What did you do today? Did you make any improvement? What progress did you make in your studies?" These are the questions of the father. I will add the questions asked by the mother, to whom a boy must render account, too. But if any forgetfulness is found, to talk about slaps is nothing: they also refuse him food.[25]

Food deprivation—or at least, barring children from the food of their choice—has always been an effective parental weapon.[26] Lucian remarked that when parents were pleased with a child's progress, they gave him food as a special reward: "By Zeus, this child has written so nicely! Give him something to eat." Or, "He did not write well at all, do not give him anything!" (*De parasito* 13). But the dining room did not only witness students' defeats. Over his meal, a young man also had the opportunity of flaunting all his learning, in the hope that his parents realized how much of it he had accumulated. Parents then were the unwilling victims of displays of useless erudition. Much of the knowledge an advanced student paraded sounded foolish to the unsophisticated ears of his relatives, who wished his teacher had provided him with more profitable notions. In a passage of Lucian it is an uncle, a simple man without much culture (*agroikos*), who laments with a teacher:

> I would have liked him to profit from you in this sort of thing rather than have all that knowledge which every day at dinner he displays to us, though we have no need of it: how a crocodile snatched a child, but promised to give him back if his father answered some question; or how surely when it is day, it cannot be night. . . . And when his mother asks him why he talks such nonsense, he laughs at her and says: "If I learn well this nonsense, nothing will stop me from being the only rich man, the only king, and the others will be slaves and trash compared with me." (Lucian *Hermot.* 81)

"Trash," *katharmata*, is a word spit out with much fury and contempt. A young man facing judgmental adults did not always use orthodox language to justify himself. The same word that this youth shouts at his mother is employed by the student Neilos in a letter to his father, when

---

[25] *Chria* 3.9, Foerster vol. 8, p. 86.

[26] On depriving children of food as a form of punishment, see Gregory of Nyssa, *De castigatione*, Migne *PG* vol. 46, p. 313.

he is fending off accusations that he is neglecting his education.[27] Libanius also uses this term in portraying the defensive attitude of a lad accused by his teacher of squandering the money he received from home to pay the tuition. This student would burst into class shouting, threatening, and calling everybody "trash" (*Or.* 3.6). Are we capturing the sound of an ancient youth jargon?

Parents must have particularly felt the urgency of monitoring their sons' instruction when the latter were studying far from home. Only the upper strata of the population—and students and teachers among them—were geographically mobile in antiquity. Leaving home was mandatory for those students who lived in outlying towns that could not offer the most sophisticated range of schooling. Some places were renowned for the specialized instruction they provided—Berytus for the law, for instance—and attracted certain types of advanced students.[28] At other times the fame of a teacher spread far and wide, implicitly bringing the promise of future brilliant careers for his students. Libanius was one such star. His students came from the most diverse regions of the Eastern world, often accompanied by their well-off parents, who did not mind undertaking the considerable expense for some years. One widowed mother—we are told—had come from Armenia with her only son, "a bright colt," and had willingly separated from him in the hope that he would learn the *logoi* ("rhetoric," *Ep.* 285). Before going back, she entrusted him to the care of a friend, who was to provide some supervision. But it was not only the need to find suitable rhetorical instruction that forced a young man to move. A similar problem was encountered when a grammarian was not available nearby. The need to find suitable teachers compelled students who lived in Egypt to travel to *metropoleis* such as Oxyrhynchos, Hermopolis, Antinoe, or to the capital. But Alexandria naturally also attracted students from abroad, who sought both grammatical and rhetorical instruction. Its prestige as educational center lasted well into late antiquity, and elite families sometimes sent more than one son there, each with different educational needs.[29]

One way to keep a vigilant eye on a son's education was through direct visits. Fathers sometimes tried to combine their business activities and

---

[27] On Neilos's letter, see below, and above, Chapter 2.

[28] See McNamee 1998.

[29] See the examples provided by Zacharias Rhetor in his *Life of Severus*, M.-A. Kugener, *Sévère patriarche d' Antioche*, *Patrologia Orientalis* 12 (1907): 7–115. In the fifth century, for instance, Severus of Sozopolis in Pisidia studied grammar in Alexandria as his two brothers were following the class of a *sophistēs*, and another student, Paralios, came from Caria, attracted by the fame of the grammarian Horapollon.

parental duties of supervision, but it was not always feasible. This is what is revealed in the papyrus letter of the student Thonis, who wrote to his father Arion saying that he was frustrated at having to keep waiting for him:

> I have written to you five times and you wrote back only once, never mentioning your health, nor have you come to visit. Though you promised me, saying, "I am coming," you have not come to find out whether the teacher pays attention to me or not. Almost every day he himself inquires about you, saying, "Is he not coming yet?" and I always say, "Yes." Thus, make sure to come to me as soon as possible so that he may teach me, as he is willing to do. If you had come together with me, I should have received my instruction long ago. When you come, remember the things I wrote to you often. Come quickly to us, then, before he leaves for Upper Egypt. I send greetings to everybody in the family, each by name, and to those who love us. Greetings also to my teachers. Goodbye, my lord and father, may you be well, together with my brothers free from harm.
> (Postscript) Remember my pigeons.[30]

This letter is a clear manifestation of a youth's malaise and homesickness. His hometown—somewhere in Egypt—and the old teachers left behind are still vivid in Thonis's memory. He had started the class of a new instructor whom his father had promised to meet, probably in order to negotiate and settle the appropriate salary. This teacher was getting impatient, complained to Thonis of missed opportunities, and even threatened to leave. Thonis could only send frantic messages. He felt abandoned. He could not even find any more comfort in his pigeons—"pets that are capable of totally capturing a boy," Libanius would go on to say, having decided to sell his own on discovering love of learning at the age of fourteen.[31]

From Libanius's correspondence, one derives the impression that fathers' visits were welcomed by teachers and students alike. Teachers could proudly display the product of their labor, assuage parents' anxiety, fend off doubts or accusations, prove that money was well spent, and take the occasion to ask for more. Students, on the other hand, claimed their rights over the siblings they had left at home, felt reassured about their parents' love, received helpful advice, and asked for money and supplies. Libanius

[30] *SB* III.6262; cf. below, p. 217. This letter has many erasures and corrections.

[31] Libanius *Or.* 1.5. The passion of children for pigeons is also documented in the mummy portraits; see, e.g., Doxiadis 1995: 46, where is represented a young boy holding a pomegranate and a pigeon.

recognized on several occasions that the visits of relatives were a necessary ingredient to good, profitable relationships. So many of his students came from distant provinces that letters alone could not always provide adequate communication.[32]

Some parents, however, like Thonis's father, resisted the pressure from children and teachers, and declined to show up. One of them was that Heortios of Heraklea Pontica, to whom Libanius sent three letters. The first is particularly eloquent in depicting the despondency of Heortios's son, Themistios, who needed money and support but felt that his father had forgotten him:[33]

> I am perhaps playing the busybody when I beg a father to take care of the son he is determined to neglect. But I saw Themistios crying, and I prefer to give you this impression than to overlook the whole thing. He did not use any harsh word, but only said that you have forgotten him. If you were in financial difficulties, I would ask you to borrow from friends to help your child. But since you are doing very well and you are among the wealthiest, I suggest that you should spend some of your money for your most valuable possession. Excessive poverty perhaps is not particularly advantageous to a young man, but in this case we are not even talking about the needs of his belly, but about this young man's books. Without them, he will be like a man learning to do archery without a bow.

Undoubtedly Libanius was capable of stinging words when he felt someone hampered his teaching mission. Even though it is not inconceivable that he hoped Heortios's visit would bring him some financial gain, nevertheless the situation depicted in this letter underlines one of the positive sides of this teacher's rapport with his students. That he was close to some of them and considered them as his own children is not only implied by his calling them "son" or "my child."[34] His letters reveal the undeniable attachment he felt for some students, and the bonding and intimacy created by daily association.[35] He continued to follow his pupils' fortunes after they left, rejoicing at their weddings and victories, and when they died prematurely, he cursed the teaching profession "because the teacher

---

[32] On the provenance of Libanius's students, see Petit 1956: 112–18.

[33] See Libanius *Ep.* 428; Norman1992, 1: 376–77, no. 10.

[34] On Libanius's use of *pais* ("child"), see Petit 1956: 33–36.

[35] A letter that conveys well the sense of how a school was a family, where teachers played the role of parents and classmates that of siblings, is *Ep.* 1165.

is the father of many young men, and when one has many children it happens easily that he is grief-stricken" (*Ep.* 1141.1). When Libanius wrote to the father of a student that he felt the pupil was really his own son because he composed marvelous discourses, we see a teacher's pride blending with a father's joyful recognition of a son's accomplishments.[36] But in spite of formidable pressure from children and teachers to come and witness the results of education, some fathers were unmoved.[37] Libanius wrote two more letters to Heortios: in one he said that he was not going to inform him about Themistios's progress by letter because he wanted to see him in person, but in the other he titillated paternal vanity by disclosing the great changes this youth had undergone.[38] But Heortios did not come.

The correspondence of Libanius with the parents of his students is so dense that one wonders whether letters from teachers discharged some formal function in education. In the modern world, report cards are issued periodically to keep families informed of a pupil's pace of learning, achievements, and ability to move to a higher class. In antiquity, readiness to pass academic hurdles rather than age determined the level at which a pupil studied.[39] When youths studied away from home, and the costs of education soared, periodic confirmations that money was well spent were a necessity. Many of Libanius's letters to his students' families seem to touch key points in the overall evaluation of a youth.[40] Thus, for instance, in a note sent at the end of the school year to the lawyer Akakios,[41] who was also responsible for the education of his nephew Philoxenos, Libanius writes, "Philoxenos has shown himself entirely worthy of your family. He worked very hard, and cared to achieve good results in his conduct as well as in his studies" (*Ep.* 60). One thinks of the lists of victors in school contests in the Hellenistic gymnasia where children obtained prizes in *philoponia* ("good work") and *eutaxia* ("discipline").[42] Philoxenos had received full marks in his work, effort, and behavior, and could enjoy his summer in peace.

[36] Libanius *Ep.* 660, written to the father of Lysimachus; see also *Ep.* 287.2 about another student whom Libanius calls his "son."

[37] *Ep.* 1352.1–2 concerns another young man who was so completely neglected by his parents that they did not even write to him.

[38] *Ep.* 547 and 549, both short notes.

[39] See Kleijwegt 1991: 90 and 117–18.

[40] See, e.g., *Ep.* 172, 600, 1005, and 1165.

[41] See the beginning of this chapter.

[42] See, e.g., *SIG* 1061.4 in Samos; Ziebarth 1914: 119–20.

Help from Home

When boys studied far from home, families had to give them some assistance in the practical matters of their new life. Even a large school such as that of Libanius, which combined at least grammatical and rhetorical education, did not offer room and board, and youths had to experiment with various solutions. On one occasion, Libanius alludes to the power that the class of innkeepers (*pandokeōn genos*) had over a professor, since they could either sing his praises or denounce him with their student guests (*Or.* 25.48). A few passing remarks in this rhetor's letters also point to students boarding in private houses.[43] But in regard to the details of students' accommodations, the papyrus letters of the Roman period are more eloquent. The following letter that Cornelius writes to his son, who is studying in Oxyrhynchos, is a good example of parental involvement in the nitty-gritty of education:

> Cornelius to his dearest son Hierax, greetings. Everyone in the household salutes you and all those with you. In regard to the man about whom you write to me so often, claim nothing until hopefully I come to you together with Vestinus and the donkeys. For if the gods will, I shall arrive quickly at the end of the month of Mecheir, since at present I have urgent affairs on hand. Take care not to offend anybody in the household, but pay attention only to your books, devoting yourself to learning, and they will bring you profit. Receive by Onnophris the white garments that are to be worn with the purple cloaks, while you should wear the others with the myrtle-colored ones. I shall send by Anoubas both the money and the monthly supplies and the other pair of scarlet cloaks. You won us over by the dainties, and I shall send the price of these, too, by Anoubas; but until Anoubas comes to you, you will have to pay for the provision for you and the people with you out of your own money, until I send you some. For the month of Tubi there is for you whatever you ask for, and 16 drachmai for Phronimos, 9 for those with Abaskantos and Myron, and 12 for Secundus. Send Phronimos to Asklepiades in my name and let him get an answer to the letter I wrote to him, and send it to me. Let me know what you want. Goodbye, my son.[44]

This letter abounds in tantalizing details concerning the life of a student in a city. Hierax was boarding in the house of some people with whom

---

[43] See Festugière 1959: 110 n. 1.

[44] See *P.Oxy.* III.531, dated to the second century C.E.

his father was probably acquainted. He must have occupied several rooms, since apparently he had moved to Oxyrhynchos accompanied by others. It is not inconceivable that siblings were studying with him, but some of the people mentioned at the end of the letter must have been servants, and one of them surely a pedagogue. Every month Cornelius sent his son an allowance of money and supplies. Hierax in turn sent from the metropolis delicacies that were much appreciated at home. The letter shows that not everything was proceeding smoothly: Cornelius was worried about some problems that his son was having with someone in the household. In order to maintain some privacy, however, not much is disclosed about the identity of this person or the nature of the disagreement.[45] Cornelius's answer to Hierax's insistent messages—wait, I am coming, do not offend anybody and study hard—is the eternal parental response to similar problems. All the details concerning clothes of various colors and the way to wear them confirm this father's participation in the life of his son. Cornelius, who wants Hierax to cut a fine figure in the new school, appears very aware of the importance of proper attire for a student. One cannot but recall the many mummy portraits of young men from the Roman period with their sophisticated good looks and refined wardrobe. Born into upper-class families, many of them must have been students. When they died, their families surrounded their portraits with gilded frames as a sign of unbearable grief.[46]

The two foremost concerns of students corresponding with their parents were money for tuition and for various expenses, and the victuals they received from home. These provisions—bread, lentils, apples, salted meat, roasted meat[47]—were not only tokens of affection but served as daily sustenance. Since often more than one sibling was pursuing advanced education, and costs of provisions in the city were higher than in the country, where some parents owned productive estates, families opted to send food through their own emissaries or took advantage of traveling acquaintances. Students reciprocated by dispatching choice items together with their letters: they were somewhat proud of their acquired status. In the second century, a student writes home:[48]

[45] Concerns with privacy and security are common in letters. Cf. *P.Col.* X.279, where the writer explicitly refers to the convention of omitting the name of a person for these reasons.

[46] For portraits of boys who were probably students, see Walker and Bierbrier 1997: nos. 30 and 31; see also nos. 32, 43, and 47, in which a gold frame surrounds the portrait.

[47] See Neilos's letter, examined below. The meat was preserved in some way, probably smoked.

[48] *P.Oslo* III.153, a letter mutilated at the beginning. The first few lines present problems of interpretation.

... Write to me about tuition for my studies and my brother's, in order that I can be informed and relieved from anxiety. Rest assured that it is not we who consume the loaves of bread, but each time they devour threefold as much as we. ... We salute Ptolema, my brothers, Theodous, and everyone in the household. I sent you by Euthenias ten eggs and two pomegranates. If you want more eggs, you have to tell me, for I have others. ...

This letter—an impromptu conversation—leaves again in the dark the identities of those people who stuffed themselves with the bread sent from home. Those loaves must have been the subject of a previous letter in which relatives wondered why they did not last longer. There was no need for the student to be more specific: doubtless the parents knew who the inconsiderate gluttons were. The hosts of the two students were probably taking advantage. It is amusing that the writer refrains from the colloquial language he used in the rest of this epistle when he reports the greed of his hosts. The term employed, "devour" (*esthein*), is a word of epic proportion, which reveals this student's crudition, as well as his indignation.[49]

A similar situation is depicted in another letter of the Roman period, which shows that provisions sent from home helped to maintain profitable contacts with acquaintances in the city, who could eventually provide some reciprocal assistance.[50] This time parents had sent apples to distribute to various people and had asked their son to buy beer for them. But a grouchy young man, Serenus, writes back to his father:

> I received through Ptolemianos sixty-three apples and another eleven from the wife of Serenus, and I want you to know that they have all vanished and I could not find any to give to the people whom you mentioned in your letter. So I bought some to have something to present to them. I also want to inform you that I go every day to Serapias, the woman who sells beer, but she does not give any to me. Every day she says "Tomorrow," and this happens every day. If Isidoros gets his hair cut, what gift do you wish me to give him? ...

Unlike the lad of the previous letter, this one had to endure by himself all the frustrations of daily living. He was probably the oldest of his siblings and the only one studying in town. Apparently his brother Isidoros had not passed puberty yet and was still sporting the lock of hair

---

[49] We would expect *phagein* ("to eat"). *Esthein* is an epic, poetic form that was used by Homer, e.g., *Od.* 5.197; cf. also in Callimachus *Hymn* 6.88, *ēsthie myria panta* ("He devoured countless things"), about the ferocious hunger of Erysichthon.

[50] See *BGU* I.38, found in the Fayum.

on one side of his head that imitated the hairdo of the god Horus.[51] But not for long. A ceremony called *mallokouria*, celebrated with a family feast and gifts, was in the making to mark this boy's first haircut and his coming of age.[52] The ceremony was an event to which friends and relatives were invited. A papyrus of the Roman period contains an invitation to celebrate the coming of age of two children: guests were invited to dine "at the banquet of the lord Serapis," a meal that was held in the temple of the goddess Thoëris.[53] The boy Serenus of our letter was getting ready for this commemoration and wondered what would be a suitable gift to give his brother. Perhaps in the near future Isidoros would join him in the city, too.

SOME BALANCE: STUDYING AND PLAYING

A frequent exchange of letters, visits, and the presence of acquaintances who could keep an eye on young men were only partial remedies to distance and lack of daily contact between parents and their children studying away from home. Some parents were always tormented by doubts about whether or not they had chosen the right school, and agonized over the treatment and instruction their children received. Over and over, teachers like Libanius had to reassure them that the situation was under control, that their children performed adequately and were well considered, and that the praises he sang of them corresponded to the truth.[54] Students were well aware that families worried about them. A papyrus letter sent by Dios, who was probably studying in Alexandria, to his father in Oxyrhynchos had the precise aim of comforting a concerned par-

---

[51] About Fayum portraits of young boys with locks, see Walker and Bierbrier 1997: no. 94; and Doxiadis 1995: nos. 26 and 77. Girls of young age wore what was called the Isis lock; see Doxiadis 1995: nos. 59–60.

[52] Since early times it was customary for youths who were coming of age to dedicate their hair to a local deity; cf. Plutarch *Thes.* 5.1 and Theophrastus *Char.* 21. Plato (*Ti.* 21b) says that on the third day of the *Apaturia*, a feast held in October, boys were presented in a cermony called *koureōtis* because their hair was cut; see Hesychios s.v. About *mallokouria* in Greco-Roman Egypt, see D. Montserrat, "Mallokouria and Therapeuteria: Rituals of Transition in a Mixed Society," *BASP* 28 (1991): 43–49.

[53] See *P.Oxy.* XII.1484, a short invitation sent by a certain Apollonios.

[54] Adamantios of Armenia, for instance, was always anguished by rumors he heard about Libanius's school, and once even asked his son Anatolius to leave. Even though his son's pedagogue went to Armenia to reassure him that Anatolius was doing fine, Adamantios never stopped worrying. See Festugière 1959: 108–9, and especially Libanius *Ep.* 129.

ent.[55] "Do not be anxious, father, about my studies; I am working hard, but I also take relaxation. All will be well with me." The remainder of this epistle consists only of salutations to a long list of people back at home. This letter was not going to bring novel messages and requests, but, read aloud in a circle of relatives, it would please many. Apparently Dios had found the formula for academic success in a proper balance of rest and study.

From the earliest times, the need to strike the right note was discussed by parents and educators alike. Plato and Aristotle recognized that play and relaxation were necessary for the hard-working person,[56] and Ps.-Plutarch maintained that "children must be given some breathing space from continuous tasks" (*De liberis educandis* 9c). Quintilian went a step further: pupils needed relaxation, not only because there is nothing in this world that can stand continuous strain, but because study depends on a student's goodwill, which cannot be secured by compulsion (1.3.9). A proper balance between work and recreation reassured parents of the physical and mental health of their children—a constant preoccupation for parents. Letters had the important function of reassuring relatives and were always welcome even when they did not communicate any real news. The primary aim of many letters from Greco-Roman Egypt, in fact, was to alleviate the concerns of faraway relatives. Silence brought anxiety—a father told his son: a letter from him had finally relieved the family's fear that he might be dead.[57] For students, dying away from home or even in a foreign land was not necessarily just a *topos*, as two inscriptions from Claudiopolis in Asia Minor show.[58] These epitaphs commemorate the student Theodoros son of Attalos, who had come to this city from the town of Agrippeia in Bithynia to study rhetoric but had died there. Even though they were composed by a teacher or fellow student with rhetorical pretensions, the laments over a young man who died "in a city that he loved" but "in alien bosoms stretching out his hands to his mother nor even clasping the last embraces of his father" go beyond the cliché. Libanius's writings reveal that illness and even death were not exceptional among students. In those trying moments, parents found some solace in the presence of pedagogues, who—if we believe Libanius—were better than nurses, rivaled mothers with respect to the care they provided to the sick,

---

[55] *P.Oxy.* X.1296, dated to the third century.

[56] Plato *Laws* 643b–c, 797–98, 819b; Aristotle *Pol.* 1337b.37–40.

[57] *P.Mert.* III.115: it is unclear whether the word "son" refers to a family relationship.

[58] See *SEG* 34.1259, first century c.e. See, e.g., similar inscriptions of students who died in foreign land, Vérilhac 1982: nos. 56, 73, and 74.

and when death occurred were inconsolable (*Or.* 58.10–11). In the latter case it is likely that, besides the fact that some of them might have grieved sincerely, they felt responsible for failing families' expectations and trust.

But distant cities also abounded with amusements and temptations. In Libanius's time, Antioch was a city as dangerous as Alexandria.[59] Many young men, especially those who had come from small towns in Armenia, Cappadocia, and other provinces, were unprepared to resist the charms of the metropolis. Concerned parents had to rely on the vigilance of pedagogues, who were often advanced in years and had to take care of their charges for the whole afternoon, when classes were over. Spectacles in the theater, mimes, horse races in the hippodrome, playing dice—there were plenty of activities that a young man could pursue instead of doing his homework, at the age when he was trying his wings. Akakios, the father of Titianos, apparently decided on a certain occasion to keep his son by his side, blaming the dangers that the theater and the large crowds—*theatra, polyanthrōpia*—represented for a young man. In approving his decision, on the grounds that Titianos could have the best teacher in his father, Libanius replied that nevertheless this young man had the strongest character and would not suffer any damage from the city's perils (*Ep.* 373).

For other, less-disciplined students, however, it was a different matter. As he grew older, Libanius found it ever harder to witness impotently some of his pupils' revelries. In an oration dedicated to his students, he lamented that some of them would rather touch a snake than their books (*Or.* 35.13). The city was teeming with distractions: going religiously to horse races, and spending the rest of the time discussing them and betting on the fortunes of a jockey, took all the energy of a lad. Libanius himself in his youth had found this kind of life attractive, but, at the age of fourteen, he had abandoned spectacles in the theater, chariot races, and gladiatorial combats for more responsible and studious behavior (*Or.* 1.5). Many of his students, however, did not feel a real passion for their studies. Oration 3 was written by Libanius to reproach pupils who showed indifference toward his regular declamations. In a fit of anger, the rhetor announced that he was no longer going to pronounce the public discourse held at the end of classes, at the beginning of the summer. This declamation, which was attended by high officials and by the students' families, was part of a ceremony that was cherished by pupils, perhaps because it marked the start of vacation. Even though the discourse of censure,

[59] On the passion of the Alexandrians for spectacles and horse races, see Dion of Prusa *Or.* 32.

epitimesis, is a well-known oratorical genre, a conventional theme of so-phistic diatribe, the picture that Libanius leaves of the indifferent and provocative attitude of some of his students rings true: it has the echo of a real experience.[60] With indignation, he reveals that when he pronounced his declamations during the year, his students behaved erratically:

> When I start declaiming, they keep on nodding to each other in regard to charioteers, mimes, horses, dancers, and past or future combats.[61] Even better, some stand up as if they were made of stone with their hands crossed, others pick their nose with both hands, others sit down even if many get up with enthusiasm, others force people who would like to get up to sit down, others start counting the new arrivals, and others are content to look at the leaves.[62] (*Or.* 3.12–13)

But the list of the students' faults goes on: they walk in the hall distracting everybody, purposely clap their hands at the wrong time, go back and forth spreading false news, and invite people to come to the baths. No wonder a conscientious father such as Akakios felt that his son was better able to concentrate at home.

Long before, in Egypt, Theon, the father of Neilos, had manifested similar concerns. Neilos seems to plead quite articulately for the cause of students left to look after themselves in a large, ancient city:[63]

> . . . You relieved us of our greatest depression by declaring that the events at the theater make no difference to you. . . . It is the depression about these things that makes us neglect our appearance, for it is not necessary for those who are not yet engaged in work to care for their persons, and especially when there are not even those who bring in money. For at one time the "useful" Heraklas—the hell with his wickedness—every few days used to bring in some pennies, but now, immediately after being shackled by Isidoros, as was right, he has run away and gone up, as I

---

[60] See Martin 1988: 84–86.

[61] It is uncertain whether Libanius refers to students' fights or spectacles in the circus. Apparently youths who followed the classes of rival sophists sometimes fought against each other (*Or.* 1.19 and 21–22). Gladiatorial spectacles had been officially forbidden by this time, but in reality they were slow to disappear.

[62] Festugière (1959: 511) thinks that the word *phylla* ("leaves") alludes to pages of a student's book; it seems more likely that these are real leaves. The building where the discourse was pronounced was surrounded by fig trees, gardens, and vineyards, and the students could see the trees from the openings; see Martin 1988: 279.

[63] *P.Oxy.* XVIII.2190; cf. above, p. 50. For other parts of this letter, see above, pp. 57–58.

guess, to you. Be aware that he would never hesitate to plot against you. For he was not ashamed first of all to spread news in the city about the events at the theater with great joy and to tell lies that not even an accuser would utter; all this even if he was not treated as he deserved, but could do everything without restraint, like a free man. But in any case, if you do not send him back, you can put him to work with a carpenter, for I hear that a lad can make two drachmai a day; or employ him at some other work in which he can make more money, so that his wages can be collected and sent to us from time to time. You know, in fact, that Diogas is also studying literature. In the meantime, while you send the little one, we shall look for a bigger place in a private house. For in order to be near Dionysios, we got ourselves into a place that is too small. We received the basket, safely containing all that you wrote . . . and I sent half a measure [of wine?] with a letter to each of the people you wrote about. I got the six measures of lentils, a Coan jar full of vinegar, 126 pieces of pickled meat, the contents of the jar, and the thirty pieces of roast. Farewell!

Apparently Theon was not an exacting father: he had reassured Neilos in regard to this lad's involvement in some disreputable events at the theater, in which his brother had had a part, too. The boys' embarrassment had been increased by the gossiping of their slave Heraklas, who had followed the two students to the city to bring them the revenues of his work and help them with their expenses. But some conflicts had arisen, in spite of the fact that the boys swore that they had treated Heraklas fairly and allowed him much freedom. There are reasons to suspect that the reality was different: Neilos's attempt to put his father on guard against the viciousness of the slave was probably caused by a bad conscience. On the other hand, Neilos felt somehow entitled to the economic benefit Heraklas would bring and did not want to give the slave up. His suggestion— offered with the tone of someone well acquainted with worldly affairs— was that his father put the slave to work with someone, and send the money to his sons.

Since the first part of this letter is concerned with Neilos's detailed justifications for not finding suitable opportunities for education, it seems that Theon offered his pardon in regard to the events at the theater, but at the same time dug in his heels about strict academic standards and the importance of education. In his previous letter, this father, exactly like Cornelius in the letter discussed above, had shown some concern about his boys' appearance. Visitors to the city or some of his Alexandrian acquaintances may have related to him that the two students were not well-groomed or wore inappropriate clothes. In attributing the cause of their neglected looks to the depression they felt about their rough beginnings in the city, Neilos also advanced the perennial excuse of a student: being still in school and not yet taking part in adult life and work, young men were not required to conform to strict dress codes. But we know that his father had a different opinion. Theon had already sent two of his sons to Alexandria: while Neilos was looking for rhetorical instruction, his younger brother Diogas followed the class of a grammarian. Since a still younger brother was supposed to come soon to the city, probably to receive grammatical instruction, new, larger quarters were necessary, and the expenses for education were skyrocketing. Theon's concerns were well grounded, since he had invested a great deal, and he had reason to suspect that his boys were wasting time.

Upper-class parents made education one of their foremost concerns, because they believed that it was a crucial factor for their children's welfare and, ultimately, for their own happiness. They were ready to go to great lengths to ensure that their financial sacrifices acquired the most qualified teachers and the best opportunities: they paid the high fees of grammarians and rhetors, gave teachers gifts on special occasions, and supported their sons when they left home. Investment in education was a top priority for families who could afford it: it was planning for a family's future and for the parent's own well-being. In Libanius's opinion, some fathers were very willing to spend all the money they had so that their children could acquire the precious possession of education (*Or.* 55.26). Exhorting one of his students not to quit school—and, of course, defending his own interests—Libanius assured him that "a father would be even happy to die for such good, so that his son could enjoy the revenues coming from education in addition to his just and natural inheritance." Even though this was an exaggeration that reeked of self-promotion, Libanius had a point. Though it is doubtful whether the acquisition of minimal literacy always brought conspicuous financial benefits, those who acquired a higher education became part of a network of power, in which they were enmeshed by their own educational achievements, personal wealth, and connections. Parents fulfilled many roles besides that of financial provider. In the educational scenario, they were far from being marginal figures. Their active presence and vigilant eyes accompanied students during their ascent of the hill of learning, making sure that they practiced their mental gymnastics.

PART TWO

*

CHAPTER FIVE

Tools of the Trade: Teachers' Models, Books, and Writing Materials

GYMNASTICS OF THE MIND

T HE CONCEPT that physical exercise was necessary for a healthy body was deeply ingrained in Greek and Roman thought. Running and the sports of the gymnasium were part of a general system of training for improvement of body and soul upheld by moralists and philosophers, and even hardworking businessmen were exhorted not to overlook their exercise in the gymnasium. Exercise was also considered useful to women, but whereas Plato advocated thorough physical training for them (*Resp.* 5), others, such as Xenophon, thought it more appropriate for women to exercise indoors by walking in the house and doing housework (*Oec.* 10.10–13). Scholars and students, however, were warned against the tiredness and lack of concentration that derived from immoderate physical exertion. The search for "exercises suitable for scholars" ranged from Galen's recommendation of handball to the suggestion of other doctors and writers, like Plutarch, who preferred vocal exercise.[1] Students who had to dedicate long hours to intellectual activities had to refrain from excessive muscle buildup. Ps.-Plutarch approved Plato's statement that "excessive fatigue and sleepiness were enemies of studies" (*Resp.* 537b) and endorsed moderate exercise for students: it was better to keep slim bodies and to have alert minds (*De liberis educandis* 8d). That these warnings often fell on deaf ears is shown by the frequent reminders of writers such as Quintilian or Libanius that male students were not supposed to spend part of their life rubbing themselves with oil and that it was counterproductive to exercise furiously as if training for the Olympics.[2]

---

[1] Galen *Small Ball Workout* (K5.905); Plutarch *Mor.* 130a–d. See A. Rousselle, "Parole et inspiration: Le travail de la voix dans le monde romain," *History and Philosophy of the Life Sciences* 5 (1983): 129–57; Gleason 1995: 88–94.

[2] *Inst.* 1.11.15; Lib. *Or.* 35.13; Plutarch *Quomodo adul.* 5d–e; Himerius *Or.* 22.7. On the necessity of both mental and bodily exercise, cf. Diogenes Laertius 6.70: the mind and the body both needed good health and strength.

All writers concerned with education, however, agreed that students had to train in mental gymnastics. Even though they do not say so explicitly, their remarks were probably also valid for those female students who underwent the same educational training as male students. As weaknesses could be overcome and skills acquired through physical training, mental powers were sharpened by educational practice. Exercises for the mind stretched natural capacities such as memory and the ability to organize and assimilate material, developed a student's analytical powers, and in the end gave the young man who studied rhetoric the means to achieve some independence by going beyond his models. The concept that faculties like muscles could be developed and strengthened by hard work was a corollary of a culture that gave exercise, *askēsis*, such preeminence, and the metaphor that captured it with precision often resurfaced in literature.[3]

On an ostracon of the second century C.E., found at a quarry in the eastern desert of Egypt, a student wrote: "Diogenes the Cynic philosopher, when asked by someone where the Muses dwelled, said, 'In the minds of those who study hard.' "[4] Sayings of Diogenes dominated education at all levels. In other quotations of this maxim, "those who study hard" are replaced by "those who are educated,"[5] but fundamentally the difference was minimal. The love of the Muses was bought at a cost: studying involved constant application and sacrifice. "The toil of studying for one day is equivalent to going around with a donkey for five days," wrote an Egyptian pupil on a Demotic ostracon.[6] Another student, who must have been personally aware that education was a slow, onerous process, wrote in Greek: "Those who want to be virtuous must train their bodies with exercises and their minds with discourses."[7] The educational training process was its own reward, even for those who received only small doses. When the end of the process was in sight, it was possible to appreciate its positive effects. After much stumbling, a student was able to spread his wings.[8] "Go with the wind and spread the sails of the ship

[3] See Kaster 1988: 16–17 nn. 10 and 11 with more occurrences. See also Lucian *Anach.* 20. On the adoption of the concept in Christian thought, see Basil *De legendis gentilium libris*, passim, particularly 2.30–31 and 8.44–45.

[4] See *O.Claud.* II.413.

[5] Thus *tōn pepaideumenōn* (in *P.Mich.* inv. 141, Gallo 1980: 325–33, and Cribiore 1996a: no. 215) instead of *tōn philoponountōn*.

[6] Bresciani, Pernigotti, and Betrò 1983: no. 12, written in Demotic, a form of the Egyptian language.

[7] Cribiore 1996a: no. 186, attributed to Antisthenes.

[8] Cf. below, Chapter 8.

and the wings of the swan," wrote Libanius to his student Leontius, exhorting him to pour into the art of discourse studious effort and all of his natural ability, his own "spring of excellence" (*Ep.* 106).

The formidable burden of acquiring an education was tolerable because it was divided into a series of steps. A student was made to progress with painstaking regularity. In climbing the hill of learning, the "athlete"[9] did not go straight up the slope but proceeded in slow circles. Each circle expanded and enriched the compass of the preceding—in addition to introducing some new material—and embraced authors and exercises that were introduced previously, but were now used with a different purpose and in greater depth. According to the metaphor of education as mental gymnastics, we may say that the same exercises were performed by using weights that became gradually heavier. It is tempting to see this view of education as a vertical ascent to be climbed in circles represented to some extent in the frequently used expression *enkyklios paideia*. This phrase is usually taken to mean "general education," with the adjective *enkyklios* ("circular") pointing to the completeness of a program that had to envelop a student. It is possible that it also hinted at the multiplicity of the educational circles involved and at the cyclic revisiting of the same texts. When I mention circles of education in what follows, the reader should visualize a student in ancient times walking up a hill along circular paths.

Instruments of Learning

In the chapters that follow I shall retrace the steps ancient students had to cover in their mental gymnastics as they went from their initial acquisition of literacy to their learning the art of discourse. But it is expedient to provide a background to the exploration of the challenges offered at each level by inquiring about the various instruments of learning of which ancient students could take advantage: the model exercises and texts prepared for them by teachers, the books that offered assistance to inexperienced readers, the extant commentaries that appear to address scholastic and not scholarly needs, and the various materials on which students wrote their work.

[9] Quintilian 10.1.4; Libanius *Ep.* 1020.3.

The general questions that this chapter addresses are fundamental to understanding the mechanics of ancient education. Insofar as they regard the organization and shortcomings of ancient schooling, they need to be considered in connection with issues already investigated. They ultimately concern pupils' dependence on their teachers, the ways in which a classroom functioned, and the limitations that the use of certain writing materials may have put on the acquisition and development of habits of literacy. But in order to investigate these areas, a magnifying glass is necessary. One begins to follow the educational journey of ancient students by learning the characteristics of the typical handwriting of teachers, the detailed geography of models, the ways in which a book meant for a general audience can be distinguished from one that addressed students' needs, and the use of materials according to educational levels. By examining minute marks that appear on exercises and schoolbooks—accents, divisions of syllables and words, or trivial notes written in the margins—it is possible to gain access to the ways in which knowledge was structured and presented in ancient education and to understand the rules that organized its assimilation.

This chapter also serves to elucidate the particular type of authority that ancient teachers exercised over their students by clarifying that knowledge often did not possess an existence independent of those who imparted it. Teachers not only were those who devised drills and taught techniques of reading and writing, but often were the very sources of knowledge of the ancient writers, whose works were inscribed in their memory. As a rule, even today, a student's engagement with a text is mediated by the teacher, who eases his or her understanding of it. But in antiquity, teachers were not only the necessary intermediaries between impenetrable texts and limited skills. Both transmission of a text and its interpretation rested with a teacher. This was particularly true at early educational stages, when students trained their hands by copying from models and learned to read from literary passages written for them by their instructors. But even when they gained some access to books, they often had to rely on the text that a teacher offered and on his assessment of it. Homer, therefore, did not have an existence separate from that conferred on him by the teacher who entrusted models with his text to a girl or boy to copy and study, or who hung them in class.

Books are now considered indispensable trappings of literacy at every level, the proper cultural instruments of the student and the educated. A statement of Ps.-Plutarch is apparently consonant with modern expectations: "It is necessary to acquire the works of earlier writers and make a collection of these, like a set of tools in farming. For the corresponding tool of education is the use of books through which we can study knowledge at its source."[10] Yet books may not have been in every circumstance the foremost "tools of education" in antiquity, the *organa tēs paideias*. Surely the need to collect the works of poets and prose writers was felt at a comparatively late educational stage. With few exceptions, primary education enabled students to acquire only very limited reading and writing ability—not much more than the ability to copy a brief text and read a list of words or a short passage from an author previously rehearsed. When the student reached the next level, his initial efforts were dedicated to reinforcing his skills. Though the student's final goal was to be able to approach with confidence the works of the poets and to interpret them in all their nuances, initially he strove to acquire a stronger writing and reading ability and the capacity to manage larger quantities of text.

From the fifth century B.C.E. on, the use of books spread, and the written word acquired a larger audience.[11] Yet books did not penetrate every milieu: social and economic status, level of literacy, and even age remained powerful determinants of the degree of familiarity readers were able to reach with written texts. Thus the outrage of Alcibiades, who hit a *grammatodidaskalos* ("elementary teacher") who did not have a book of Homer, is hardly justifiable.[12] It is to be expected that elementary teachers did not always possess books of the authors they used so sparingly, and, when they did, that they did not always bring them to class. At every level, teaching was geared to fit the condition of the ancient classroom, which, if it was provided with seats at all, contained only benches.[13] Most of the time, ancient students had only their knees on which to rest a text and were likely unable to cope with the format of books and their relative fragility.[14] When their skills were still rudimentary and the text to be studied relatively short, making "textbooks" was the responsibility of teachers.

---

[10] Ps.-Plutarch *De liberis educandis* 8b. There is a clear echo of Plato *Laws* 1.643b–c, where children are supposed to have *organa smikra* ("small tools") to rehearse for their future roles in life. The grammarian Palladas (*Anth. Pal.* 9.171) calls books "tools of the Muses," *organa Mousaōn*.

[11] See Kenyon 1951; Turner 1977; Thomas 1989: 32–33; Turner 1980: 74–88 and 204.

[12] Plutarch *Alc.* 7.1.

[13] On benches, see Small 1997: 150–55.

[14] Books were in a roll format, but around the second century the codex came into use, particularly for Christian texts; see A. Blanchard, ed., *Les débuts du codex*, *Bibliologia* 9 (Brepols, 1989); on the advantages a codex offered for teaching and learning, C. H. Roberts and T. C. Skeat, *The Birth of the Codex* (London, 1987), 45–53 and 67–74.

THE TEACHERS' MODELS

The principle of imitation inspired ancient education from beginning to end. From the time students learned to wield a pen to when they composed their first declamation, they measured themselves against an exemplar that was either in front of their eyes or inscribed in their memory. "In everything that we teach, examples are more effective even than the rules that are taught in the schools. . . . The elementary study of every branch of learning is directed by reference to a definite model that is placed before the learner." These statements of Quintilian (10.1.15 and 10.2.2) had universal validity. A boy or a girl who formed his first letters or copied a short passage to improve his writing skills looked for constant confirmation from a model. The mechanical support a model provided with regard to letter shapes became, as a pupil advanced, a validation of the correctness of a passage. When a male student started to compose, a model did not lose its power: instead of reproducing it exactly, the writer attempted to vie with it.

Students learned efficient management of extensive texts relatively late in their school careers, well after entering grammar school: in their early education, they never had to confront handbooks of theory or whole works of an author, nor did they need to check references. In primary school and upon entering the class of the grammarian, a male or female student could expect the teacher to furnish both the necessary theoretical knowledge and passages from poetic texts written down for class use. The presence of teachers' models in the ancient classroom—an efficient way to deal with existing teaching conditions—is attested in the visual and literary sources.[15] Quintilian (1.1.27 and 35), who describes models that beginners followed in learning the alphabet, also alludes to models used at a later stage, from which students copied short passages. The presence of models in the classroom is also attested in the *Hermeneumata*, in which students are shown copying from models onto their waxed tablets. The activity of reading, which is described rather confusingly as being based on a model text, in one version appears to be centered on a book.[16] The student is asked to read five pages from a book (called *analogeion* and glossed as *manuale*), certainly not an elementary text, judging from the

---

[15] See, e.g., a cup by Douris, above, and Fig. 2. Columella *De re rustica* 10.251–52; Cassian *Conlatio* 10.5, where a model is called *protypium*; Clement *Strom.* 5.8.48.4–9, 49.1, 359.1–9, 360.3; and Seneca *Ep.* 94.51. On the various terms applied to models in antiquity, see Cribiore 1996a: 122–23.

[16] See Goetz 1892: 225; and Dionisotti 1982: 99 ll. 20 and 27.

lengthy reading. The book, in any case, appears to be held by the teacher, who calls the pupil up to read it.

The school exercises of Greco-Roman Egypt amply confirm the reliance of ancient students and teachers on models. They include about sixty exemplars written by teachers on several materials—ostraca, tablets, and occasionally papyrus. Some are accompanied by the student's copy underneath; others can be identified by various characteristics.[17] It appears that in the initial phases of learning, teachers tended to write model alphabets on clay sherds that were easily passed from pupil to pupil for copying. For their first copying exercises, pupils needed a smooth surface and a model from which they could reproduce the text letter by letter. Wooden tablets—plain or covered with wax—were ideal: they were sturdy enough to endure damage and mishandling and were reused as the need arose.[18] For instance, a tablet from the second to third century C.E. discovered in the Roman cemetery of the village of Tebtunis was the prized possession of a boy or girl whose penmanship needed improvement. On top of the tablet, a teacher had written a model with a hexameter line: "Begin, good hand, beautiful letters, and a straight line," which was completed by the exhortation, "Now, you imitate it!"—one of the few times in which the voice of an ancient teacher rings loud.[19] The student copied the hexameter five times, each time awkwardly writing down the final recommendation. The text deteriorated progressively as it proceeded down the tablet, as if this pupil followed in turn the previous attempt and listened to his or her own voice—"Imitate it!"—instead of looking up at the model. Since this beginner was apparently unable to read and therefore to correct mistakes, errors of every kind proliferated.

The next challenge, learning to read, was also met with the help of models. When students learned syllables, most of the time the various syllabic combinations were inscribed by teachers on tablets and ostraca. A teacher might even employ two different sherds that consecutively contained a series and functioned as separate pages—an example of how inventively writing materials were exploited.[20] The papyri have also preserved three examples of early Byzantine schoolbooks containing syllabaries that had been produced professionally. It is to be expected that books such as these, inscribed in formal, elaborate hands, made of fine papyrus, and provided with page numbers, were used sparingly and only by students of the upper class. They were fragile and expensive and could

[17] Cribiore 1996a: 123–28, with references to specific models.
[18] On a tablet with a model, see above, pp. 39–40.
[19] Cribiore 1996a: no. 136.
[20] Ibid.: no. 91.

not go into everybody's hands.[21] Models continued to be useful when a pupil was required to recognize syllables in whole words: teachers wrote lists of words on ostraca and tablets, some in which the words were divided into syllables, others in which words were separated from each other. Students used these models not only to practice reading and writing whole words, but also to memorize their contents. Thus, when a teacher wrote a long list of names mostly from the *Iliad* in alphabetical order on a very large ostracon, this was used as a mythological reference that was always at the student's disposal.[22]

Models continued to be of practical use when students confronted passages from literary works. Though this process started in the last stage of primary education, a pupil upon joining a grammarian's class still needed considerable assistance in decoding words written in continuous blocks— *scriptio continua*. Since books for beginning readers were not produced on a regular basis, models prepared by teachers fulfilled an invaluable function. Homer and Isocrates were transcribed on tablets with words separated, with some lectional signs (such as occasional accents and breathings), and sometimes with syllables separated by one or two dots. When a passage was exhausted, the teacher transcribed another. Let us look closely at a model tablet inscribed on both sides with consecutive lines from Book 2 of the *Iliad* (Fig. 16).[23] The word groups (nouns together with articles, prepositions, etc.) were separated by oblique strokes, and sometimes by spaces. The date by month and day at the end referred either to the time when the passage had been written or to the day by which it was supposed to be read and perhaps memorized. The general effect of this text resembles that of a printed page in its attractive regularity: as in the case of most models, legibility was the foremost concern. Models such as this formed an indispensable transition to texts written by scribes without division of words.

The ancient sources are almost entirely silent about the question of how models were used and handled, but the dimensions and shapes of the models from Greco-Roman Egypt suggest some answers. The manageable size and sturdiness of most indicate that they could be used by individual students and could circulate in class with a minimum of inconvenience. In this respect, there is a striking similarity between these models and the hornbooks that were indispensable educational tools for children from the sixteenth to the eighteenth century and that continued to exercise an

---

[21] Ibid.: nos. 81, 84, and 97. On medieval books containing syllabaries, see Bischoff 1966: 75 n. 12. Cf. below, pp. 172–74.

[22] Cribiore 1996a: no. 113.

[23] Ibid.: no. 296.

Figure 16.   Tablet with verses from the *Iliad* written by a teacher as a
model, third to fourth century C.E.

influence on primers until the beginning of the twentieth century.[24] In trying to picture the activity of copying in an ancient classroom, modern
Koranic education in northern Africa is also useful (Fig. 17).[25] Children
sit in the sand copying Koranic verses from models. They still use reed
pens, ink made with water, charcoal, and gum arabic, and wooden tablets.
Stains, mistakes, pondering over the model: this is learning as it always
was. These children copy letter by letter, as do modern students in Egyptian schools, who are given a book from which to write. They copy what
is written without necessarily understanding it.[26]

   The sands of Egypt have also preserved other models of a particularly
large size. It is conceivable that large wooden boards functioned somewhat like modern blackboards. Models inscribed on ostraca of large proportions, however, were extremely unmanageable, being either fragile and
difficult to handle when of clay, or heavy and hard to move when on
limestone.[27] It is likely that models such as these rested somewhere in the
classroom and were used by students and teachers alike as works of reference from which to copy Homeric verses or gnomic texts. Let us look, for

[24] See A. W. Tuer, *History of the Horn-Book* (London, 1986). Most hornbooks were
small slabs of wood with letters, numbers, and a prayer.

[25] "Education in Niger," *National Geographic* 195, no. 3 (March 1999): 18–19.

[26] See Abu-Lughod 1993: 142.

[27] See Cribiore 1996a: nos. 311, 315, and 319.

Figure 17. A contemporary school in Niger: children copy from a model.
Their writing implements are the same as in antiquity.

instance, at a large model found in the same military outpost of Mons
Claudianus where the student mentioned above, who was aware that the
Muses befriended the hard-working, lived and studied (Fig. 18).[28] The
model contained a list of disyllabic words in many columns, a hodgepodge
of elements drawn from local reality, and mythological reminiscences. Besides the seven columns of writing, a large male bearded face was drawn
in black and red—Pluto, the god of the Underworld. The text was written
around the neck and shoulders of a tall jar, and the model probably stood
for display in the classroom, being at the same time a decorative object
and a work of reference. One thinks of the vignette of Diogenes the Cynic,
who entered a school that had few pupils but was adorned by many statues
of the Muses, or of the statues of the "dear Muses" who witnessed the
flogging of Kokkalos.[29] But in this Egyptian classroom Pluto stood guard
in less elegant, and somewhat threatening, fashion.

[28] *O.Claud.* II.415: the hand displays some irregularities, probably due to the coarse surface. A teacher may have asked a student to prepare a model for the class.

[29] Diogenes Laertius 6.69; Athenaeus 8.348d. In the *Didaskalos*, Metrotime refers to the
Muses as *haide* ("these") as if they were materially present in the classroom and hopes they
can see her son with bound feet; cf. Mastromarco 1984: 34.

Figure 18.   A large ostracon from Mons Claudianus that might have
sat in a classroom (*O. Claud.* II.415, second century C.E.).

BOOKS AND GRAMMARIANS

In his ironic account of the day of an ancient student, Lucian says that on
his way to school "with eyes bent down and without facing the gaze of
anyone he meets, he is followed by an orderly band of attendants and
pedagogues who grip in their hands the revered tools of virtue . . . many-
leaved writing tablets or books that preserve the excellence of ancient
deeds." After toiling zealously (*enathlein*) in exercises of the mind, the
boy turns to bodily exercises (*Amores* 44–45). This passage, which praises
the "virtuous" life of a schoolboy in contrast to the impure life of a courtesan, piles up with sarcastic zeal the ingredients of a successful schooling.
In reality, the average student of the grammarian may have had only one

attendant, one pedagogue, and probably a single book that followed him to class, even though he was probably able to consult more books once there. Plato describes how teachers in class handed students books of poets to read and memorize, once they were able to understand written texts (*Prt.* 325d).

The papyri testify that books were common ingredients of school life in Greco-Roman Egypt at an intermediate level. Some letters allude to books used by students: a reading book for Heraidous,[30] a geometry book for a student obsessed with schoolwork,[31] and books that Hierax was supposed to study diligently.[32] It is also likely that the student Ptolemaios, who had reached Book 6 of the *Iliad*, had done so with the help of books rather than with models.[33] Identifying texts that were used in or for class, however, is not an easy enterprise: in most cases they were virtually identical to the books—rolls and codices—that were at the disposal of educated individuals—a fact that should make us very cautious when drawing conclusions about the reading assignments of students. There was not a large market for texts provided with special features, since models usually covered the stage at which a reader needed serious help in decoding words. Sometimes, however, it is possible to identify books used by learners, either because they exhibit particular characteristics in the presentation of the material or features intended to facilitate reading, or because the student who read them or the teacher who used them to prepare his class left marks and annotations.

A papyrus with a fragmentary text on the Labors of Heracles provides a fitting example of a text geared to instruct and entertain an inexperienced reader (Fig. 19).[34] The piece that is preserved regards the Labor of the Nemean Lion and consists of an elementary text written in simple style and diction and crude meter. Though the large handwriting was fairly easy to read, further assistance was provided in the form of gaps between some words. The story is accompanied by simple sketches that represent different moments of the Labor.[35] Only traces remain of the color that the

[30] Cf. above, Chapter 3.

[31] Cf. above, pp. 41–42.

[32] Cf. above, p. 115.

[33] Cf. above, Chapter 2.

[34] *P.Oxy.* XXII.2331 (third century C.E.).

[35] These are of great interest, because literary papyri are rarely illustrated. About illuminations, Pliny 25.2.4–5; Martial 14.186; E. Bethe, *Buch und Bild in Altertum* (Leipzig, 1945); K. Weitzmann, *Illustrations in Roll and Codex* (Princeton, 1947), and *Ancient Book Illumination* (Cambridge, 1959); U. Horak, *Illuminierte Papyri, Pergamente und Papiere* (Vienna, 1992).

Figure 19.   Papyrus text concerning the Labors of Heracles with drawings
(*P. Oxy.* XXII.2331), third century C.E.

artist used in plenty: the hero had yellow hair and garments, the ground
was green, and the lion and the club tawny. This was an attractive text
that targeted a young audience. But books such as this, striking in its
modern features of easy readability and appealing presentation, must
have been quite rare.[36] More common were books used for didactic purposes that presented the textual material in a less sophisticated way than
those aiming at the general public.[37] An example is provided by a papyrus
with sayings of Diogenes.[38] The repetitious presentation of the sayings—
each one introduced by the constant formula "The philosopher Diogenes
said . . ." or "The philosopher Diogenes, on being asked . . ., said . . ."—
would hardly be appropriate in a text for the general public.[39] A teacher,

[36] Another such book might be a papyrus that presents the story of the mouse and the
weasel in dramatized form, S. Daris, "Esercizio scolastico," *Aegyptus* 52 (1972): 91–96. Cf.
Cribiore 1996a: no. 263 for an exercise on the same subject. See also H. S. Schibli, "Fragments of a Weasel and Mouse War," *ZPE* 53 (1983): 1–25, and "Addendum," *ZPE* 54
(1984): 14, about a mock-epic poem on the conflict between mice and a weasel.

[37] See P^2 240 (G. A. Gerhard, *Sitzb.Heid.Akad.* 1912, Abh. 13), a papyrus of the third
century B.C.E. containing a collection of maxims of Chares of Lampsacus with a plain arrangement that were addressed to a child (the word "child," *pai*, appears in [a], line 3). See
also two late texts with Menander's maxims in Greek and Coptic translation, Hagedorn
and Weber 1968; cf. below, p. 200.

[38] *P.Mich.inv.* 41 (first century C.E.), Gallo 1980: 325–33.

[39] In a moral treatise or in a biographical work, the sayings would be incorporated into
the text, while in a *gnomologium* they would be introduced by the pronoun *ho autos*, "he."

however, could utilize this presentation, in which each saying is complete in itself, for he could ask his students to copy directly from the book.

Sometimes books addressed the needs of uncertain readers through consistent word separation. Part of a hexameter poem about Hero and Leander is preserved on a papyrus in which the words are separated by spaces and the handwriting is large and remarkably clear.[40] The text, which seems to refer to Leander's final journey, contains an appeal to the stars not to shine and to the Evening Star to assist Leander as he swims back to the other side of the Hellespont. It testifies that Alexandrian literature and poetry of pathetic appeal and aetiological character was of interest in educational contexts. Another text confirms that the Isocrates of the *Cyprian Orations* was a favorite in ancient schools. Though the school exercises usually preserve Isocratean passages of limited extent, a papyrus roll contains about half of the *Ad Nicoclem*, in which dots consistently divide the words, particularly in places where doubts might arise in reading.[41] This was an abridged edition, for the title of the whole work appears at the end of the shortened text.

But since Homer was the subject of constant study at many levels, it is among Homeric papyri that books used in schools are most often found.[42] A good example is provided by a codex that contained Book 20 of the *Iliad*, in which the words are consistently separated by vertical dashes in the shape of acute accents.[43] In another papyrus, which originally preserved the first six books of the *Iliad*, there is some use of dots to separate words, and an unusual wealth of lectional signs, such as accents, breathings, apostrophes, and marks of quantity.[44] The text was written on the right-hand pages of a codex, leaving ample space for annotations. One is reminded of Quintilian's advice to leave blank pages in manuscripts for additions (10.3.32). The codex format was particularly handy for educational purposes, since a text could be consulted more easily, a reference

[40] *P.Ryl.* III.486 (P^2 1783, first century C.E.); *SH* 951. The myth was the source of Ovid *Her.* 17 and 18 and of the poem of the fifth-century grammarian Musaeus.

[41] See P^2 1254 (third to fourth century C.E., A. Schoene, *Mélanges Graux* [Paris, 1884], 481–504), Isocrates *Ad Nicoclem* 1–30. Cf. Worp and Rijksbaron 1997; and below, p. 203.

[42] On the use of Homer in schools, see below, Chapter 7.

[43] *MPER N.S.* III.3, P^2 971, fourth century C.E. The same feature is found in a few Homeric codices from the sixth century from Hermopolis, H. Maehler, "Fragmente antiker Homer-Handschriften," *Festschrift zum 150 Jährigen Bestehen des Berliner Ägyptischen Museum* (Berlin, 1974), 370–71, 387–88, 390–92, nos. 7 (*Il.* 7), 23 (*Il.* 21), and 26 (*Od.* 10).

[44] P^2 634 (*P.Lond.Lit. 5*), third century C.E. See also Turner 1987: 40 no. 14. On the specific shape that these signs have in the papyri, see Cribiore 1996a: 84–86.

could be found in less time, and a codex could hold a longer text than a roll, which could accommodate a maximum of two to three Homeric books.[45] In this case, some of the blank pages were used to copy a modest grammatical handbook, a short outline of the parts of speech in which words are regularly separated by spaces.[46] In the class of a grammarian, where the Homeric text was scrutinized, it was convenient to have a book that also included a grammatical treatise. Several grammatical handbooks have been found that addressed the needs of students at this level.[47]

Unusually profuse accentuation in texts other than lyric[48] can also be an indication that a book was written for or used in school. A case in point is a fragment from what was probably the fourth book of the *Catalogue* of Hesiod in which nearly every syllable has an accent.[49] Though Homeric papyri frequently present abundant accentuation, the presence of this feature accompanied by many lectional signs that indicate a regular punctuation strongly points to a book used in education.[50] Moreover, when a wealth of accents was added not by the original scribe but by the reader, one strongly suspects that a student was engaged in an accentuation exercise. Thus, a beautifully written text of *Iliad* 24, the "Bankes" Homer, which also presents elementary marginal annotations, is disfigured by numerous accents grossly written by a second hand: a student marked the book with an energetic disrespect for the written word.[51] Other texts that show signs of school use combine an unusual amount of accentuation with marginal notes written by the reader: a carefully written text of *Iliad* 5, to which plentiful accents and other lectional signs have been added— this time more gently—by a student, also exhibits numerous marginal annotations of an elementary nature.[52] Asked to distinguish the narrative

[45] See Kenyon 1899: 122, and 1951: 65; Lameere 1960: 168.

[46] P^2 1539 (*P.Lond.Lit.* 182), not compiled from a work by the famous grammarian Tryphon but taken from various school handbooks, V. Di Benedetto, *Ann.Pisa* ser. 2, 27 (1958): 191–96. See also Wouters 1979: 61–92.

[47] On *technai*, see below.

[48] Accents were traditionally written on verses in difficult dialects.

[49] *P.Oxy.* XXIII.2355 (P^2 528, first to second century C.E.).

[50] See, e.g., *P.Michael.* 2 (P^2 997, *Iliad* 23, first century C.E.); P^2 943 and 944, *P.Rain.Cent* 20 (*Il.* 17, second century C.E.); *PSI* VII.747 (P^2 708, *Il.* 4, second century C.E.); all belonging to the third century: *P.Mert.* I.3 (P^2 915, *Il.* 14); *P.Oxy.* III.541 (P^2 678, *Il.* 2); *Pap.Flor.* XIX, pp. 111–15 (*Il.* 7). In most of these texts, the accents were marked by a second hand.

[51] *P.Lond.Lit.* 28 (P^2 1013, second century C.E.); Turner 1980: 90–91.

[52] *P.Oxy.* II.223 (P^2 733, third century C.E.); see also *P.Lond.Lit.* 6 (P^2 643, *Iliad* 2, first century C.E.). Consider also the exemplar of *scholia minora* to the *Iliad* and the codex of this poem owned by Dioskoros of Aphrodito in the sixth century, where notes, lectional signs, and corrections were added in Books 10 and 11 by one or more readers, probably his

parts of the book from the speeches, this pupil wrote in the margin the names of various speakers and the indication "the poet" in a rough hand.[53] That such an exercise was needed is shown by the evident uncertainty in identifying the poet's voice. In any case, one should not feel too sorry for such ancient books in disgrace. It is likely that an expensive book copied accurately in a formal hand by a scribe landed in the hands of a student only at the end of a useful life spent in the service of more respectful readers.

Comprehension of Homeric diction was furthered by glossographical works that presented "translation" of difficult terms. *Scholia minora*, which were often compiled by students and teachers, also circulated in book form.[54] Other tools of exegesis were texts that concentrated on mythological, paraphrastic, and explanatory material. In elucidating the texts of other poets, ancient grammarians drew heavily on school commentaries. These handbooks differed from scholarly commentaries insofar as they concentrated on mythological material and on a type of exegesis geared toward rendering the text more easily approachable. Though learned points from erudite commentaries occasionally crept in, much of that information was omitted in favor of a concentration on notes of grammatical character, brief paraphrases, and glossographical material. Moreover, the compilers of these handbooks (the grammarians themselves?) often added other elementary observations and literary parallels. An example is a late codex with notes to the *Phoenissae* of Euripides that exhibits trivial information, careless language, and confused presentation of the material.[55] Other authors for whom school commentaries are extant are Aratus, Aristophanes, Pindar, and Theocritus.[56] Thus, for instance, the text of the *Phaenomena*, the astronomical poem of Aratus

---

students; see Fournet 1997. In *P.Mert.* II.52 (*Od.* 2.404–16, 431–34; 3.1), peculiar dashes were added at the end of verses by a student who also wrote a mathematical exercise.

[53] A few Homeric papyri present this feature; see Haslam 1997: 57. On this expression applied to Homer, see Kindstrand 1973: 99–100; A. M. Harmon, "The Poet κατ'ἐξοχήν," *CP* 18 (1923): 35–47.

[54] See, e.g., *P.Freib.* I.1c, *P.Schub.* 2, and *P.Ryl.* I.25.

[55] *P.Würzb.* 1; see Maehler 1993: 109–11.

[56] See K. McNamee, "An Innovation in Annotated Codices on Papyrus," *Akten des 21. Internationalen Papyrologenkongresses* (Berlin, 1997), 669–78; McNamee 1994, on *P.Rain* I.23. Zuntz (1975) showed that marginal notes in late codices of Aristophanes derive from school handbooks; see, e.g., *P.Oxy.* VI.856 (third century C.E.) and *P*² 142 (G. Zuntz, *Byzantion* 13 [1938]: 635–57, fourth century C.E.). For Theocritus, see, e.g., a commentary from the second century, *BKT* V.1.56 (*P*² 1496) and the marginal notes in *P.Oxy.* XVI.2064 + L.3548; cf. Maehler 1993: 99–101.

(ca. 315–240 B.C.E.), which was linguistically approachable by students because it drew mainly from Homer, presented cryptic astronomical lore: a papyrus handbook from the third to fourth century was geared toward making this text intelligible.[57] While handbooks of this kind betray their educational nature, a more difficult question to answer is to what degree extant learned commentaries were employed in school, for teaching purposes, rather than in advanced scholarship.

BOOKS IN HIGHER EDUCATION

On moving to higher stages of education, assessing the value of books versus teachers' contributions becomes even more challenging. At the earlier levels, the teacher was omnipresent and omnipotent. The transmitted school exercises are precious skeletons of ancient instruction, mere shadows of what went on in the classroom. They reach us as if in a vacuum, almost always deprived of the voice of the teacher who explained an assignment, read a mythological account, or lectured on a poet. Teachers' contributions are most apparent in the models that allow us to verify how they made the work of an author more accessible or that reveal the material they chose to have their class study. Moreover, a teacher's voice may still echo in the notes written in the margins of some papyri, for students might simply have jotted down what they heard in class and what came to them through their teacher's mediation and voice, *apo phonēs*. At the same time, however, students had to rely heavily on books, for the demands that reading made on them were challenging.

It is customary to associate rhetoric with oral discourse and live speech. Even though rhetors often followed the example of Isocrates, who produced speeches meant only for reading,[58] rhetoric remained tightly connected with impromptu performance, at least in theory.[59] When Quintilian stressed the superiority of the live example furnished by the teacher over written discourses,[60] his remarks were directed at what he regarded as the problem of the increasing intrusion of the written word. But although he may have justly complained about an excessively bookish approach, reading and writing were undoubtedly also essential at this stage.

[57] M. Maehler, "Der 'wertlose' Aratkodex P.Berol inv. 5865," *APF* 27 (1980): 19–32.

[58] See, e.g., *To Philip* 25–27.

[59] But see Philostratus *VS* 2.8, about a rhetor delivering the same showpiece in various places as an extemporaneous speech.

[60] See, e.g., 2.2.8.

When a student joined a rhetorical school, he was lectured by his teacher on rhetorical theory. It is likely that some of the rhetorical treatises transmitted by the papyri not only served the needs of instructors but also circulated among students.[61] Particularly interesting is a papyrus (*P.Oxy.* XVII. 2086) that combines theory with a teacher's contribution. It apparently contains notes jotted down during a lecture, rather than the guidelines of a set treatise. As Quintilian testifies, students made frequent annotations that sometimes circulated in public and reproduced a teacher's work to its detriment (1 Preface 7–8 and 2.11.7).

Much of a student's energy, moreover, went into reading prose works, since he did not encounter them in the class of the grammarian. Whereas Demosthenes[62] and other orators were constantly perused, the fifth-century historians Thucydides and Herodotus were also the object of intense study aimed at capturing and assimilating their style and vocabulary.[63] Besides erudite commentaries on Thucydides, scholastic handbooks that concentrated on glossographical material and treatment of individual questions were available.[64] The texts of the prose authors were studied initially as a preparation to rhetorical school. The same texts, moreover, were studied and memorized during the school year and in the course of summer vacations.[65] Among the written works that students were supposed to study were the discourses of Libanius himself (*Or.* 3.17). In their splendid country houses, with "trees, waters, and breezes as consolation to their fatigues," students spent much time memorizing (*Ep.* 419.1). Libanius testifies to his use of Thucydides in class (*Or.* 1.148–50). A copy that he particularly cherished, so small that he could take it to class himself without the help of a slave, was stolen and sold in the second-hand market. Since the purchaser happened to be a student, Libanius recovered it "like a long-lost child unexpectedly restored."

As a rule, Libanius refers quite casually to the use of books in school. Students are constantly exhorted to pay attention to their books (*Or.* 35.12–13 and 25). When they go to school, they are in the company of slaves who carried their books, which were bulky and quite heavy (*Or.*

---

[61] See, e.g., *P.Yale* II.106; *P.Oxy.* III.410, XVII.2086, and LIII.3708.

[62] Libanius complained that sometimes Demosthenes was not studied enough, *Or.* 3.18. For a book that may have served the needs of a student, see, e.g., a papyrus codex, *BKT* I.78–82 (*P²* 317) with a lexicon to a single speech of Demosthenes, *In Aristocratem*.

[63] On books read in Libanius's class, see Libanius *Ep.* 1036, and Norman 1964. On reading authors in order to acquire a stock of words, see Quintilian 10.1.8–9.

[64] See O. Luschnat, "Die Thukydidesscholien," *Philologus* 98 (1954): 14–58.

[65] See Festugière 1959: 135; cf. Libanius *Ep.* 379.5 and 9, 894.2, and *Or.* 34.12.

25. 50 and 54. 31).[66] When books were made of parchment, they were even bulkier and harder to transport—and well suited to serve as weapons in fights with other students (*Or.* 4.18 and 58.5). Books could also be the origin of a family crisis. Olympios, an advocate of Antioch, lent a book to his son, a student of Libanius, but the lad gave it in turn to some fellow students who never returned it (*Ep.* 1375). In terror at the idea of confronting his father, the youth ran away to a distant city. Money budgeted for purchasing schoolbooks is considered by Libanius to be as important as money spent for tuition, as a letter quoted above shows.[67] Books were amply used in rhetorical schools when youths had to acquire a ready familiarity with the authors of the past. But undoubtedly, when students learned to deliver their own declamations, the example of their teacher and contact with the living tradition were of foremost importance.

The role of books at more specialized levels of education, such as schools of medicine, architecture, engineering, and philosophy, is also of interest, even though the brief remarks here may seem to border on the superficial. It is likely that books sometimes lost ground in favor of the direct instruction of teachers. Galen testifies to an ambivalent attitude toward books in medical teaching.[68] Although he recognizes their usefulness in disseminating certain works—particularly among a nonspecialized public—he shows the customary distrust of the skilled craftsman toward the written word. The word of the teacher and his practical demonstrations were sovereign, but then it was up to the teacher to publish a written version of a lecture. Certain skills could not be learned from books alone, and when the necessity arose, it was better to read a book with the assistance of a teacher. In this field, therefore, books maintained their usefulness,[69] even though the living voice (*zōsa phōnē*) of the teacher was the primary means of instruction. In philosophical teaching, books were useful in transmitting the doctrines of the past and as "reminders" of direct teaching.[70] Though the voice of the teacher also had the function

---

[66] Norman 1960: 124–25. See also Augustine *Enarrationes in Psalmos* 40.14; Vössing 1997: 360.

[67] *Ep.* 428. See above, p. 113.

[68] L. Alexander, "The Living Voice: Scepticism towards the Written Word in Early Christian and in Greco-Roman Texts," in *The Bible in Three Dimensions*, ed. D.J.A. Clines, S. E. Fowl, and S. E. Porter, *Journal for the Study of the Old Testament*, suppl. ser. 87 (1990): 221–47; Mansfeld 1994: 123–26 and 148–76. See Galen *Libr. Propr.* 11, Kühn 19.42; *De antidotis* 1 Pref., Kühn 14.6; *De compositione medicamentorum* 6 Pref., Kühn 12.894.

[69] See, e.g., *P.Mil.Vogl.* I.15 (P² 2340), a catechism for a medical student.

[70] Seneca *Ep.* 6.5 and 33.9; Lucian *Hermot.* 2.

of presenting and interpreting the received tradition, it was essential in expounding a new doctrine. In this respect, written texts were secondary to oral instruction: they functioned as records of the instruction given and could be interpreted and modified at any time. It is in this light that the well-known criticism of Plato of the role of books and the written word in the *Phaedrus* should be interpreted: Plato is not concerned with books in general but with the oral and written word in the context of the schools (274c–277a). There, the continuous interaction of teacher and pupil was fundamental, and only in those conditions could a student reach a state of philosophical illumination (*Epistula* 7.341c).

Where did one get schoolbooks or, in any case, copies of authors that were probably the ancient equivalent of our paperbacks? A letter from the second century provides some suggestions:[71] "Iulius Placidus to his father Herclanus, greetings. Deios came to see us and showed to us the six parchment codices. We did not choose any of them but we collated eight others for which I gave a deposit of 100 drachmai." Deios was a traveling bookseller who went door to door to offer his books and had developed his own clientele.[72] It is conceivable that his books were not all first quality since the letter's writer did not approve of what he was being offered. Iulius Placidus must have developed in the class of a grammarian some literary expertise that allowed him to compare different manuscripts. Another letter alludes to one Demetrios, a "bookseller" (*bibliopōlēs*) in Oxyrhynchos, though it is unclear whether he had a real bookstore or he left his books in a shop in the city to be picked up by customers.[73] This letter offers a very suggestive picture of a circle of friends who eagerly bought books, exchanged them, had them copied, and anxiously looked for others. "Should you find any, apart from those which I possess, make copies and send them to me," says one of the writers. The two specific books that are mentioned—a work on the prosopography of comedy and another on the myths of tragedy—would not have been out of place among a grammarian's possessions.[74]

[71] *P.Petaus* 30; J. van Haelst, "Les origines du codex," in A. Blanchard, ed., *Les débuts du codex, Bibliologia* 9 (1989): 21–23.

[72] Cf. Lucian *Ind.* 4. See R. J. Starr, "The Circulation of Literary Texts in the Roman World," *CQ* 37 (1987): 213–23; T. Kleberg, "Commercio librario ed editoria nel mondo antico," in Cavallo 1984: 27–80.

[73] *P.Oxy.* XVIII.2192, second century C.E.

[74] On the educational use of such collections, Norman 1964: 165; and, e.g., Libanius *Or.* 64.83.

This letter also testifies to the habit of members of the upper class of keeping private scribes to serve the needs of the household.[75] Thus, when students still lived with their families, it is likely that they could take advantage of a slave or freedman in the house to have a book copied. Different arrangements had to be made when they left home to pursue advanced studies. Libanius, who always had one or more slaves to act as copyists for him during his career as rhetor,[76] used the services of a copyist (*biblographos*) when he was a student in Athens (*Or.* 1.43). Having someone to copy books was most convenient for those students who could afford it. Since families apparently provided their children with a retinue of people whose functions are not specified, one wonders whether a slave who would copy schoolbooks was part of a student's entourage.

WRITING MATERIALS AND IMPLEMENTS

The writing materials used in schools—papyrus, ostraca, wooden and wax tablets, and, more rarely, parchment—were the same as those employed for various writing purposes in everyday life. What was different were the uses to which these materials were put, the texts inscribed on them, and the frequency with which some of them were employed. But observing all the characteristics of usage is not enough: important questions remain about the social and economic status of the people who handled them, the availability, cost, and practical employment of the writing materials, and the limits—if any—that these factors imposed on an individual's ability to learn to read and write. It has recently been argued that the scarcity and high cost of good writing materials, and the great inconvenience of those easily available, hampered the acquisition and spread of literacy.[77] It is with this in mind that we review the evidence.

Although allusions to materials used in various circumstances are frequent, it is unknown whether the ancients regarded them as cheap or expensive, comfortable or cumbersome to use—an indication that they accepted them as part of their life. The question of the cost of papyrus in antiquity has often been debated: expensive for a farmer or a villager, papyrus was nevertheless quite affordable in more elevated social mi-

---

[75] See McDonnell 1996: 477.

[76] See, e.g., *Or.* 1.184–85 and 232.

[77] See Harris 1989: 94–95 and 193–96.

lieus.[78] Papyrus was a material often employed in education. The fact that a poor schoolboy might have had some trouble acquiring a papyrus roll does not affect the general conclusion that the cost of papyrus for educational uses was irrelevant. Students needed fresh papyrus rolls relatively late in their school careers, at a stage hardly ever reached by students of the lower classes. Most often students employed recycled papyrus.[79] When they were learning to write, they preferred to use the front of papyri, where they could follow the horizontal fibers as guidelines and where the surface was smoother; they did not need large pieces but could take advantage of small unwritten scraps cut off from used papyri.[80] Occasionally, when the need for a large piece was felt—for instance, to write a syllabary—it was possible to wash off a previously written surface. A student who was not looking for elegance did not worry if some traces of previous writing remained, and the underlying writing on these palimpsests is clearly visible. Many school papyri betray the fact that they were reused at the end of a long life. Though occasional repairs and patchings done to strengthen a piece beforehand add to its general coarse appearance, sometimes the rough look of a papyrus is a mark of production and of cheap quality: thick papyri with a coarse surface were more likely to fall into the hands of pupils.

Though it was possible to wash off a papyrus with a sponge, a more common way to reuse a papyrus was to inscribe its clean back. This would provide a student with large pieces for copying long passages of prose and poetry. When the soldier Terentianus tells his father in a letter that he is sending him "two papyri for school use" (*chartas scholares duas*), he is probably referring to papyri that had been used only on the front sides.[81] Relatively large sheets were needed when students no longer had serious problems with the technical side of writing: at this stage, the inconvenience of having to write against the fibers was minimal, and the act of writing unchallenging. The practice of using the backs of papyri whose fronts contained obsolete documents or literary texts that no longer interested the owner is observed in daily life and naturally flourished in schools, where most of the work done was ephemeral. Since school exercises did not need to be saved and were in fact found discarded in dumps,

---

[78] The most recent assessment, with bibliography: T. C. Skeat, "Was Papyrus Regarded as 'Cheap' or 'Expensive' in the Ancient World?" *Aegyptus* 75 (1995): 75–93.

[79] Cribiore 1996a: 57–62.

[80] Cf., among many examples, Cribiore 1996a: no. 240, where the student tried to fit a passage from Euripides in a precut papyrus.

[81] See *P.Mich*. VIII.468.

reused material—the ancient equivalent of scrap paper—was appropriate and convenient. In the same way, papyrus acquired a new life through recycling, ostraca were written on and thrown away, and tablets were washed.

Ranting against the pretensions of the uneducated man who advertised his literacy through the possession of many books, Lucian declared that his attempts to appear cultivated would all be unsuccessful, even if he pasted all his rolls together and walked about wrapped in them (*Ind*. 4). Surely, such a bizarre dream was out of reach of most ancient students, who did not have many chances to amass large quantities of papyrus or parchment. This is also shown by the diminutive sizes of the few school notebooks in codex form found in Roman Egypt, which contain various types of exercises, often in order of difficulty. Thus, for instance, one of them, made of eleven leaves, displays several lists of words, sayings of Diogenes, maxims, and a prologue to the *Fables* of the second-century writer Babrius (Fig. 20).[82] The contents of the notebook, which was penned by a student who wrote rather fluently, or perhaps by a teacher, addressed the needs of someone in the last phase of his elementary education, who would have been pleased by those talking creatures of the Golden Age: the pine tree, the leaves of the laurel, the fish who spoke to the sailor who had befriended it, and the sparrows who conversed with the farmer. As in other cases, the size of this schoolbook is striking: it could fit in a hand—the equivalent of those *codicilli* or *pugillares* used in Rome for schoolwork or for writing epistles.[83] Small and even tiny notebooks must have been part of school tradition. They were still used in the Middle Ages, at least in fourteenth-century Florence.[84] In all times, students have preferred having their own instruments of literacy, however modest. In Greco-Roman Egypt, the student who stumbled upon a used papyrus roll or a codex unwritten in some parts was not content to write an exercise right there, but opted to cut off individual pieces or to stitch them together.

Education was a constant process of moving ahead and refreshing and renewing one's knowledge. Old school exercises were not kept after a certain amount of time. Rather than store old schoolwork somewhere in the house, a student stored its contents in his memory: the cubbyholes of

---

[82] Cribiore 1996a: no. 393.

[83] See, e.g., Pliny *Ep*. 1.22.11, and Catullus 42.5. In the *Hermeneumata* a slave hands the student his tablets (*pinakidas*), glossed as *pugillares*; Dionisotti 1982: 99 line 22. See also pocket rolls of poetry found in Egypt, such as *P.Oxy*. LIV.3723, with some bibliography.

[84] Gehl 1989: 392.

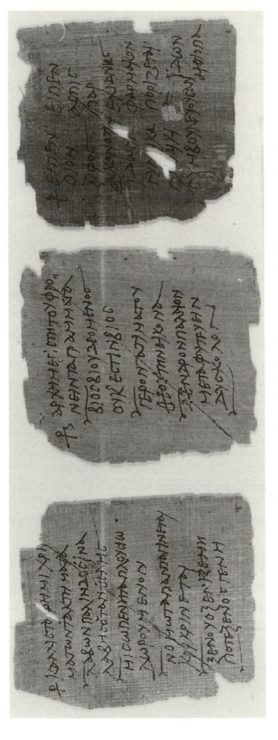

Figure 20. Pages from a papyrus notebook (fourth century C.E.) with maxims and sayings: "A literate woman is sharpened like a sword" (*P.Sorb.* 826).

his mind contained the syllabaries of the past, the lists of mythological figures, and the works of the poets he had scrutinized. Problems of physical storage of schoolwork did not trouble ancient students until they began to possess relatively advanced textbooks. Thus, doubts sometimes raised by modern scholars about the inconvenience of storing and handling potsherds are baseless.[85] Not only were most ostraca used in education relatively small, but they had a brief life. Pieces of broken pots or, more rarely, slices of white limestone could be picked up anywhere. It is curious to imagine an ancient student standing before a pile of ostraca lying on the ground, pondering the size and shape of the ostracon he needed. But this is probably what happened. As a rule, the size of school ostraca appears correlated to the length and type of exercise that a student had to inscribe on them, with the writing often following the shape of the piece and assuming the whimsical aspect of some modern poems. Another modern doubt about the convenience of ostraca, that is, the difficulty of transporting them, is also groundless, since potsherds of small size were generally used. The large and cumbersome pieces sometimes employed to write models rested somewhere in the classroom.[86]

The advantages of ostraca for students and teachers are quite obvious. Available in plenty anywhere, they provided an unlimited source of writing material. Their sturdiness and durability were also particularly appreciated at elementary levels, when sherds were able to stand students' abuse and were stained or dropped to the ground without much regret. Though the somewhat rough surfaces of ostraca were not ideal for calligraphic exercises, they proved invaluable for receiving alphabets, lists of words, texts of a few lines to be learned by heart, and notes of various kinds. Was cost a principal reason for their employment? The superiority of a material that costs nothing over another that costs something is obvious, particularly when performance is equal; but to say that ostraca were preferred by students "in the poorest circles" is misleading.[87] Availability, convenience, and even school tradition were powerful reasons why they were used. It was not only disadvantaged students who used them, but all students, for certain kinds of exercises. Diogenes Laertius, who wrote on philosophy in the third century C.E., reports that the philosopher Cleanthes, who became the successor of Zeno as head of the Stoic school in the third century B.C.E., used ostraca to write down Zeno's lectures

---

[85] This also applies to ostraca used for other purposes, such as tax receipts, which, being generally small, could be stored anywhere.

[86] On ostraca used for models, cf. above.

[87] Bonner 1977: 165.

Figure 21. A poem of Sappho written on an ostracon (*PSI* XIII.1300), second century B.C.E.

"through lack of money to buy papyrus" (7.174). On evaluating this testimony, however, one has to take into account not only the proverbial poverty of Cleanthes but also the fact that he was then a student following a well-established school tradition of using ostraca. The employment of sherds for writing, in fact, was not confined to elementary educational stages. For instance, the student who took down on an ostracon, from dictation, the poem of Sappho that describes a shrine of Aphrodite was at the grammatical level (Fig. 21).[88] The seventeen lines of the poem are written as if in prose and follow the shape of the sherd, which tapers toward the bottom. The rough and somewhat faded surface and the occa-

[88] Sappho 1, Voigt 2; Cribiore 1996a: no. 247. Cf. nos. 233–37, ostraca written at advanced levels of education.

sional mistakes and omissions still allow us to sense the beauty of those apple branches.

Compared to the writing materials considered so far, commonly available and regularly recycled, tablets had to have been somewhat more costly. Wooden tablets written in ink, and those whose hollow surface was covered with wax, were made for school use.[89] Occasionally the wood was found locally, but most often it was imported, and this contributed to escalating costs.[90] This drawback was compensated for by the fact that both types of tablet could be erased easily. The surface of a wooden tablet was covered with a coating that made it smoother and easier to erase, and to obliterate the writing on a wax tablet it was enough to smooth out the wax with the back of the stylus. Not that wax tablets were maintenance-free. In Herodas's *Didaskalos*, Metrotime dutifully rewaxes the tablet of Kokkalos once a month, even if it was always left "orphaned" in a corner of the room (15–18): not only did she periodically renew her hopes that her son would learn to write, but she also performed a necessary act, since otherwise the wax, used or unused, would harden. A student in the *Hermeneumata*, in fact, appears to be distressed that the wax on his tablet is hard and, therefore, difficult to write on.[91] Naughty Kokkalos may have also fiddled with the wax of his tablet in the same way as did Lucian, who admits modeling cattle, horses, and men out of the wax scraped from his tablet (*Somn.* 2). Though Lucian's father was rather proud of these creatures, which enraged his teachers, Lucian's tablet must have needed constant maintenance.

Both wooden and wax tablets could be bound together in a notebook, containing up to ten tablets. Euripides alludes to tablets tied together—carrying a letter—with the suggestive expression "the many-doored folds of tablet" (*IT* 727)—a definition that captures the very nature of a notebook, in which writing was hidden inside and each hard surface provided an entrance door to it.[92] Although codices of tablets were used at all levels of education, and many have been preserved, it is likely that some extant

[89] Tablets were sometimes used in everyday life for certificates, wills, accounts, and the like. For a description of tablets, see Cribiore 1996a: 65–69; Worp and Rijksbaron 1997: 9–21, with bibliography.

[90] On tablets made of local acacia, see Worp and Rijksbaron 1997; for tablets made of various imported woods, see R. Pintaudi and P. J. Sijpesteijn, *Tavolette lignee e cerate da varie collezioni* (Florence, 1989), 203–11.

[91] Goetz 1892: 71, 25–29: "The wax is hard, it must be soft" (*cera dura est, mollis debuit esse*).

[92] When a codex of tablets contained important documents, it could be bound shut.

Figure 22.   Attic cup showing a girl with tablets; ca. 460–450 B.C.E.

individual tablets were used separately: students like Kokkalos did not need more than a single tablet. On Athenian vases of the classical period, students are portrayed as carrying their tablets tied together with strings, or in what appears to be a case, by its handle (Fig. 22).[93] Two early Byzantine school tablets provided with bronze handles hinged directly onto the tablet have been preserved: they were transported like modern briefcases (see Fig. 4).[94]

Usually when several wax tablets were bound in a notebook, the work inside was protected by the raised edges of each one, but sometimes the same effect was obtained by placing a small wooden cube in the middle

[93] See, e.g., Beck 1975: pl. 11, 58, 59, and 60.

[94] Cribiore 1996a: no. 310, and a tablet containing a Coptic alphabet, P. Cauderlier, "Deux tablettes parisiennes en provenance d' Égypte, pour illustrer l' apprentissage des lettres grecques," *Mélanges Étienne Bernand* (1991): 143–48.

Figure 23.   Shrine with the portrait of a boy with writing
materials, first half of the third century C.E.

of a tablet. This is visible in one tablet of the diptych that is represented
next to a student in a Fayum portrait of slightly coarse and provincial
style (Fig. 23).[95] This teenager,[96] whose portrait, framed by a wreath, is
included in a small shrine, appears surrounded by all his writing materials.
The two small tablets on the right are hinged along the long sides, as was
usually the case, and on the left is represented a roll from which the split
tip of a reed pen emerges. The often-remarked-upon awkward propor-

[95] Doxiadis 1995: 108, no. 78; M. Capasso, "L' *instrumentum scriptorium* in un ritratto
conservato al museo egizio," *Rudiae* 5 (1993): 69–72.

[96] Cf. the well-developed pectoral muscles consonant with the contemporary fashion of
a tanned, well-exercised body, Walker and Bierbrier 1997: 15.

tions of the two objects derive from the fact that these are writing materials and implements especially fashioned to be used in school. Thus the small size of the roll, which was cut from a larger piece and already used on the back, is accentuated by the large size of the pen. When this young man died, the writing materials he handled in school were considered most appropriate for defining his identity.

Tablets were suited by their nature to schoolwork that needed to be rewritten and corrected often or that necessitated an even surface. They were popular at all levels of education for different kinds of exercise. In the initial stages of learning, they provided an ideal surface. The painful struggle of novices hesitating at every stroke is still trapped on the surface of many school tablets, where we capture learning at its tender beginning. Further exercises of calligraphy benefited from the even writing surface that offered no resistance to the pen. At the grammatical level, there was still plenty of work that required much rewriting, such as tables with declensions of nouns and conjugations of verbs, and so-called *scholia minora*. Tablets followed students to rhetorical schools, where they were used for note-taking and for exercises of composition. Quintilian recommended them warmly not only because they could be erased often, but also because they allowed a student to write quickly, without having his stream of thought interrupted by dipping the pen: only the student with poor eyesight had to avoid them (10.3.31–33). In Quintilian's opinion, tablets should not be unduly wide, so that the overzealous student would not feel the temptation to write excessively long compositions. Libanius mentions that writing discourses on a tablet to be corrected by the teacher was part of school routine (*Ep.* 911.1). He speaks of young men "filling their tablets with the writings appropriate to rhetoric many times a month" (*Or.* 35.22).[97]

Although durability and sturdiness were among the major characteristics of tablets, the written sources have transmitted curious examples of their being broken by angry pupils. Violence generated violence in the schoolroom.[98] In the second century B.C.E., the Roman playwright Plautus mentions students who would no longer endure their instructors' abuse and broke their tablets over the heads of their teachers, with their fathers' approval (*Bacch.* 440–43). Likewise, the fourth-century Christian writer Prudentius, on describing the martyrdom of Saint Cassian by his angry

---

[97] Cf. *Ep.* 886.

[98] Cf. above, Chapter 2. See also below for a *stylus* used as weapon. Cf. Juvenal *Sat.* 7.213–14: the orator Rufus beaten by his pupils. See the formulaic graffito "breaking teacher's bones" in schoolbooks of fourteenth-century Florence, Gehl 1989: 397–98.

students, says that "some throw their fragile tablets and break them against his face, the wood flying in fragments when it strikes his brow, the wax-covered boxwood splitting with a loud crack, as it is dashed on his blood-stained cheeks, the broken slab wet and red from the blow" (*Perist.* 9.47–50). The description appears slightly exaggerated, since tablets were sturdy and most of the ancient examples have been preserved intact. Yet the Christian writer Basil of Caesarea in the fourth century also associates angry students and broken tablets, showing children who, when reproached by their teacher, broke *his* tablets in anger (*Homilia dicta tempore famis et siccitatis* 67c).

Basil's testimony is particularly interesting because it confirms the evidence of the tablets of Greco-Roman Egypt: tablets were not always the private possessions of students but might belong to a teacher. It is conceivable that an individual who possessed some literacy and owned some tablets fulfilled the basic prerequisites to set up a school. Though most of the tablets appear to be written by a single student, sometimes several pupils seem to be at work in the same notebook. Three students, for instance, wrote exercises in a codex of seven wooden tablets: fractions, the conjugation of a verb, a rhetorical paraphrase, and the text of a psalm in Coptic.[99] This evidence is particularly suggestive: not only does it evoke a picture of a classroom where the teaching of Coptic stood side by side with the teaching of Greek,[100] but it presents students at different levels of ability sharing the same material.

Writing on papyri, ostraca, and wooden tablets was done with a reed pen.[101] An epigram applies to the pen (*calamos*) the metaphor of culture and education as an initiation into the mysteries of the Muses.[102]

> I was a reed, a useless plant, bearing neither figs, nor apples, nor grapes. But a man initiated me into the mysteries of Helicon, fashioning thin lips for me and excavating in me a narrow channel. Ever since, when I drink black liquor, I become inspired, and utter all manner of words with this voiceless mouth of mine. (*Anth. Pal.* 9.162).

The Greeks adopted the reed pen from the ancient Egyptians, but whereas in pharaonic Egypt thinner reeds were used (their ends were frayed to function as brushes), in Greco-Roman times reeds were thicker, pointed,

---

[99] See Cribiore 1996a: no. 388.

[100] See R. Cribiore, "Greek and Coptic Education in Late Antique Egypt," *Akten 6. Internationalen Koptologenkongresses*, July 1996 (publication forthcoming).

[101] For a selection of reed and metal pens, see Bonner 1977: fig. 14.

[102] On culture as an initiation into a mystery, see Kaster 1988: 16.

and split, with the shape of medieval quills. They could be resharpened many times until they became short stumps, and sometimes the life of a pen was prolonged by sticking a piece of wood into its end.[103] Of course, the younger the student, the more clumsily he employed a pen, forgetting to resharpen it, writing with a stubbed nib, and allowing the pen to "drink black liquor" too often.[104] To cancel writing—something that was supposed to be done by expunging dots or by carefully sponging off the wrong text—students often employed the timeless method of the finger wet with spit.

A pen (*stylus*) made of metal, ivory, or bone was used to write on wax tablets. Iron and bronze were the metals most frequently employed, but expensive styli were not unknown, made of silver and gold, or elegantly fashioned with a figurine at one end.[105] The sharp point of the stylus served to scratch the letters into the wax; the other end was usually flat and was used to smooth out the wax for corrections or erasures. It is not unusual for ancient writers to allude to the stylus and its use,[106] but ironically the most detailed description appears in the account by Prudentius mentioned above of the murder of Saint Cassian at the hands of his angry students (*Perist.* 9). The body of the saint is presented as a writing surface, and the act of piercing it with countless pricks of styli is described as the studious effort of his pupils. The rhetorical implications are carried to an extreme, with pupils asking their dying teacher to examine and correct the lines they are writing on his body. Another unorthodox way to use the stylus can be glimpsed through an anecdote reported by Plutarch in which Roman children appear tormenting an elephant by pricking its proboscis (*De soll. an.* 968e).

From what precedes, it appears that in the Greek and Roman world, the technology of manufacture was not a restrictive factor with respect to literacy. Ostraca, for instance, far from being a deterrent to literacy, encouraged certain types of informal writing with their common availability. The need to employ a large quantity of papyrus came at a rather

---

[103] See Winlock and Crum 1926: 94.

[104] Carbon black ink was mixed with some chemical compound to produce a brown color, starting from the fourth century C.E. Simple inkwells of round shape made of terracotta were most common, but luxury ones were sometimes used in wealthy households; see Metropolitan Museum of Art 1977.11.8, a Hellenistic inkwell with a relief with a frontal head and a snake.

[105] The Metropolitan Museum of Art in New York has a gold *stylus* apparently found in Ptolemaic Egypt (26.7.1361), and another of Roman date with a small figure of a boy at the flat end (23.160.88).

[106] See, e.g., Ovid *Met.* 9.521, *Am.* 1.11.23; and Martial 14.21.

advanced level of education: since mainly upper-class students reached that level, cost was not an issue.

It is important to analyze the past in its own terms, visualizing the informality of most of the writing that was done in ancient schools and in the ancient world at large. The extemporaneous and casual quality of Greek and Roman writing technology successfully counterbalanced the limiting and intimidating factor that strongly characterized it in ancient Egyptian and medieval times and that created definite problems of access to writing. In early medieval England, writing was an art in itself that required a laborious technology and much time and ability.[017] Putting a pen to parchment was the affair of scribes, and of monks who had to sustain this humbling fatigue; meanwhile, common laymen did not feel confident enough to pen a letter or even to sign. The only form of writing was the dictation of a text to a professional, a skill that was an extension of speaking and was taught in school.

The overall picture of literacy in Greco-Roman Egypt is strikingly different. A taxpayer who needed a receipt for which he was supposed to provide the writing material[108] simply picked up an ostracon and gave it to the official in charge to inscribe. A man or a woman who hardly knew how to wield a pen did not shrink from signing a document or from attempting to write an epistle in quivering but somewhat empowering characters. These were habits acquired in school. In the following chapters, we shall see how they were formed and developed.

---

[107] See Clanchy 1993: 114–44. Using quills required laborious training; M. Finley, *Western Writing Implements in the Age of the Quill Pen* (Carlisle, Cumbria, 1990).

[108] N. Lewis, *Life in Egypt under Roman Rule* (Oxford, 1983), 166–67.

The First Circle

The first letter was a circle with a navel in the middle;
then two straight rules yoked together,
while the third resembled a Scythian bow;
next to that lay a trident on its side;
then mounted on one rule were two slanting lines;
the last was again like the third.

THUS, IN THE *Telephus* of the fifth-century B.C.E. tragic poet Agathon, an illiterate man tries to describe to the audience the spelling of the name Theseus (ΘΗCΕΥC; fr. 4 TrGF). In doing so, Agathon imitated a similar speech in the *Theseus* of Euripides, in which an illiterate herdsman looking out at sea saw a ship carrying these letters on its sails.[1] It is uncertain whether these passages presuppose the existence of a somewhat literate audience in which everybody was able to follow the spelling with anticipation.[2] Yet they certainly refer to the very first step in the acquisition of literacy, when the combined visual images of the letters correspond to a real entity, a name. Agathon's account is more imaginative than Euripides', since he describes the letter shapes at a glance by comparing them to familiar images. The success of the scene was due partly to its correspondence to a universal experience.[3] In antiquity, the accomplishments achieved at an elementary stage of instruction ranged from this embryonic form of "reading" the letter shapes to the moment when the letters, articulated into words and sentences, were read with an increasing degree of understanding. This chapter covers the first circle of instruction, in which a male or female student had an initial taste of what lay ahead.

All the elements of knowledge approached in the first circle were in tight connection not only with each other but also with contents intro-

---

[1] Eur. fr. 382 Nauck². For another imitation, Theodectas fr. 6 TrGF. The whole account is in the collection *The Learned Banquet* of the second-century C.E. writer Athenaeus, 10.454b–f.

[2] See Turner 1952: 8–9; Harvey 1966: 603–4.

[3] P. Horner ("The Development of Reading Books in England in 1870," in Brooks and Pugh 1984: 81) mentions a primer, *Reading without Tears* by F. L. Mortimer, that started by likening the letters to familiar objects, such as "*A* is like a hut with a window upstairs."

duced at later educational stages. Education was a world folded in upon itself; it reflected what came before and prefigured what lay ahead in an endless process of reduplication. Of course, elementary education built the foundations of technical skills on which further knowledge rested. But instruction at the first level already contained in embryonic form elements that were to be developed in further stages if a student continued in the educational process.

This was the stage of "skills and drills" that required an inflexible intellectual gymnastics in order to compensate for the general deficiency of teaching aids and texts for inexperienced readers, and a lack of word divisions and lectional signs in the texts that were available. Even though the models prepared by the teachers addressed some of the initial difficulties, it was felt that a student should be prepared for an "unfriendly" environment of learning. Contents followed a rigorous order in which the links of a chain that extended up to the rhetorical level were connected by similarity. From the beginning, a student learned to distinguish as many similarities as possible within the presented material and to extrapolate from there. Identifying and mastering the alphabetical order, for example, led to recreating new combinations, and the understanding of the basic order governing a syllabary led to reproducing it through a proliferation of ever more abstruse sets of letters.

It is important to recognize, however, that at all levels of learning, although an order[4] was always followed in introducing new elements, that order was not invariably the same. In higher education, degree of difficulty was not always the principle that dictated the choice of authors read; tradition, authority, and usefulness for further study were also fundamental. As a rule, primary education proceeded from shorter to larger links, from one unit to the juxtaposition of many. Concerns with gradual increases in difficulty did not always apply, however. Lists of words on which a student practiced reading, writing, and memorization, for example, often strictly followed an organization according to number of syllables, even though monosyllabic words included abstruse terms that were less familiar and harder to remember than other longer words learned afterward. In the same way, reading and writing did not always conform to an identical process governed by the same rules. Past historians of ancient education have envisaged both reading and writing as following identical laws of rectilinear movement, with a progressive building upon

---

Now a four-year-old of my acquaintance spells aloud his name, *T-O-M*, as "the umbrella, the sun, and the two peaks."

[4] The ancient writers called this the *ordo docendi*, the order maintained in teaching.

the initial link—the letters of the alphabet—that led to syllables, words, and sentences. The school exercises from Greco-Roman Egypt reveal instead that a different sequence might sometimes be privileged, and that teachers who valued handwriting made students copy sentences, maxims, and brief passages when they had not yet mastered syllables and could not read. These students, therefore, skipped the links of the individual syllables and single words: they learned according to an order that was based not on comprehension but on reinforcing writing skills.

It should be noted that the network of rules that governed learning at this stage had the capacity of increasing and sanctioning a teacher's authority. I have identified in previous chapters why a teacher's position in antiquity was weak—for example, the lack of financial security and the punctilious control exercised by parents. But insofar as teachers were the individuals who knew, and could apply and transmit, the rules of knowledge, their authority was above that of parents. The rules conferred to them an external, unobjectionable power, and in the rules they trusted.

It is difficult to specify with precision the length, limits, and characteristics of the training of elementary education. Among the literary sources, only Plato speaks in exact quantitative terms when he envisions that a ten-year-old would need three years to learn letters, but his remarks may not refer to the whole period of elementary instruction (*Laws* 7.810a). The contradictory opinions that historians of education sometimes venture in this respect derive from a complex reality.[5] We have seen not only that elementary teaching was a function of local needs and expectations, but also that the duration of the available course oscillated according to students' demand and teachers' availability.[6] Both length of schooling, and quality and quantity of notions imparted, must have depended a great deal on environment, students' social status, and the degree of professionalism of accessible teachers. Though some pupils may have assimilated only the most basic principles of reading, writing, and reckoning, others may have exhausted their primary teacher's treasury of learning. Not all students took advantage of the entirety of what was available. I shall concentrate on the most basic skills that an elementary student must have acquired from the course.

Of course, elementary education left tangible traces on many more people than did subsequent stages of learning. There is, therefore, great inter-

[5] See Marrou 1975, 1: 227 and 2: 64. Vössing (1992) maintains that Roman elementary schooling lasted longer than it does today, but he considers mainly the personal experience of Augustine.

[6] Cf. Chapter 1.

est in investigating the ways in which male and female students approached writing and reading, how they coped with the tasks required, how beneficial an initial knowledge of the letters was, and what kind of an advantage literacy brought to their lives.[7] Education is usually presented as a self-sufficient microcosm with its own laws, dogmas, and boundaries.[8] Jeremiads over its rigidity and inability to instill any practical knowledge are frequent. Since the connections between knowledge imparted by elementary education and the demands of daily life in ancient society are not often explored, it is worthwhile to investigate whether there were channels of communication between real life and the somewhat unreal world of learning.

In Egypt, with the advent of Alexander of Macedon, writing, which in pharaonic times was the almost exclusive province of specialized priestly and scribal circles, acquired new functions.[9] Not only did the extent of documentation and the volume of writing increase considerably, but the old scribal elite ceased to be a segregated body. Though scribes retained the specialized task of penning legal and administrative documents, people could show and exploit the skills they had learned in schools by drafting epistles, daily lists, and accounts, or by testifying to the authenticity of a document by adding to it anything from a full-length subscription to a signature. Members of elite and scholarly circles used writing with varying degrees of sophistication for literary purposes. What made Greco-Roman Egypt a literate society, in spite of the fact that the mass of the population was illiterate, was that even people who did not have direct access to writing had to reckon with it in their daily lives, and they recognized the framework of conventions and expectations that governed it.[10]

In this society, a lack of writing skills did not engender stigma and disdain: illiterate people, who had to have recourse to a network of literate individuals—relatives, friends, or the omnipresent scribes—were not looked down upon, because illiteracy was too common a condition.[11] But the fact that semiliterates—those called in the documents "slow writers" (*bradeōs graphontes*)[12]—cared to exhibit their very modest attainments rather than use other strategies shows that "knowing letters" engendered

---

[7] On literacy in antiquity: Stock 1983; Street 1987; Harris 1989; Thomas 1989 and 1992.

[8] For education in Rome, see the new approach of Frasca 1996a and 1996b.

[9] Ray 1986; Thompson 1994.

[10] Bowman and Woolf 1994a; Bowman 1991; Hanson 1991; Cribiore 1996a: 3–11.

[11] On literates and semiliterates, see Youtie 1971a and b, 1975b.

[12] Cf. the *oligogrammatoi* in Justinian's *Novellae* 73.8 (*Corpus iuris civilis* III, 1899, ed. Schoell-Kroll).

pride and a sense of accomplishment. Personal literacy carried some prestige, a positive reinforcement of identity, a badge of belonging to a literate society, and a shield against fraud. Direct examples of illiterate people purposely victimized or deceived are not many, but in reality lack of writing and reading skills must have put people at risk: abuses of the confidence of illiterates and semiliterates must be at the heart of many of the petitions that people addressed to the authority.[13] A single example will suffice. In the third century B.C.E., a father appealed against the fraud perpetuated at the expense of his young son Sopolis by a courtesan with the suggestive name Demo, "the common one."[14] This woman persuaded the youth to sign a paper in which he declared that he had borrowed from her a large sum of money. The paper remained as proof of a loan that apparently had not taken place. Sopolis's meager attainments in literacy may have partly contributed to his victimization.

THE ALPHABET AND MEMORY

Elementary instruction started with the relentless gymnastics of the alphabet. The sands of Egypt have preserved alphabets written by students and teachers alike, as well as exercises in which groups of letters were practiced without an alphabetical order. Though models containing alphabets are the only teaching aids that we know of directly, the literary sources describe other kinds of support and incentives used to entice reluctant beginners to learn. In the Roman world, apparently, a wealthy child was given ivory alphabet blocks and ivory or boxwood letters to play with, and models were used in which the letters were carved into the wood so that a novice tracing the letter shapes was forced to stay within their limits.[15] The authors also mention little cakes in connection with the alphabet, but it is unclear whether these were shaped in the form of letters or whether, more likely, they were only incentives or rewards.[16] The fact that real knowledge was internalized knowledge resulted in medieval times in cakes decorated with the alphabet, tablets in which the written

---

[13] See Youtie 1975a: 205–7. Other examples of persons victimized because of illiteracy might be found in *P.Oxy.* I.71, and *P.Enteux.* 1 and 50.

[14] *P.Enteux.* 49. The age of this young man is uncertain, A. P. Christorilopoulos, *Mikra Meletemata* (Athens, 1973), 90–93; Legras 1999: 218. Cf. A. Arjava, "Die römische Vormundschaft und das Volljährigkeitsalter in Ägypten," *ZPE* 126 (1999): 202–4.

[15] Quintilian 1.1.26–27; Jerome *Ep.* 107.4.

[16] Cf. Horace *Sat.* 1.1.25–26; Jerome *Ep.* 128.1.

text was covered with honey and then licked by the learner, and hard-boiled eggs inscribed with the letters of the alphabet.[17]

But eager parents apparently could go overboard when trying to force their unwilling children to learn. The plutocrat and sophist Herodes Atticus (ca. C.E. 101–177) devised an extreme remedy to help his son, who is described in the sources as "foolish, bad at letters, and of a dull memory," where *dysgrammatos* is the likely equivalent of the modern "dyslexic" (Philostratus *VS* 558). He employed twenty-four young slaves, each with the name of a letter of the alphabet, who were supposed to be with his son at all times.[18] The story is tantalizing. One cannot help but try to go beyond the bare account, imagining a slightly grotesque pantomime: slaves singing aloud their names, forming a single row, reversing its order by starting from the end, making up short rows by skipping letters in between, pairing themselves into syllables, or even forming words. The school exercises show that this is how a beginner learned his letters. Was Herodes inspired by the fifth-century B.C.E. Athenian poet Callias, who had composed a play, an "Alphabet Show" (*Grammatikē theōria*), in which the twenty-four letter-women forming the chorus sang the alphabet back and forth and moved then to a syllabary made up of letters in pairs?[19] The consistency of methods used in antiquity to master the letters is remarkable. The pedagogic use of songs, which started in the preschool years, continued when beginners sang the alphabet aloud in school.[20] Even today, "Sesame Street" and the loud alphabetical songs booming out of modern Egyptian primary schools testify to the usefulness of associating letters and rhythm.

Since pure rote knowledge of the alphabet was discouraged, beginners were taught to follow every kind of alphabetical sequence, such as proceeding from the bottom up or skipping a fixed number of letters. Exercises of this kind, which appear a bit contrived to the modern eye, required memory and concentration. Pupils were not always up to them. A school exercise from Roman Egypt, for instance, shows that a student was asked to write on an ostracon two alphabets, one in regular and one in reversed order, by pairing the first letter (*alpha*) with the last (*omega*), then the second with the second to last, and so on.[21] But this pupil had some trou-

[17] See Harvey 1978: 73–75; Manguel 1996: 71 and n. 9.

[18] This is not a story with a happy ending. Herodes' son grew up as an alcoholic philanderer and was finally disinherited.

[19] Athenaeus 10.453d–f; Svenbro 1993: 183–86.

[20] Jerome (*Ep.* 104.4) mentions an alphabetical song (*canticum*).

[21] Cribiore 1996a: no. 44.

ble following the required order. One wonders whether he or she was able to convince the teacher that the exercise had been done as instructed. Certainly this student does not fool the modern papyrologist, since the letters and the ink reveal that the first alphabet was written in its entirety, and then the pupil proceeded to the reversed one starting from the bottom, thus following again the order, *alpha*, *beta*, and so on. A curious device used to enforce command of the letters was the tongue-twister, *chalinos* ("gag"), which consisted of alphabets in scrambled order that joined together letters that were difficult to pronounce.[22] Thus, for instance, when beginners wrote and sounded out aloud the made-up word *knaxzbrikh*, they practiced the letters and, supposedly, improved their pronunciation. These "words" used in school practice passed into Hesychius's *Lexicon* with pseudo-meanings.[23]

The insistence of ancient teachers on enforcing a confident command of the letters by practicing them in various combinations is a good demonstration of the passion with which they clung to rules and order, but this approach was also justified by the fact that the alphabet was used as a mnemonic device and organizational tool. Memory was the foundation of all knowledge in a world that could not rely on easily consulted books, tables of contents and indexes, library catalogues, and electronic search tools.[24] Exercises of mental gymnastics practiced at every level of education aimed at strengthening the student's natural capacity for retention to levels unheard of in the modern world. Higher education was particularly concerned with developing a student's "artificial" memory, thus not only improving his ability to memorize content word for word but also strengthening his capacity to build rapid and effective systems for learning. The art of memory created by Simonides and Aristotle was adopted by the Romans: arguments and subjects were located under "places" in the mind (*topoi*, *loci*), such as buildings or settings.[25] The ancients' experience of these memory-images was much more vivid and intense than our own.

Whereas mnemotechnics were taught in rhetorical schools as an aid to the future orator, who would need to deliver long speeches with unfailing accuracy, concern for improving memory and retrieval showed at every stage of education. A more capacious and elastic memory had to be nour-

---

[22] Quintilian 1.1.37; Clement *Strom.* 5.8.48.4–9 and 8–9; 49.1; 359–60. In this group were also classified pseudo-epic hexameters with all the letters of the alphabet used in scribal training.

[23] R. Merkelbach, "Weisse KNAΞXBI-Milch," *ZPE* 61 (1985): 293–96.

[24] On memory in antiquity, Small 1997; Carruthers 1990; Yates 1966; and Blum 1969.

[25] See Small 1997: 81–116.

ished with tender care from the early years of childhood. Early education was not so much concerned with developing artificial memory, but rather with nurturing the natural memory of children: memory was the "storehouse of education" and had the capacity to create and foster.[26] It was essential to master the alphabet in the early years for its immediate and future gains. Alphabetical and numerical orders were tools used to organize materials, concepts, and subjects to be stored in the mind and retrieved when necessary. The various exercises nurtured a student's ability to glide quickly through the alphabet and created the mental agility necessary for using and assimilating all sorts of letter combinations.

Mastery of the alphabet was the point of departure for all future learning. Pupils developed a peculiar ability to "calculate" with the letters that is unknown in the modern world. Thus the alphabet became as flexible a tool as numerical order for organizational purposes. The maxims that the students had to memorize and copy letter by letter at the next educational stage were sometimes organized in alphabetical acrostics.[27] Syllabaries combined vowels with each consonant in turn: sets made of multiliteral combinations required some dexterity to juggle the letters. Similarly, the lists of words that students had to write and read were often included in alphabetical entries: teachers stored under each letter words that were taken from different contexts and whose initials were the only sign that they belonged to a specific category.[28] Thus the letters distinguishing each set and the number of the items filed under each entry were used together as mnemonic devices.

First Steps in Literacy

The school exercises show that at the same time that students were learning to juggle the letters of the alphabet, they had to apply their new expertise by learning to write their personal names. The ability to write one's name—a recognized achievement for young children even today—was even more meaningful in antiquity. Even when one did not progress much further, this limited knowledge brought immediate practical advantages. Adults who were only signature literates often appear in documents from Greco-Roman Egypt as they append their names to a transaction: they

[26] Quintilian 1.1.19; Ps.-Plutarch *De liberis educandis* 9e.
[27] See Cribiore 1996a: no. 316.
[28] See, e.g., ibid.: no. 390.

Figure 24.   An ostracon with letters of the alphabet.

are not schoolboys—or schoolgirls[29]—any more, but their performance does not rise above that of young learners. The *Hermeneumata* directly link writing one's name to a school practice: after entering in class and saluting teachers and classmates, an elementary student gets down to work by writing his name.[30] From the school exercises it appears that pupils combined somewhat mechanically the letters that formed their names when they still had only a shaky grasp of them. An ostracon of the Roman period provides a good illustration of the mechanics of learning at its tender beginning (Fig. 24).[31] A boy, Kametis, was asked to write his name, followed by the first four letters of the alphabet in regular and reversed order—ΑΒΓΔ and ΔΓΒΑ. That he had trouble doing this is shown by the second sequence, ΔΒΓΑ, in which a thickly traced Δ—the hinge on which the exercise revolves—is wrongly followed by Β, whereas Γ looks like a Τ. The letters at this point were only strokes coming together without meaning. The achievement of the five-year-old son of the emperor Constantine, who was able to validate decisions by writing his name, was celebrated with admiration by the panegyrist Nazarius.[32] The exercises show that this was not an exceptional performance. But everything is

[29] See, e.g., the almost illegible signature of a woman such as Sentia Asklatarion in *P.Soter.* 18–21.

[30] Goetz 1892: 381.2–3.

[31] Cribiore 1996a: no. 51. Some of the exercises show that students kept on writing their names at later stages in order to identify their work.

[32] *SEG* 19, no. 37.

relative. In the sixth century, the historian Procopius alludes to illiterate kings forced to use wooden models with letters incised into them: like children, they had their hands guided by another's through the letter shapes (*Historia arcana* 6.15–16). King Theodoric apparently used a thin gold-plated model that allowed him to write subscriptions: four letters were cut into it, forming the Latin word *LEGI* ("I have read").[33] But even though there have been suspicions about the king's literacy, Theodoric was able to write: the model was only an aid in forming letters in Byzantine chancery style.

The practice of teaching beginners who barely knew the alphabetical characters to write their names goes unmentioned in modern histories of ancient education, according to which letters always and only led to syllables. Modern historians in fact follow rigidly the accounts of the ancient educational theorists, who apparently perpetuated an inflexible order of learning. The concept that teaching followed a progression of difficulty (*ordo docendi*), that easier material had to be inculcated first and foundations had to be built in order for education to be successful, is common to these accounts.[34] According to them, a beginner who mastered the letters learned to combine them into syllables, joined the syllabic combinations into words at a later stage, and finally was able to build up sentences. Learning was encapsulated into a few pills that had to be swallowed according to an inflexible prescription. On the strict basis of these accounts, writing one's name or copying a sentence were not appropriate goals at the initial stage.

Some of the extant school exercises follow the order advocated by the literary sources, others do not. Some writing exercises in fact indicate that immediately after learning the letters, pupils were made to copy very short texts, such as maxims or individual verses, that they were apparently unable to read.[35] Even though these texts probably had been explained or memorized, the great number of mistakes committed, the inability of a student to correct himself or herself once an error was made, and the passive dependence on a model—the teacher's model or the student's own first copy—all show that pupils copied a text letter by letter, trying to reproduce the shape of the characters but unable to connect words into real units of understanding. These students' shaky handwriting, moreover,

[33] Anonymus Valesianus 61 and 79; Riché (1995: 53–54) discusses the culture of Theodoric, with full bibliography of the question in notes 36 and 37.

[34] Augustine *De ordine* 2.7 (24); Ambrose *Ab Abraham* 1.30; Manilius *Astronomica* 2.755–64; Jerome *Ep.* 107.4 and 128.1; Gregory of Nyssa *De beneficentia* 5–13.

[35] See, e.g., Cribiore 1996a: nos. 136, 160, 202, 383, and 403.

is a further indication of extreme immaturity, since it reveals the basic uncertainty of the recent learner, who "was at a loss about the shapes of the letters."[36] A definite improvement in writing skills shows in other exercises, such as some of the syllabaries and lists of words, where students' hands appear more secure and betray more training and maturity.

How to reconcile the rigid accounts of learning given by the ancient writers with this picture of a more flexible practice? A recent discussion of the copying method exemplified by the exercises maintains that this method was used to train only lower-class students and slaves, who were not going to progress in their educations and needed only to achieve rudimentary copying skills.[37] The evidence, however, suggests that this practice was more widespread. The few syllabaries and the many lists of words written in the hands of students display handwriting more practiced than that of complete beginners. These students, who did not quit immediately after learning some copying but followed the regular progression of steps toward reading and proper writing (letters, syllables, words, sentences), had already made considerable progress in penmanship. Even though some of these word lists might belong to higher educational circles, it would be perverse to think that the writers were all students of grammarians. With regard to students' social backgrounds, moreover, it should be noted that in one case, it is certain that the teacher who signed a model for a student on a tablet was not a *grammatodidaskalos* ("elementary teacher") but a grammarian.[38] The pupil in question, who reproduced the letters of the text painfully and one by one, without any knowledge of syllabic division, presumably belonged to the upper class. This grammarian, therefore, cared that his pupil achieved good copying skills before engaging in the usual training to start writing and reading.

One should not be too surprised that the ancient sources do not speak explicitly of the initial practice of copying that emerges from some of the school exercises. Most likely, such sources were not interested in the minor strategies that teachers used in their classrooms. On reading the various accounts that describe the teaching process, one is struck by their uniformity, as if they were all imitating one another, or perhaps going back to a common source. The rigid sequence of learning became a sort of *topos* that maintained its validity for a long time not only on account of its attractive and straightforward structure, but also because it addressed the essential stages by which reading and writing properly were

[36] Quintilian 1.1.21: *haesit circa formas litterarum.*

[37] K. Vössing, "Schreiben lernen, ohne Lesen zu können? Zur Methode des antiken Elementarunterrichts," *ZPE* 123 (1998): 121–25.

[38] See above, pp. 39–40, and Chapter 2, note 62.

taught. The rest fell through the cracks. The attention of ancient writers was caught by the linear coherence of a process that rested on the virtually universal assumption that little things are more easily learned than big ones. The practical details of how teachers tried to enforce good handwriting did not concern them in the least.

What the ancient sources describe is in fact the sequence of principal steps followed in antiquity to learn reading and writing properly—not only copying. Up to the early Middle Ages, reading was taught in the Greek and Roman world by a system of building blocks, a so-called synthetic method that constructed the progressive rings of a chain starting from the letters, then forming syllables, words, and sentences. The process of learning to read bears a strong resemblance to that of learning spoken language, and the synthetic reading method imitated to some degree what was viewed as the spontaneous process of language-learning. As of the sixteenth century, all the various teaching methods known today had been suggested or practiced occasionally—syllabic, whole words, whole sentences, and phonic—but the synthetic method that builds on letters has dominated the reading field.[39]

Writing, in the sense of putting together elements in combinations of varying length to achieve communication, followed the same approach. But writing is a multifaceted activity that requires a minimum level of competence at its basic stage, when it consists only of the physical act of forming some characters or copying passively. Copying a sentence and writing one's own name do not require the same building up of structural elements or the same process of mental maturation as composing. Achieving good copying skills was more vital than it is today. Legible and relatively competent handwriting was necessary not only to someone who thought of embarking on a scribal career, but also to the student who progressed further in his schooling and to the adult who needed writing for everyday use and for copying his own texts. Personal hands catch the eye of the palaeographer who looks at literary and epistolary texts on papyrus.[40] They do not have the smooth flow of scribal handwriting at its best, which resembles modern printing, but are nevertheless the product of skill and application. In antiquity, personal handwriting was recognized and valued as a symbol of identification in legal and official transactions, even when the name of an official or a clerk was not given.[41] Teaching, therefore, was structured to serve the needs of a vast pool of students.

---

[39] See Pidgeon 1988.
[40] See Schubart 1925: 146–55.
[41] On personal handwriting, Libanius Or. 1.232 and Ep. 44.7–8.

Moreover, for students who would attend only one or two years of elementary instruction, basic copying skills and the ability to produce a signature represented coveted tools of practical utility. The example of Petaus and countless other men and women in the same condition is illuminating in this respect.[42] Petaus, a town clerk on the verge of illiteracy who tried to pass himself off as literate, has become exemplary of the struggle of "slow writers" in Greco-Roman Egypt because some details of his personal story are known. Not only do some documents in the archive of papers he collected show his signature in tortured letters, but a writing exercise has been preserved in which he practiced writing, over and over, his name, title, and a verb, "I submitted"—the whole arsenal he needed to subscribe the documents that he passed on to higher authorities.[43] Petaus's practice sheet reveals that he was copying passively from the line immediately above, using his writing as a model, and he could not recover his bearings once he made a mistake. That he was able to keep his official post in a society highly dependent on paperwork was due to his skillful covering of his meager accomplishments and his dependency on scribes in his employment. Apparently, however, his brother Theon had reached an entirely different level of literacy, since he could produce the whole text of a loan of money that he and Petaus had contracted.[44] When Petaus wrote his short subscription to this deed of loan, he must have copied it from a model that his brother made for him. Since Theon and Petaus came from the same moderately wealthy middle-class family, the different packages of skills they possessed may cause some surprise. But more than nowadays, length of school attendance, personal predisposition, and frequent practice of skills acquired in childhood played a part in the degree of literacy an adult was able to achieve.

READING READINESS

The next goal of a student who was covering the first educational circle in his journey up the hill of learning was the acquisition of basic reading and writing skills. The calisthenics of reading readiness were precise, relentless, tedious, and unhurried. In some cases they were also nonsensical and failed to target the real needs of learners. The exercise of the syllabary was done by reciting the various syllabic sets inscribed on teachers' models

[42] See Youtie 1966 and 1971a; Turner 1973: 36–47; Hanson 1991: 171–74.
[43] *P.Petaus* 121.
[44] *P.Petaus* 31.

and by writing down letter combinations according to a system. A student who started, for instance, with biliteral combinations of one consonant with all the vowels in turn (*ba-be-bi-bo-bu*), and proceeded through all the alphabet, could be asked to form triliteral or quadriliteral sets (such as *bras-bres-bris-bros-brus*) and to go on to exhaust all the possibilities. Though the building of syllabic sets further reinforced alphabetical skills, it did not always address a student's need to be familiar with components of words that he or she will encounter in the future. Why was a student who would never have to decode most of the words that contained these combinations made to practice the bizarre *bras-bres* series mentioned above?[45] But Quintilian fully approved of this practice: all the syllables, even the most abstruse, had to be learned by heart (1.1.30). The exercise was painstaking and pointless to some degree, a game that tested a student's patience and concentration, as the many mistakes committed in the process indicate. A student writing a Greek syllabary under the burning Egyptian sun might be deceived by the mechanical nature of the exercise. His capacity for using the letters as numerical units might go to extremes, and he might perform his drills thoughtlessly, indulging in bizarre productions, like the pupil who treated the vowel *i* (*iota*) as a consonant and wrote *iai, iei, iii*—combinations that hardly appear in any word.[46]

The tyranny of the syllables continued to rule learning when whole words were introduced. Most exercises at this level show words divided into syllables by means of bars or dots or included in sets according to number of syllables, that is, monosyllables, disyllables, and so on. Starting from the first century C.E., moreover, sets of words were ordered according to the alphabetical sequence. Most, but not all, lists presenting these characteristics are connected to exercises of reading and writing readiness. It is conceivable that those lists which are organized by subject—such as birds, gods, rivers, or historical and mythological figures—served as works of reference or were memorized in order to build a vocabulary.[47] This insistence on categorizing the world by means of bare sequences of words seems to suggest that they were used as cultural symbols,[48] even though one should take into account that their message might

---

[45] See Cribiore 1996a: no. 78.

[46] Cribiore 1996a: no. 83.

[47] About the use of lists in Mesopotamian and ancient Egyptian education, see Nissen, Damerow, and Englund 1993: 105–6; Brunner 1957: 93–98; and Eyre and Baines 1989: 94–95; for lexicographical material, see Kramer 1983. Some lists, however, might have originated in the class of the grammarian; see below, p. 193.

[48] Morgan 1998: 101–4.

be fleshed out by the missing voice of a teacher. In any case, the effectiveness of building on syllables to teach reading and writing was not questioned throughout antiquity.[49] Only in the ninth century do we begin to see signs of a different approach that taught reading through whole words, until reading by syllables acquired a definite stigma at the end of the Middle Ages.[50]

The unremitting enforcement of the syllabic method was grounded on the need for school to prepare a beginner for the texts that were in general circulation. As a rule, in fact, texts were written in continuous blocks of letters without word separation (*scriptio continua*) and without pauses between major sections. In Greek schools, a clear concept of a word per se was not instilled, but words were conceived as chains of syllabic units. Concentrating on a limited number of syllables was necessary when the eye and the mind were not ready to handle long strings of them. Thus a word was conceived as a "piece of speech" rather than a single independent entity.[51] When teachers wrote model passages that provided word separations, these divisions were convenient pedagogic measures for ordering the material rather than an attempt to instill into a pupil the concept of a word as a strict language unit. In these passages, in fact, marks of separation do not distinguish single words but word groups, that is, words considered together with articles, prepositions, and other particles.

The ancient sources agree that learning to read was a slow process that depended on the solid buildup of mnemonic and mechanical skills together with proper eye coordination. In the first century B.C.E., the writer Dionysius of Halicarnassus, for instance, says that it was only after the lapse of a considerable time that children were able to put together coherently the different messages they had received (*Comp*. 25). According to Quintilian, teachers were not supposed to press students to read continuously but had to guide them through the syllables. Nothing could be gained by hurrying: reading had to be secure at first, and it became connected with time. The theory of looking to the right to anticipate what was coming next was valid as long as it was accompanied by constant practice (1.1.30–35). The Greek word for "reading" itself, *anagignōskein*, emphasizes the cumbersome process of recognition: reading consisted of "knowing again, recollecting" what one had surveyed at a glance.

Testimonies about the struggle of beginners in learning to read are sparse—another proof that ancient society did not regard children as wor-

[49] See Reynolds 1996: 9–10; and Small 1997: 24–25.
[50] See Saenger 1982: 384 n. 91.
[51] Cf., for a similar situation in Vai culture, Goody 1987: 227–28.

thy of full attention.[52] Two passages, however, should be considered. Naughty Kokkalos in Herodas's *Didaskalos* had reached the level of learning to read and write syllable by syllable, but, in his mother's words, he could not even recognize "an *alpha* syllable," and he misspelled the simplest words (22–36). At the same time, he was compelled to memorize tragic speeches in school; when asked to recite, however, he could not produce a passage fluently but "let it trickle out as if from a sieve." It seems that the way in which this boy was learning to read—by breaking sentences into units—had some reflection upon the way he retrieved a passage from memory. The experience of Kokkalos reproduces that of innumerable other ancient students in dealing with repetitive and demanding practices. In the *Shepherd of Hermas*, a Greek text written in Rome in the second century C.E., the sense of loss a beginner felt in front of a text written as a sequence of letters without distinctions is vividly expressed. This text consists of revelations made to a young man, Hermas, by the Church, who appeared to him as a lady reading out from a little book. Hermas asked the lady to give him the book so that he could copy it. He says, "I took it and went away to a certain place in the country and copied everything letter by letter, for I could not find the syllables" (Vision 2, 3–4). Since the text appeared to be a formidable mass of letters, Hermas resorted to a practice typical of a novice: passively copying it letter by letter. The irony is that just when he was expected to have a deep understanding of the message he had to divulge, he was in the darkness of ignorance.

Bilingualism provided an additional hurdle for the learner. In Rome and in the rest of the empire, people were exposed to more than one language. The Roman student who learned Latin at home was taught literacy via his weaker language, Greek, which he acquired in school.[53] Likewise, many provincials in the eastern part of the empire, who also functioned in their indigenous language, reinforced their Greek through formal schooling. In many cases, moreover, bilingualism did not correspond to biliteracy, and in some circles the language of acquisition became the dominant one because the written and oral registers met there. In Egypt this problem was even more pronounced, because for centuries Egyptians were unable to read and write their own language, and Demotic—like its predecessors, hieroglyphic and hieratic—always remained the script of a specialized minority because of its complexities. In the east-

---

[52] On the marginality of children, Wiedemann 1989: 176–79.
[53] Quintilian 1.1.12. Cf. the difficulties experienced by Augustine (*Conf.* 1.13).

similar to that described in histories of education as followed in medieval Christian schools, where there was a definite priority of reading over writing.[61] It is not unusual for scholars to refer to comparative case-studies, such as those on medieval or seventeenth-century England, in order to support their claim that reading skills were more widespread than writing ability. There is no doubt that the advent of Christianity fostered reading of the Scriptures, while in early medieval Europe, strong expectations developed about the quality and professionalism of writing, discouraging common laymen from practicing even its most rudimentary forms. Thus individuals who could read a Christian text or dictate a letter refrained entirely from copying and writing, since the proper use of parchment and quills was difficult and intimidating. Schooling was not even in charge of enforcing signature literacy, because seals or the simple cross—symbol of a promise made in the name of God—replaced personal signatures.[62] This disparity between writing and reading continued in later times. Instruction in schools in Tudor and Stuart England rested on the full mastery of reading skills; writing was introduced in later years. It has been shown that at that time, the ability to sign one's name was a sure indication of social status, since only children of relatively prosperous condition could remain in school for the length of time necessary to learn this skill.[63] But literacy skills in medieval and early modern Europe cannot be the basis for maintaining that an analogous precedence of reading over writing was the norm in Hellenistic, Roman, and early Byzantine times. Quite the opposite: conditions and expectations were actually so dissimilar as to strengthen the case for the teaching of some writing skills at an early stage.

A Minimal Cultural Package

At the primary level, the content of instruction revolved around a limited selection of texts, the knowledge of which was to be enriched as a student's education progressed. Since ancient society considered children to be miniature adults without tastes and talents of their own, it is no surprise that with very few exceptions, not only the formats but also the contents of books and instruction were identical to those offered to an adult public. Even fables were not exclusively connected to childhood, but also aroused the interest of adult ancient readers. Maxims and sayings, which remained

---

[61] Marrou 1975, 2: 160.
[62] Clanchy 1993: 232–33 and passim.
[63] Cressy 1981; Spufford 1981.

the basis of learning in medieval schools,[64] were examples of the first language of authority that a student encountered. They were deeply ingrained into ancient society because they embodied popular wisdom. But it was not enough for a beginner to have an initial taste of them in the first educational circle, using them in exercises of penmanship and memorization. Students were supposed to chew them over and over at every level, making collections of them and expanding their content in writing until, as adults, they would be able to spit them out on occasion as cultural symbols.[65] When a man such as Timaios, in writing a letter on papyrus to his master Heroninos, added two Homeric verses in the margin to emphasize that Heroninos should take care of a certain matter in a hurry, "All the other gods and men, lords of chariots, were sleeping the whole night through, but Zeus could not have sweet sleep" (*Il.* 2.1–2), one wonders whether he had a good knowledge of the *Iliad* or only remembered popular quotations from it.[66] The independent life of these verses is confirmed by the fact that Libanius proposes them as a theme for "preliminary exercises" (*Progymnasmata* 8, pp. 106–17 Foerster).

Some Homer, a bit of Euripides, and some gnomic quotations from Isocrates formed the cultural package of students at the primary level; elementary instruction appropriated these texts in successive phases. A pupil's initial taste of one of these authors, gained by copying a short text as an exercise in penmanship, was enriched when he attempted to read the same text with syllables and words separated.[67] As the example of Kokkalos in the *Didaskalos* indicates, these basic pieces of a Greek education proved a student's cultural involvement and showed progress in the eyes of parents. These bits of knowledge were coveted talismans of culture, magical formulas that could open some doors. When the ancients attributed magical power to the tongue-twisters called *chalinoi* that were sung in chorus by the children and common people of the city of Miletus to cause a plague to abate, they apparently understood the intrinsic nature of these educational symbols.

But what about texts that originated from and referred to a local Egyptian reality? Were they entirely absent from the cultural scenario of a primary student? Greek culture, which maintained a high regard for the venerable religious traditions of the country, was practically impermeable

[64] See D. Alexandre-Bidon, "Quand les maîtres parlaient par proverbes," in *Les Cahiers du C.R.I.S.I.M.A.* 1 (1993): 23–43.

[65] See Quintilian 1.1.35; Seneca *Ep.* 33; Barns 1950–51.

[66] *P.Flor.* II.259.

[67] See, e.g., Cribiore 1996a: no. 182 (Eur. *Tro.* 876–79, divided into syllables), and in no. 379 the short passages from Eur. *Phoen.* and *Ino*.

to indigenous culture in other respects. The scope of education was to instill Greek ways of thinking and highlights of Greek culture; thus an almost total disregard for anything that was not Greek is to be expected.[68] An example of a late text popular in primary education is highly significant.[69] Aesop's *Fable* 48 from the sixth century B.C.E. reported the story of someone who murdered another man and, pursued by the dead man's relatives, ran to the river Nile, managed to escape from a wolf, climbed a tree on which there was a serpent, and, in a last attempt to escape from his lot, threw himself into the Nile, where he was devoured by a crocodile. As the moral said, there was no escape for people polluted by bloodshed. But this is not exactly the version that teachers gave their pupils:

> A son who had killed his own father, fearing the law, took refuge in a desolate place, but when he reached the mountains, he was pursued by a lion. Since the lion chased him, he mounted a tree. But he saw a serpent lying on it and, unable to climb further, he was killed. The evil man never escapes from God, for the divine leads evil people to justice.

The transformations are all interesting. Pupils must have felt some horror at the murder that the protagonist, one of them, committed, and must have shared in the relief of the Christian ending. The animals of the original fable were reduced to two, with the lion really taking the lion's share and acting as a righteous instrument of punishment. A few of these exercises even show drawings with lions that smile in a friendly way. But what about the Nile and the crocodile? One may suppose that these details were what had originally attracted the attention of Egyptian teachers. Yet they were made to disappear so that the story would become less localized and more Greek.

NUMERICAL LITERACY

A complete picture of the benefits that a student derived from an elementary education requires a brief excursus on numerical literacy. The fact that arithmetic was a subject offered in ancient primary schools is usually considered a given and treated with broad generalizations,[70] but the de-

[68] See Cribiore 1996b. The few exceptions mostly involve Egyptian gods that appear in lists, due to the syncretism that characterizes religion in Egypt. Cf. Bowersock 1990.

[69] See Cribiore 1996a: nos. 230, 231, 232, 314, 323, 409, and 412. See also a schoolbook with the same text, J. Diethart, J. Kramer, and P. J. Sijpesteijn, "Ein neuer Zeuge der 'Vater-Mördergeschichte' " *Tyche* 3 (1988): 33–37.

[70] See Marrou (1975, 1: 236–38) and Bonner (1977: 180–88), who both relied on the evidence of only a handful of Greek school exercises. See also Frasca 1996a: 277–78. On

tails of the picture can only be filled in by the evidence of the mathematical exercises from Greco-Roman Egypt. So far, the general assumption has been that students learned to perform and wrote down arithmetical operations and fractions in elementary schools. Since the Greeks used the letters of the alphabet with three additional signs to represent numbers, it is usually inferred that pupils learned the alphabet and the numbers at the same time. Of course, one has to take into account the oral component of ancient learning: it is possible that numbers were memorized mostly by recitation at this stage. In fact, the preserved written work generally shows that students began to write down lists of numbers after learning the alphabet and reinforcing their penmanship, as they were getting ready for reading. Thus not only do exercises with simple sequences of numbers appear in conjunction with syllabaries or lists of words, but students' handwriting seems to have progressed beyond extreme clumsiness.[71]

The quality of handwriting of students who wrote down additions is further improved—another sign that written arithmetic probably should not be correlated with an initial stage of learning. But the fact that exercises with this numerical operation are extremely rare calls for some explanation.[72] In fact, even though the absence of addition from the papyrus roll called *Livre d' écolier* has been considered with some surprise,[73] an examination of other mathematical exercises all but confirm that this numerical operation was seldom written down. A number of factors may account for this. Since Augustine relates that simple additions were recited by schoolchildren in monotonous chants that he calls "hateful" (*odiosa cantio, Conf.* 1.13), it is conceivable that they were performed mostly orally at this stage. It is also likely that students were taught to do this simple operation on their fingers or on the reckoning board, called *abacus*.[74] The *Hermeneumata* and a school exercise on papyrus provide some suggestions. In the *Hermeneumata*, fingers and pebbles are mentioned in connection with counting, and an abacus and beans are included among school objects.[75] In Roman Egypt, moreover, at least one student was aware of the usefulness of the abacus. After writing a maxim about the

---

mathematics in antiquity, see Fowler 1987; Dilke 1987; and O. Neugebauer, *The Exact Sciences in Antiquity*, 2d ed. (Providence, R.I., 1957).

[71] See, e.g., Cribiore 1996a: nos. 379 and 118; *MPER N.S.* XV.144 and 148.

[72] See, e.g., *MPER N.S.* XV.150 and 151; *O.Claud.* II.416. No addition tables used for commercial purposes are preserved.

[73] Cribiore 1996a: no. 379; Bonner 1977: 180–81.

[74] J. H. Turner, "Roman Elementary Mathematics: The Operations," *CJ* 47 (1951): 63–74, 106–8. R. Merkelbach, "Die Zahl 9999 in der Magie und der Computus Digitorum," *ZPE* 63 (1986): 305–8 n. 4 with bibliography.

[75] See Goetz 1892: 382 ll. 40–42; and Dionisotti 1982: 99 line 22.

happiness of rich people, this pupil added two drawings to illustrate its message: a human figure that may represent King Midas—the wealthy man par excellence—and what appears to be an abacus.[76]

The next stage of instruction in arithmetic was represented by multiplication and fractions.[77] Multiplication did not present unusual difficulties: multiplication tables closely followed the format of addition tables by pairing numbers. The Egyptian system for treating fractional quantities as sums of parts was cumbersome, however, and had to be learned with some accuracy. Fractions were used extensively in documents because properties were often divided into diminutive portions, and familiarity with fractions was an absolute necessity for the accomplished scribe. Many tables of fractions have been found, but the long and systematic ones that are written proficiently are ready reckoners that were probably hung in the offices of government workers, lawyers, and businessmen for easy consultation.[78] Even the less coherent or isolated tables that appear to have originated in schools do not seem to represent the written work of primary students. Though some smattering of multiplication and fractions was certainly imparted to elementary pupils, this was mostly done through memorization of tables compiled by their teachers. Teachers' models, in fact, also played a crucial role in inculcating a simple knowledge of arithmetic after students had acquired some literacy. When tablets containing mathematical models also include students' work in other areas, it appears that these pupils either had already acquired good handwriting or were doing exercises in reading readiness.[79]

In specialized scribal schools, however, a deeper knowledge of multiplication and fractions, exemplified by students' compilation of extensive and complicated tables, appears to have been an integral part of the curriculum. It is generally assumed that individuals who aspired to a scribal career needed specialized training in proficient scripts and in the legal and bureaucratic jargon and syntax of the trade.[80] Though scribes seem to have been generally male, women sometimes received the same training, as is shown by the fact that Origen in Alexandria used numerous women to copy his books.[81] Next to nothing is known, however, about the ages

---

[76] See Cribiore 1996a: no. 210.

[77] Tables of fractions are sometimes called "tables of divisions."

[78] See, e.g., *P.Bad*. IV.64 and *P.Mich*. XV.686.

[79] See Cribiore 1996a: nos. 383 and 395. Cf. also *Pap.Flor*. XVIII.4, a model prepared by a teacher for the student Phaustus.

[80] On scribes as technicians, see Pinto 1974: 166.

[81] Eusebius *Hist. eccl.* 6.23.

of students in scribal schools, their level of ability when they were first admitted, or the duration of this specialized education.[82] The evidence does show that it was in these professional schools that individuals practiced extensively the multiplication tables and fractions that were going to be useful for their future activities. Several exercises compiled by students during their professional training are preserved.[83] They are usually included in notebooks, and their script consists of fast cursives, sometimes provided with flourishes, that show a quality of execution that appears to be the mark of apprentice scribes. Part of the instruction in these schools also dealt with metrological expertise: apprentices had to become familiar with weights, measures, conversions, and the monetary system.[84]

The evidence shows, therefore, that the notion that students learned the numerical operations in elementary schools needs to be qualified. Numbers were introduced after a student reinforced his knowledge of the letters of the alphabet through copying. Although addition exercises were rarely written down in either elementary or scribal schools, multiplication and fractions were usually learned by the elementary pupil with the aid of models drawn by the teachers. Systematic and extensive written work with arithmetical operations, however, was part of the curriculum of specialized schools. Are we to believe, therefore, that Petaus and other "slow writers" did not learn to count during their one or two years of schooling? Though the written numerical literacy of these men and women must have been very deficient, once school was left behind, life itself may have schooled some of them. At any rate, even students who walked the entire path of elementary schooling do not seem to have dedicated much effort to writing numerical operations. At this level, numerical literacy remained mostly in an oral and practical dimension, as Plato had advocated centuries before: mathematics was to be learned "by way of play and fun, dividing up apples and crowns" (*Laws* 7.819b).

Picture now ancient students at the conclusion of their first educational circle: what were they able to see from the plateau reached in their climb up the hill of learning? By modern standards, not much. Elementary education aimed at modest and circumscribed goals through the acquisition

---

[82] Many exercises of apprentice scribes that presuppose specific notarial training are included in *MPER N.S.* XV.

[83] See, e.g., *MPER N.S.* XV.152; B. Brashear, "Holz- und Wachstafeln der Sammlung Kiseleff," *Enchoria* 13 (1985): 13–23; and P. Cauderlier, "Cinq tablettes en bois au musée du Louvre," *RA* (1983): f. 2, pp. 259–80.

[84] See, e.g., *P.Ryl.* II.64 and III.538.

of mechanical skills and rote learning, with minimal concern for developing critical thinking and creative ability. The limited knowledge that it imparted was systematized and shackled by iron rules. It was through the learning and application of rigid rules that students started to glimpse a world of higher literacy, of which most of them would not become part. Knowledge of the set of rules necessary at this stage and of a very limited selection of authoritative texts were the only prerequisites for elementary instructors.[85] The acquisition and imparting of precise rules engendered pride and a sense of accomplishment in both students and teachers. The passive application of strict formulas, embodied first in syllabaries, carried over to the stage when words were introduced. Bizarre exercises that produced words invented to exemplify a certain number of syllables or the association of consonants with all the vowels in turn show that realism was secondary to the uniform exactness of drills.[86]

And yet, in the precarious conditions of teaching and learning in antiquity, what was accomplished was not minor. Students who would go on to pursue more ambitious goals had a taste of what awaited them and, through rigorous mental gymnastics, began to develop the skills needed to overcome the hurdles that lay ahead. Not less were the attainments of those whose education ended at the elementary level. The possession of a modest cultural package and of basic techniques in the art of decoding writing engendered a strong sense of distinction from the uneducated. Being able to cite from memory a *bon mot*, to copy a short text, to sign, to jot down a phrase, and to read words from documents of the central government posted in large clear letters[87] were not small accomplishments. Primary education was geared to serve the needs of both types of student: for all its rigid immobility, it never completely lost touch with reality.

[85] On the ancients' scorn for primary teachers, see above, Chapter 2.
[86] See Cribiore 1996a: nos. 100 and 124.
[87] See *SB* XIV.12144.13–14; *P.Oxy.* VIII.1100.2; *P.Hib.* I.29; *P.Oxy.* XXXIV.2705.10.

The Teaching of the Grammarian:
Content and Context

Grammatikē is an *empeiria* ("acquired expertise") of the general usage of poets and prose writers. It has six parts: first, accurate reading with due regard for the prosody; second, explanation of the literary devices contained; third, the provision of notes on phraseology and subject matters; fourth, the discovery of etymology; fifth, the working out of analogical regularities; sixth, the critical study of literature, which is the finest part of the *technē* ["art"].

THUS WROTE the grammarian Dionysius Thrax around 100 B.C.E. in the initial section of his grammatical treatise, the only part whose authenticity has never been disputed.[1] Though the discrepancies between this introduction and the whole treatise have caused some ancient and modern scholars to doubt that the rest of the work, as it is preserved, was composed at the same time and to prefer a date around the third century C.E. or even later, this definition of *grammatikē*—that is, "grammar" in a broad sense, which covered the full area of expertise of a grammarian—remained the basis of all subsequent definitions.[2] Grammar intended in a restricted sense as the study of language had a hard time finding its own identity and distinguishing itself from other disciplines, such as philology, philosophy, and rhetoric, particularly because the various aspects of the work of grammarians were inextricably tied together in education. Dionysius's definition, which applied to *grammatikē* at a time when a strict systematization of linguistic facts had not yet taken place, covered all the skills that an ancient grammarian possessed and taught his students. It is in fact conceivable that a part of Dionysius's treatise was a study of the activities of grammarians as well as a technical treatment of aspects of

[1] Cf. *Grammatici Graeci* 1.1, p. 5, 1–5. Part of this definition is preserved in a school notebook of the fifth century, Cribiore 1996a: no. 405.

[2] The question of the authenticity of the text is hotly debated; see Di Benedetto 1958, 1959, and 1973; Wouters 1979 and 1995; Schenkeveld 1993; Law and Sluiter 1995. I am inclined to consider the body of the *Technē* as a product of late antiquity.

language.[3] Since his definition conveniently embraces the range of the work covered at a secondary stage of studies, I shall follow it step by step.

According to Sextus Empiricus, who around C.E. 190 wrote a work critical of professors of higher learning, the definition of *grammatikē* given by Dionysius was immediately perceived as referring to several aspects of the activities of grammarians.[4] In the first century B.C.E., Asclepiades of Myrlea had distinguished three areas of study: the "historical," the "technical," and the "special."[5] The "historical" part embraced all the contextual and historical questions arising from literary texts, such as mythological or geographical information, and glossographical notes. The "technical" part of *grammatikē* consisted of a study of language, such as sounds, word classes, orthography, and correct Greek (*hellēnismos*). But Dionysius considered the highest skill that grammarians practiced the "critical study of literature" (*krisis poiēmatōn*), that is, exegesis, textual criticism, aesthetic evaluation, and judgment of the authenticity of a text. Though I shall cover in this chapter the first two aspects of the grammarian's teaching, I shall not expand on the *krisis poiēmatōn*, the specific branch where a grammarian showed the fullness of his expertise. His students, however, merely sampled his most sophisticated and erudite work.

Hotly debated in antiquity was the fact that Dionysius defined "grammar" as an *empeiria*—an expertise acquired through practice and experience—while at the same time calling it a *technē*—that is, "an art or science."[6] What appears a contradiction (which raised the objections of ancient grammarians, who feared that he was selling the subject short) finds its proper collocation within the realm of education. Calling "grammar" an *empeiria*, Dionysius stressed a methodological approach that pointed to the active work of students in applying the teachings they received, and not only to their passive reception of notions. By closely working on texts, a pupil acquired a systematic method of study. But "grammar" also consisted of a body of transmitted notions. Through his teacher's instruction, and thanks to the personal work of discovery, a student began to understand the underlying principles of the "art of grammar," a *technē*.

In this chapter, the tension between description and argument will somewhat favor the former, since my aim is to verify systematically the

[3] Schenkeveld 1993: 269.

[4] See D. L. Blank, *Sextus Empiricus: Against the Grammarians* (Oxford, 1998).

[5] Sextus *Math*. 1.91–94 and 252–53: *historikon, technikon, idiaiteron*. The date of Asclepiades is uncertain.

[6] On this problem, see Robins 1996: 6–10.

multifarious sides of the teaching activities of a grammarian. Although we are well acquainted with the theoretical aspects of grammarians' work, the details of their pedagogy are less well known, though not irrecoverable.[7] This chapter will elucidate the tools employed in educational gymnastics, the ways in which they were used and their respective effectiveness, the intensity of the training, and the goals achieved.[8] In the class of a grammarian, a student attained the mental fitness and the sense of identity required to be recognized as a person of culture: for the elite, education at this level was closer to a common experience than was rhetorical education.[9]

At this point in the journey, the hill of learning has already lost the majority of its climbers: the male students who could not afford the high fees that education commanded, and the vast majority of female students, for whom the basic principles of reading and writing—if even that level of learning applied—were considered a sufficient achievement.[10] It should not be forgotten, however, that a few girls of the upper class were able to reach instruction at this level and followed the course for one or two years, if not in its entirety.[11] The student who arrived at the grammatical stage was well aware that all the elements of knowledge fitted precisely into a grid, that knowledge consisted of an accumulation of points that were in a relation of similarity among themselves, and that *paideia* ("education") proceeded in a circular motion, by revisiting previous material. After following all the steps required for fluent reading, a student had to learn to dissect parts of the texts of the authors, distinguishing all their components. A passage, which was a thing closed in upon itself, was at the same time a dense cluster of interwoven linguistic and "historical" elements. It could swell up *ad infinitum*, becoming a microcosm of erudite, fragmented knowledge. When the grammarian pointed out to his class glosses, figures, tropes, relations of elements of language, similarities with other parts of an author's work or the work of other authors in a proliferation of exegesis, a text became a perfect model to which other

[7] The picture presented by Marrou 1975 and Bonner 1977 needs to be updated. Kaster 1988 did not cover grammatical instruction. Morgan 1998 combined the reading of literature at primary and secondary levels.

[8] Here, the literary sources will be used only for comparison and verification. Bonner (1977: 189–249), who used almost exclusively the literary sources, investigated only the theoretical side of the work of grammarians.

[9] Cf. Kaster 1988: 26.

[10] The vast disproportion between male and female pupils justifies the occasional use of masculine pronouns here.

[11] Cf. above, Chapter 3.

texts had to conform. All this specialist knowledge was the patrimony of the grammarian, who administered and transmitted it from the height of his authority.

A difficulty one encounters in attempting to characterize accurately the mindset of a student of a grammarian and the benefits derived from instruction at this level arises from the fact that not all students completed the course. Though some stayed long enough to assimilate the kind of exclusive education that was a mark of distinction, others received only partial instruction, leaving the class with superficial knowledge of the poets and grammar.[12] Thus, it is instructive to consider at the outset how different amounts of such an education influenced two students of different milieus. It will be useful to remember these young men, and others like them, in what follows. One was Epharmostos, the younger brother of the businessman Zenon, who received a refined education in Alexandria in the third century B.C.E.[13] Even though only glimpses are afforded of his education, they are enough to show that he took advantage of full instruction at the hands of a grammarian. His handwriting—as he jotted down a playful hexameter that he might have composed himself and a formulaic phrase from Demosthenes—betrays an advanced student.[14] From a list of books that were supposed to be sent to him, it appears that Epharmostos was interested in the collection of material characteristic of the Peripatetics.[15] Education served Epharmostos as a platform from which he could launch a prestigious career in state service.

Another young man who savored some literary education but did not progress very far into it was Apollonios, the brother of Ptolemaios, who went to school intermittently in the Sarapieion of Memphis:[16] after copying a personal anthology, he characterized it as "the lessons of Ariston, the philosopher [or learned man]." This anthology, which includes verses from Euripides, Aeschylus, and Menander,[17] was copied with many blunders on the front of a papyrus that contained on the back verses written

[12] Kaster 1988: 26–28 and passim.

[13] On Epharmostos, see above, p. 48. Zenon belonged to a circle of educated people, cf. *Pap.Lugd.Bat.* XX.14–16; *P.Cair.Zen.* IV.59532; Clarysse 1982: 43–61; I. Cazzaniga, "Pap.Zenon 59532: Epigramma in distici per la morte del cane Tauron," *Eirene* 11 (1973): 71–89.

[14] Cribiore 1996a: no. 175.

[15] *P.Col.* IV.60 mentions a work by Kallisthenes on "proxeny treaties" and another on "embassies."

[16] On Apollonios and the literary tastes of both brothers, see Thompson 1988: 245–65. About a syllabary and a list written by Apollonios, see Cribiore 1996a: nos. 78 and 98.

[17] Cribiore 1996a: no. 244; P^2 31, 401, 1320.

in stilted handwriting by Ptolemaios.[18] On another papyrus where Ptolemaios wrote an account, Apollonios clumsily copied part of the Prologue of Euripides' *Telephus*.[19] Both brothers were familiar with Egyptian language and culture, even though they could write only Greek: Apollonios wrote down a folktale, the "Dream of Nectanebos," from a Greek translation of an Egyptian exemplar.[20] Moreover, the back of a papyrus with an astronomical work[21] contained official and formal private letters that might have provided the brothers with models of style and language in their many epistolary endeavors.[22] But how did a smattering of literary education serve Apollonios? This young man, who came from a Macedonian military family, ended up first enlisting in the army, and then becoming the assistant of the chief of police on the necropolis. A literacy that extended somewhat beyond the primary level allowed him to draft letters to officials and to read police files.

READING WITH UNDERSTANDING

Not surprisingly, the first item in the list of prescriptions given by Dionysius Thrax was "accurate reading." Since all the teaching of the grammarian rested on understanding and interpreting poetic texts, a sound knowledge of reading was a *conditio sine qua non*. A student like Apollonios, who had superficially approached the technique of reading with the primary schoolmaster, had to build his reading ability at this level of studies. Though Quintilian maintained that a boy was ready for the grammarian as soon as he had learned to read and write (1.4.1), his statement needs to be qualified. Not only was a student in primary education exposed only to copying and dictation, but his reading ability was also somewhat limited at the end of the course. The skill of reading was a complex affair, fragmented into a series of acquisitions that aimed at understanding a text thoroughly. Ancient manuscripts did not make many concessions to readers. A passage made of words written without separation in continu-

---

[18] *P.Didot* 1 (H. Weil, *Monuments grecs publiés par l' Association pour l' encouragement des études grecques en France* [Paris, 1879]); A. W. Gomme and F. H. Sandbach, *Menander: A Commentary* (Oxford, 1973), 723–26. See also *P.Didot* 28–34.

[19] Cribiore 1996a: no. 246.

[20] Ibid.: no. 245; P[2] 2476. Cf. K. Ryholt, "A Demotic Version of Nectanebos' Dream (P. Carlsberg 562)," *ZPE* 122 (1998): 197–200.

[21] *P.Paris* 1 (P[2] 369). Ptolemaios read it and jotted down some notes.

[22] *P.Paris* 63. Cf. above, p. 20, and below, p. 216.

ous blocks and containing almost no punctuation was only an ensemble of letters in need of interpretation. Reading at first sight was practically impossible: a text needed to be scrutinized beforehand to identify the relationship between the elements of a sentence and to understand their function in conveying meaning. It was only in the early Middle Ages that a thorough and consistent system of conventions was devised to help readers readily extract the information contained in a written text: word separation, features of layout, and a number of graphic symbols to help decode meaning.[23] But all these conventions of a "grammar of legibility" formed slowly in the classes of ancient grammarians.[24]

When a student was still quite inexperienced, his teacher gave him concrete help by preparing texts that were "user-friendly,"[25] in which syllables and/or words were separated and a minimum of conventions was respected: the coincidence of verse-units with the written line,[26] the enlargement of initial letters of a verse, and the use of an apostrophe to mark elision. Since the boundaries between educational levels were blurred, it is difficult to be sure whether these models served to strengthen the skills of elementary students or whether they were still used by beginners in a grammarian's class. These teaching aids formed a necessary transition to the demanding texts that were in general use, which the grammarian read together with his students. A first step consisted of a preliminary reading done by the teacher—called *praelectio* in Latin—in which appropriate emphasis was placed on diction, phrasing, and pausing (Quintilian 1.8.13). Even though it is now recognized that silent reading was practiced in antiquity more often than once believed, primarily because it allowed a reader to manage larger quantities of text,[27] in the schools of both the grammarian and the rhetor the practice of reading aloud was universally observed, since eloquence was the final aim of the educational process. In articulating the phonemes, a student simulated the oral-aural process of live communication.

[23] See Parkes 1993.

[24] The term "grammar of legibility" was coined by M. B. Parkes, *Scribes, Scripts, and Readers* (London, 1991), 2. On punctuation and lectional signs used in school, see Cribiore 1996a: 81–88.

[25] On models, cf. above, Chapter 5.

[26] On the early practice of writing verses without regard for colometry—a frequent habit of ancient students—see Turner 1987: 12 and n. 57; Cribiore 1992: 259–63; and Cribiore 1996a: 87–88.

[27] On silent reading and reading aloud, see Balogh 1927; Knox 1968; Saenger 1982; Svenbro 1993; Gavrilov 1997; M. F. Burnyeat, "Postscript on Silent Reading," *CQ* 47 (1997): 74–76; further bibliography in Cribiore 1996a: 150 n. 65.

Rhetorical teaching stressed punctuation as reflecting the periodic structure of a discourse, but grammatical analysis was concerned with its application in order to identify the boundaries of a sentence and its constituents. Students were taught, both in practice and in theory, the function of the prosodic signs that could offer some assistance, and they learned to mark their texts themselves. School exercises testify to the frequent use of the *paragraphos*—a horizontal stroke written in the left margin—to mark changes of speakers in dramatic texts, to divide sections in hexameter poetry, and to separate the different components of an anthology.[28] Diaeresis, apostrophe, breathings, marks of quantity, and dots for emphatic punctuation also occur in texts written by students together with occasional accents, especially when doubts could arise in reading. But sometimes grammarians focused on specific exercises of accentuation. A student might be asked to add regular accents to the Homeric text he was copying[29] or to add a consistent accentuation to a book he was reading.[30] Prosodic signs could also be learned theoretically with the help of grammatical handbooks that listed them in order. Grammarians made use of such systematic treatment of the signs indicating difference in pronunciation, and in fact the treatise transmitted with the name of Dionysius Thrax was provided in the fourth century with a useful supplement containing the prosodic signs. Manuals reinforced the notions a student was learning to apply, particularly because their content was often memorized. Thus, for instance, a grammatical treatise (*technē grammatikē*) that was copied or written from dictation around the third century c.e. by a student of a grammarian in Hermopolis must have had this function.[31] This handbook, which started with a treatment of the prosodic signs and deviated from the usual order, was compiled by a grammarian who responded to the actual needs of his students. Even though as a rule it is somewhat unrealistic to visualize grammarians located away from Alexandria as composing their own manuals, it is nevertheless likely that when necessary, they could introduce some adaptations of the material.

Students also acquired a knowledge of the rules of punctuation and the ability to identify the various constituents of a sentence— which was reinforced through the "technical" part of *grammatikē*—as their teacher guided them through the literary texts. A grammarian's teaching was

---

[28] On the function of the *paragraphos* in prose texts, see W. A. Johnson, "The Function of the Paragraphus in Greek Literary Prose Texts," *ZPE* 100 (1994): 65–68.

[29] See Cribiore 1996a: no. 340.

[30] Cf. above, pp. 140–41.

[31] See Cribiore 1996a: no. 368; and Wouters 1979: 188–97.

composed of elements that in practice were interdependent. Even though it is necessary to unravel the various strands to investigate them, the many different activities in which the grammarian engaged in his classroom went on simultaneously as a student read through the texts of the authors. But let us listen to the real voice of a teacher emerging from the past: "Read this, and mark the main points." This assignment, written in the neat handwriting of a teacher on a small piece of parchment, involved an exercise in punctuation, or perhaps the distinction of sections according to "speakers"—the poet and the various characters.[32]

Contents of Reading

In the opening statement of his work, Dionysius says that *grammatikē* was based on the study of poets and prose writers. Though a good knowledge of prose writers was part of the cultural baggage of a grammarian, his students actually approached literature almost exclusively through poetic works. Education had always been strictly connected to criticism and interpretation of the poets. According to Plato, the sophist Protagoras in the fifth century B.C.E. stated that "the greatest part of a man's education is to be skilled in poetic works, that is, to be able to judge in what they say what has been rightly and what wrongly composed, and to know how to evaluate it" (*Prt.* 339a). Such a program would have been approved by most of the later grammarians. Protagoras, who also made some specific contributions to linguistics, considered the study of language to be inextricably tied to criticism of the poets.[33] His discussion of a poem by the lyric poet Simonides, for instance, exemplifies a typical grammarian's literary evaluation, based as it is on subtle points of semantics, distinction in the usage of particles, quotations from other poets, supporting arguments from the poem's context, and interpretation through paraphrase (339a–347a). In later centuries, students of grammarians continued to approach literary texts from all these perspectives.

Establishing the authors included in the Greek menu of the banquet of literature, where, according to Quintilian, one filled oneself first with the best writers and turned next to minor authors for the sake of variety (10.1.58), is not an easy enterprise. The information provided by the liter-

---

[32] See *P.Köln.* II.114, from the fifth century. Cf. above, Chapter 5, note 53.

[33] See Sluiter 1990: 7–11; D. Fehling, "Zwei Untersuchungen zur griechischen Sprachphilosophie," *RhM* 108 (1965): 212–29.

ary sources is theoretical in some respects.[34] Data derived from the school exercises, which reflect the reality of ancient education,[35] are also biased to a degree. The criteria employed to identify student exercises tend to isolate those that stand out because of unpracticed handwriting and various mistakes in execution, missing the work of students who wrote with confidence.[36] The exercises, moreover, provide partial clues about what was actually read. They consist of passages singled out in some way, such as similes or descriptions to be copied for penmanship, memorized, or analyzed. It is incorrect to infer from these written passages that the students' view of literature was fragmented to such an extent.[37] It is also difficult to trace with precision the reading patterns of students at this level because they often read the same books that circulated among the cultivated public. One can reach a somewhat more balanced—albeit far from complete—view by taking into account information derived from the few books that show signs of having been used in schools[38] and from those elaborate lists of words with a consistent literary flavor that are likely to reflect readings done at advanced levels of education. More important, one should place the information extrapolated from various sources within the frame of the literary tastes of the educated public.[39] Many of the authors mentioned below were already familiar to a student from primary education, and only a few were approached for the first

[34] See Quintilian 1.4.4 and 1.8.5–12. The long list of authors to be covered in rhetorical education in 10.1.46–131 addresses the ideal needs of a highly cultivated person, the orator with a leading role in society. See also Statius (ca. C.E. 45–96) *Silvae* 5.3.146–61; his father was a grammarian in Naples, an area of Greek influence.

[35] For a list of exercises, Cribiore 1996a: 173–284 and 1997b.

[36] It is difficult to distinguish good students' copies from those of educated individuals; see, e.g., *P.Genova* I.4.

[37] Morgan (1998: 100–119) reaches unrealistic conclusions.

[38] On books used in school, see above, pp. 138–43. Of course, many more were read even though no traces of their educational use survive.

[39] The figures about the literary papyri found in Egypt are derived from W. H. Willis, "A Census of the Literary Papyri from Egypt," *GRBS* 9 (1968): 205–24; P. Mertens, "Vingt années de papyrologie odysséenne," *CE* 60 (1985): 191–203, and "Les témoins papyrologiques de Ménandre: Essai de classement rationnel et esquisse d' étude bibliologique," *Serta Leodiensia Secunda* (Liège, 1992), 331–56; J. Lenaerts and P. Mertens, "Les papyrus d' Isocrate," *CE* 64 (1989): 216–30; D. Marcotte and P. Mertens, "Les papyrus de Callimaque," *Pap.Flor.* XIX (Florence, 1990), 409–27, and "Catalogue des Femmes et Grandes Éoées d' Hésiode," in *Storia, poesia e pensiero nel mondo antico: Studi in onore di Marcello Gigante* (Naples, 1994), 407–23; Bouquiaux and Mertens 1992; and the database compiled by W. Clarysse, *Leuven Database of Ancient Books* (Leuven, 1998). I also benefited from communications from P. Mertens.

time at this stage of education. The range of authors covered, in any case, was limited: as the Roman writer Pliny the Younger advised a student in the second century C.E., one was supposed to read the same selection of authors again and again, expanding one's comprehension of them (*multum legendum esse, non multa*, Ep. 7.9.15).

"THE POET"

According to Sextus Empiricus, "The grammarian appears to interpret the writings of the poets, such as Homer and Hesiod, Pindar and Euripides, and Menander, and the rest" (*Math.* 1.58). Starting from Homer is mandatory, since he was considered in antiquity the poet par excellence, a moral and religious authority, and the teacher who inspired reverence from the early years of study.[40] About a thousand Homeric papyri have been discovered, with the figures assuming some significance from a comparison with papyri of Euripides—the next favored author—which are roughly one-tenth as voluminous. There is a striking disparity between the number of copies of the *Iliad* and the *Odyssey*, the former being about three times more numerous than the latter. It appears, moreover, that not all of the *Iliad* was read with the same intensity: the first six books are represented in over half of the total papyri, whereas the first twelve books cover about three-fourths of the whole. The figures sharply decrease on proceeding to the second half of the poem, where some books in particular—14, 19, 20, 21—were the least favored.

A comparison with data deriving from school exercises and schoolbooks shows a partial convergence of findings. It is not surprising that the first two books of the *Iliad* attracted the most attention: whereas Book 1 introduced the main theme and characters, Book 2 appears to have been enjoyed in its own right, and not only because of its proximity to the previous one.[41] Even though ancient teachers concentrated on the beginning of an author's work—a trend generally remarkable in ancient scholiography—all of Book 2, including the Catalogue of Ships, earned much favor. Fondness for Book 2 can be traced throughout antiquity: in the third century B.C.E., the poet and legislator Cercidas, who asked to have Books 1 and 2 buried with him at this death, legislated that children of Megalopolis in the Peloponnesus had to learn the Catalogue by heart,[42]

[40] Plato *Resp.* 10.595b–c and 606e.
[41] See Cribiore 1994: 4–5.
[42] Photius *Bibl.* 190.151a.14 Henry; and Eustathius *Iliad* 2.494 (p. 401.36 M. van der Valk).

and likewise the Catalogue was memorized in second-century Egypt.[43] In the last centuries of Byzantium, moreover, there were countless manuscripts written for school use that contained the first two books of the *Iliad*, two or three plays, and selections of other poets.[44]

All of the first six books, in any case, were the objects of close scrutiny, even though a grammarian's commentary became more sparse as he proceeded.[45] The student Ptolemaios, who was reading Book 6 with his private teacher, must have progressed slowly through the preceding books.[46] This cluster of books was tightly constructed and contributed greatly to the monumental plan of the poem by presenting themes and figures and preparing crucial battles. But indications survive that students continued to read and work upon the rest of the first half of the epic. Book 11, for instance, was commented on closely, line by line, and in the sixth century the students of Dioskoros of Aphrodito annotated it heavily.[47] The most advanced students continued to read the *Iliad* to its end. It is significant that isolated passages from the second half of the poem—such as could have been written by the least experienced pupils—have not survived. What remains are some textbooks used in school that reproduced whole books, and paraphrases and glossographical notes—*scholia minora*—written in relatively advanced handwriting. It is noteworthy that those books that the educated public appreciated the least—Books 14, 19, 20, and 21—were not ignored in school.[48] The general public may have lacked appreciation for them because they presented an "unheroic" side of Achilles and aspects of the divine that people found offensive and lacking in dignity.[49] But students were not entitled to choose.

Ancient readers strongly preferred the *Iliad* over the *Odyssey*, since Homer was identified with the more tragic epic of doomed human limitations that better represented the Greek heroic view. When in a papyrus letter a man, Capiton, asked a friend what kinds of murals he would like

[43] Cribiore 1996a: nos. 193 and 201.

[44] Browning 1992: 137.

[45] For a book used in school that includes the whole group, see above, Chapter 5, note 44. Book 5, with the *aristeia* of Diomedes and a celebration of heroic nature at its highest, was particularly appreciated; see above, Chapter 5, note 52, and especially Cribiore 1996a: no. 340.

[46] On Ptolemaios, cf. above, pp. 48 and 54.

[47] Cf. Cribiore 1996a: nos. 342 and 329; and above, Chapter 5, note 52. After the first six, this was the book preferred by the general public.

[48] See Cribiore 1996a: nos. 274, 326, 334, 345; cf. above, Chapter 5, notes 43 and 50.

[49] Book 14, with the deception of Zeus, was the least popular. For the ancients' reservations about it, see, e.g., Plato *Resp.* 3.390c; and Plutarch *Quomodo adul.* 19f. Cf. R. D. Lamberton, *Homer the Theologian* (Berkeley, 1986).

on the walls of his house—scenes from the *Iliad* perhaps?—for "the place demands it," one catches a tangible glimpse of the place this epic occupied in the lives of provincials in the eastern part of the empire.[50] Knowledge of the *Iliad* was mandatory for understanding other epic, lyric, and tragic poetry, as well as history. In his epigrams, the grammarian Palladas indicated that "pernicious wrath" was the beginning and substance itself of *grammatikē*, whereas the only time that he mentioned the *Odyssey* was to bring together somewhat unfairly "Helen's adultery" and "Penelope's chastity" as both being causes of death.[51] Not enough indications survive from passages written in school and from schoolbooks about which parts of the *Odyssey* teachers preferred.[52] The lack of retrievable information may be due to the fact that this epic was considered more advanced reading; nevertheless, there is no doubt that it was not approached with the same intensity as the *Iliad* and that it was not read in its entirety. The favor that the *Iliad* enjoyed is even indirectly shown by the parts of the *Odyssey* preferred by ancient readers. The overall figures from the papyri indicate that the two books of the *Odyssey* that were most read were 4 and 11, which both brought back key figures from the *Iliad*, whom Telemachus met during his voyage and Odysseus encountered in the Underworld. Readers of the War of Troy, who were eager to revisit its protagonists, did not care as much for the folktale travels of Odysseus. This can be interpreted in the light of the taste for sequels, the desire to read the end of a story, and the reluctance to forsake some beloved literary figures that also contributed to the strong favor enjoyed by the *Phoenissae* of Euripides.

The evidence of the school papyri and the papyri in general about the popularity of Homer in education finds confirmation in the indications offered by Homeric quotations in ancient writers. Studies of exact quotations and paraphrases of the Homeric text together with allusions to it found in writers as diverse as the second sophistic writers Dio of Prusa (first to second century), Maximus of Tyre, and Aelius Aristides (second century), Plutarch, and Lucian show a remarkable correspondence.[53] In very few instances, in fact—such as when the specifically philosophical

---

[50] *SB* III.6823.

[51] *Anth. Pal.* 9.165, 166, 168, 169, 173, and 174.

[52] See, e.g., Cribiore 1996a: no. 335, with *scholia minora* and summaries of the first three books. Only two texts, which contained Books 10 and 2, can be identified as being used in school; cf. above, Chapter 5, notes 43 and 52. To the exercises on the *Odyssey* cited in Cribiore 1997b: 58, one should add P^2 1210 (J. Schwartz, *BIFAO* 61 [1962]: 173–74), an ostracon with excerpts from Book 9.

[53] See Kindstrand 1973; Hembold and O'Neil 1959; Bouquiaux-Simon 1968; F. W. Householder, "Literary Quotation and Allusion in Lucian," diss., Columbia University, New York, 1941. In comparing these figures with the data emerging from the papyri, it is

concerns of Dio and Maximus made them read the *Odyssey* with particular care—were reading choices dictated by individual interests. In general,
the *Iliad* was preferred on a ratio of two to one and was read in its entirety.
Metrical quotations that refer to memorized passages encompass all of
the *Iliad*, but the first half was best known, as was the first half of each
book. Books 1 and 2 were by far the favorites, and quotations abound
particularly from the Catalogue of Ships. Books 5 and 6 were well known,
even though Dio quotes 6 less than the others writers, and books such as
14 or 19, which were disliked by the public in Egypt, found almost no
favor. Figures concerning the *Odyssey* deserve particular attention. This
epic was less known, and metrical quotations missed many books; more
important, however, the first books were not particularly cited. Book 2,
for instance, was the least known of all. The *Odyssey*, therefore, received
a different treatment in comparison with the *Iliad*. The writers cited above
must have known parts of it from anthologies or approached it through
selections done by teachers in their youth, as students undoubtedly did in
Egypt. Moreover, like readers in Egypt, they longed to meet again in the
Odyssey figures known from the *Iliad* and read Books 4 and 11 with
special attention. These correspondences between the choices of writers,
cultivated people, and students in Egypt are not due to chance. Education
must have played a fundamental part in exposing people to certain works
and generally shaping their tastes.

HESIOD, EURIPIDES, AND MENANDER

Hesiod must have been familiar to students: he was often quoted by Plutarch as an inspiring guide for young men.[54] Lucian mentions him as being
read in school together with Homer (*Menippus* 3) and as being closely
scrutinized and "picked utterly to pieces" by grammarians, exactly like
Homer (*Hesiodus* 5). This epic poet occupied a special place in the pantheon of Greek authors as the poet laureate whose utterances were di-
vinely inspired (*Hesiodus* 1). The large number of papyri that preserve
his work are an excellent index of a popularity that must have originated
in the schools, probably at high educational levels.[55] For some reason,
however, the text of Hesiod was rarely considered an appropriate copy-

---

essential to keep in mind the tastes of these writers, which were more refined than those of
educated people in general.

[54] Plutarch *Quomodo adul.* 22f, 23e and f, 34d and e, 24f, 28b, 34b, and 36a.

[55] Well over one hundred papyri are preserved. According to Libanius, "Homer, Hesiod,
and the other poets" were on the reading list of the educated person, *Ep.* 1036.4.

book.[56] Though advanced pupils must have approached his work through books that do not betray many indications of scholastic use,[57] in one case we are able to verify Hesiod's presence in the classroom through a school text.[58] Another sign of Hesiod's prominence in school is the frequent occurrence in lists of mythological and heroic genealogies drawn from his work that were used in fairly advanced education. The compiler of one of these, for instance, appears to have perused the *Theogony*, excerpting whole passages from it, as when he gave a list of the Nereids, of the rivers born from Tethys and Oceanus, and of the daughters of the couple.[59] Likewise, passages and entries from mythographic works written by students ultimately go back to Hesiod.[60]

Tragedy was an area in which ancient readers manifested strong preferences. The papyri generally show that members of the cultivated public were very fond of Euripides; they read Aeschylus rarely, and Sophocles even more infrequently. School papyri confirm this, showing an absolute preference for Euripides and only two excerpts dated to the Ptolemaic period from Aeschylus's tragedies.[61] The usual caveat applies, however: the two more demanding tragedians, and particularly Aeschylus, with his majestic and often obscure diction, may have sometimes been approached at a level of expertise where it is difficult to distinguish material read or written by students. Yet Euripides enjoyed such favor in school not only because he was linguistically more accessible but also because a good knowledge of his work—and particularly of his most rhetorical plays, *Phoenissae*, *Orestes*, *Hecuba*, *Medea*, and *Alcestis*—was fundamental for the student who continued to rhetorical education, as Quintilian and Libanius testify: a grammarian must have taken that into account.[62]

The tragedy of Euripides that was by far the favorite in and out of school was *Phoenissae*. Not only was this the text most represented among the literary papyri of Euripides, but it also enjoyed a very strong

[56] Cribiore 1996a: no. 386. No. 234 was part of an anthology and may have served the same purpose.

[57] But see, e.g., fragments from the *Catalogue* that might have been used in school: *P.Tebt.* II.271, III.690; *MPER* III.5 and 6.

[58] Cf. above, Chapter 5, note 49.

[59] Cribiore 1996a: no. 390, with, among others, names drawn from Hesiod *Theog.* 240–64, 337–63.

[60] See *P.Oxy.* LXI.4099, mythographic lists and sentences from the Seven Sages copied by a clumsy hand, Huys 1996.

[61] Cribiore 1996a: nos. 244 and 250. No. 219 is the only papyrus containing a line possibly from Sophocles.

[62] Quintilian 10.1.67–68. About Libanius, see Norman 1964: 163–64.

favor among the cultivated public in the Greek and Roman world, as quotations by ancient writers such as Plutarch, Lucian, and Athenaeus reveal.[63] The popularity of this drama, which does not particularly appeal to modern sensibility, is usually regarded with some puzzlement. This is not the place to examine in detail all the aspects of this question.[64] It suffices to say that the themes of *Phoenissae*, the treatment of the Oedipus legend, the abundant gnomic material,[65] and the opportunity to expand on the background of the myth and to compare treatments by other trage-dians must have been at the heart of the grammarian's choice. It was remarked above how ancient readers and students enjoyed sequels of tra-ditional stories and favored the books of the *Odyssey* that brought back key figures from the *Iliad*. This over-full play, in which one could enjoy Euripides the "pyrotechnician" at his best,[66] presented the panorama of the royal house of Thebes with all the characters of the original myth as well as new creations of the poet. Education appropriated this text at every level, from the time when it was used as a copybook to improve penmanship to the point when a student engaged in a composition exer-cise.[67] *Phoenissae* ended up permanently engraved upon the mind of a student, who continued to revisit it even when the school years were over.

In a papyrus from the third century C.E. that preserves a list of books that might represent the inventory of a private library or a record of books to be acquired, there is a note next to the names of Homer, Euripides, and Menander: "All that one can find."[68] The numerous witnesses of Me-nander preserved from Greco-Roman Egypt—well over a hundred—testify to a popularity that was due, among other things, to his representation

[63] See Bouquiaux-Simon and Mertens 1992; Bremer 1983; and Hembold and O'Neil 1959.

[64] See R. Cribiore, "The Grammarian's Choice: The Popularity of Euripides' *Phoenissae* in Hellenistic and Roman Education," in Yun Lee Too, ed., *Education in Greek and Roman Antiquity* (Leiden: Brill, forthcoming).

[65] The *gnomai* ("maxims") in this play underline themes of longing for one's fatherland, exile, power, and injustice. They are particularly numerous in the first part; in the rest of the drama, the action itself develops these themes with sufficient clarity.

[66] See A. J. Podlecki, "Some Themes in Euripides' *Phoenissae*," *TAPhA* 93 (1962): 356.

[67] Cribiore 1996a: no. 130: a student copies from a model line 3 of the play. *PSI* XIII.1303: the debate of Eteocles and Polyneices in front of their mother is chosen for an exercise of imitation, a much shorter reworking in iambic trimeters.

[68] M. Norsa, "Elenco di opere letterarie," *Aegyptus* 2 (1921): 17–20, ll. 28–30. About other library inventories, see P. J. Sijpesteijn and K. A. Worp, "Literary and Semi-Literary Papyri from the Vienna Papyrus Collection," *CE* 49 (1974): 324–31; *P.Vars.* inv. 5, G. Manteuffel, "De novo quodam librorum inventario," *Aegyptus* 13 (1933): 367–73; and *P.Turner* 9.

of actual life and to the fact that his language was relatively accessible.[69] The exercises show that maxims from his plays were very popular at all times: they were used for writing practice in elementary education and were still collected and memorized at higher levels because students needed to have them at their fingertips in rhetorical school, where they learned to develop themes.[70] In circulation, for the convenience of students, were books with collections of Menander's *gnomai* ("maxims") and similar maxims from Euripides and later writers.[71] In the grammarian's classroom, students like Apollonios copied excerpts from his comedies. A play that enjoyed popularity both among the general public and in schools was the *Misoumenos*: though an exercise presents the opening scene of this comedy,[72] more important is the testimony of a papyrus codex that preserves extensive parts of it.[73] This was either a textbook of cheap quality or the copy of an advanced student: its scholastic nature is confirmed by the presence of a table of fractions.

The need to copy whole plays in one's own hand was sometimes felt by advanced students as well as by scholars who could not always afford *éditions de luxe*. The *Bodmer* papyri exemplify this tendency: whole codices containing Christian works and Menander's comedies were copied, with mistakes and corruptions of every kind, by students—or perhaps sometimes by teachers—in fluent but somewhat unprofessional handwriting. These texts originated in a Christian school of advanced learning in Panopolis, where religious works were studied side by side with traditional authors.[74] That they did not belong to a monastic library is indicated by the discovery of an elementary rhetorical exercise in the *Codex of Visions*, an *ēthopoiia* ("exercise of impersonation") of Christian content.[75] Menander is represented by a triad—*Samia*, *Dyskolos*, and *Aspis*— a codex of sixty-four pages in all. This book was heavily used, as the subsequent attempts to rebind it show. It is intriguing to find that the author of a school list mentioned above that probably also originated in

[69] On the popularity of Menander, Blanchard 1997.

[70] See Barns 1951: 12–13. See also Y. Z. Tzifopoulos, "Proverbs in Menander's *Dyskolos*: The Rhetoric of Popular Wisdom," *Mnemosyne* 48 (1995): 169–77.

[71] See Hagedorn and Weber 1968; cf. above, Chapter 5, note 37.

[72] See Cribiore 1996a: no. 290, likely to be the fragment from a much longer piece.

[73] See *P.Oxy.* XXXIII.2656, third to fourth century C.E.

[74] See J. van Haelst, *P.Bodm.* XXXVIII, pp. 118–19. The hypothesis of a monastic library defended by J. M. Robinson (*The Pachomian Monastic Library at the Chester Beatty Library and the Bibliothèque Bodmer* [Claremont, 1990]) is much less likely. Cf. Blanchard 1991 and Fournet 1992.

[75] See Fournet 1992. On *ēthopoiiai*, cf. below, pp. 228–29.

Panopolis[76] drew heavily from this triad of Menander, utilizing notes taken during the reading.[77] Another list from the same period confirms that this triad was used in school contexts.[78]

MORE POETRY AND LITTLE PROSE

During the Byzantine period, Menander fell out of favor in schools, and consequently started to fade among the general public. Though his *sententiae* enjoyed continued popularity, he otherwise disappeared from the scholastic curricula. As a result, most of his plays do not survive. Byzantine schoolmasters considered Old Comedy, and Aristophanes in particular, linguistically more interesting.[79] Undoubtedly, however, this feature of Aristophanes' plays, compounded with the heavy references to figures and events of his own times, relegated Aristophanes to advanced education in the Greco-Roman period. Libanius, for instance, had a good acquaintance with the plays of Aristophanes that are extant, a fact that aroused the admiration of Eunapius.[80] The *Acharnians* was one of the plays that he read with his grammarian, Didymos, during those five years of grammatical instruction to which he returned before committing himself seriously to rhetorical education. Although no specific passages copied in school from Aristophanes can be identified, his presence in advanced education can be verified through some papyri that contain notes taken from elementary commentaries on his text.[81]

"I am selling Callimachus and Pindar, and all the cases of grammar," wrote the grammarian Palladas in distress, complaining that the profession of grammarian brought him only poverty (*Anth. Pal.* 9.175). Like Aristophanes, these authors must have been read at advanced levels, where it is harder to identify traces of educational activity. A good indication of the presence of both authors in school is the conspicuous number of papyri preserved with their texts: some of them must have passed

[76] Cribiore 1996a: no. 390; see above, note 59.

[77] See Blanchard 1991: the author of this list apparently also had access to another triad containing the *Epitrepontes*.

[78] Cribiore 1996a: no. 393.

[79] See Cavallo 1986: 119; Parsons 1982: 188; N. Wilson, *Scholars of Byzantium* (London, 1983), 20. Easterling (1995) attributes Menander's lack of popularity to changes in moral attitudes that rejected his views on virginity and chastity.

[80] E.g., *Or.* 2.48; Eunapius *VS* 16.2, 3; see Norman 1964: 159 and 165; Schouler 1984.

[81] These notes are fundamentally different from learned *scholia*, Zuntz 1975. Cf. above, Chapter 5, note 56.

through the hands of students.[82] Otherwise, the influence of Callimachus is directly attested by fragments of the *Hecale* that are preserved in a tablet, and his name and reference to the *Hymns* appear in two lists.[83] A knowledge of Pindar was an essential part of the cultural baggage of rhetors, as the works of Libanius testify.[84] His presence in secondary education is attested by the extensive annotations in a late copy of *Pythian* 1 that were written by a student or a teacher: the linguistic notations, the references to other authors popular in education, and the punctilious but irrelevant details point to the class of a grammarian.[85]

Very few clear traces survive of the use of other poets in education: a little Theognis, some Hipponax, an elegy of Sappho written from dictation with mistakes and omissions.[86] Since ancient philologists had started to pay attention to contemporary Alexandrian poets already in the Hellenistic period, education could not completely ignore them, as is shown by commentaries—on Aratus and Theocritus in particular—that presented their material in a simplified way for the use of students.[87] A knowledge of the Hellenistic epic poet Apollonius Rhodius is implied by the names taken from his work that appear in the elaborate list mentioned above, and an elegy of the third-century B.C.E. epigrammatic poet Posidippus was transcribed by a student with mistakes resulting from faulty memory.[88]

No prose was read in a grammarian's class except for fables and gnomic—that is, didactic and moralistic—works by Isocrates.[89] Like other texts that ancient education habitually revisited, fables, especially those of Aesop and Babrius, were approached at many different levels: they were copied as initial writing endeavors, served the grammarian as a training ground to instill some notions of grammar, and were the basis of the first *progymnasmata* (preliminary rhetorical exercises) in rhetorical school. From classical times, fables not only were deemed appropriate for early childhood but were ingrained in grammatical instruction: in a telling

[82] About seventy papyri of Callimachus and fifty of Pindar are preserved. Cf. Cameron 1995: 287.

[83] Cribiore 1996a: nos. 303, 379, and 590.

[84] See Schouler 1984: 505–9.

[85] Maehler 1993: 114–21; McNamee 1994.

[86] Cribiore 1996a: nos. 234, 235, 237, and 247. Theognis, an elegiac poet, and Hipponax, an iambic poet, both belonged to the sixth century B.C.E.

[87] See F. Montanari, "Filologi alessandrini e poeti alessandrini: La filologia sui 'contemporanei,' " *Aevum antiquum* 8 (1995): 47–63. Cf. above, Chapter 5, notes 56 and 57. Both Aratus and Theocritus lived in the third century B.C.E.

[88] Cribiore 1996a: nos. 381 and 590.

[89] On the study of prose in rhetorical schools, cf. below, Chapter 8.

scene in the *Phaedo*, Socrates, awaiting death, decides to put some fables of Aesop into verse, reverting to a stage of his cultural education—*mousikē*, that is, the study of literature—that he had failed to develop (60b–61b).[90] That versified animal fables were still enjoyed in Roman Egypt is shown by the dramatized story of the mouse and the weasel that appears in an exercise and in a schoolbook.[91]

The Cyprian Orations were the only works attributed to Isocrates read in the class of a grammarian. The popularity among the general public of these relatively undemanding orations, which consisted almost entirely of gnomic material, is shown by the fact that they make up about half of all the papyri of Isocrates. These orations were addressed to two young men, Demonikos and Nikokles, as models of style and good conduct: moral precepts were for the soul what physical exercises were for the development of the body (*Ad Demonicum* 12). The usual phenomenon of appropriation of the same author at subsequent educational levels also applied to Isocrates. While individual maxims served as exercises of penmanship in elementary education, and teachers copied short excerpts of these orations with words and syllables separated for students who were learning to read, some teachers' models presented longer excerpts in *scriptio continua* that addressed relatively advanced students.[92]

At a later stage of learning, entire orations were studied with the help of books written by professional scribes[93] or of copies made by advanced students themselves, as for Menander. Such is the recently published book of tablets that contains the three Isocratean orations, short *hypotheseis* ("summaries") of the *Ad Demonicum* and *Ad Nicoclem*, and elementary notes to the beginning of the former.[94] Written by three different hands with some lectional signs, frequent word separation, mistakes, and corrections, this book is certainly connected to teaching and learning, even though the circumstances of its preparation are not completely clear: did a teacher ask some advanced students to copy it as part of a school library, or does it consist of a series of exercises? At any rate, the quality, density,

---

[90] E. A. Havelock (*The Muse Learns to Write* [New Haven, Conn., 1986], 116) wrongly associates the scene, in my opinion, with reverting to an oral stage.

[91] Cf. above, p. 139n.

[92] See, e.g., Cribiore 1996a: nos. 204 and 298.

[93] See P[2] 1254; cf. above, Chapter 5, note 41. See also P. Schubert, "P.Bodmer LII: Isocrates, *A Nicoclès* 16–22," *MH* 54 (1997): 97–105 and bibliography in n. 17; and the fragments of a codex that was perhaps used in education: it contains words from *Ad Demonicum* and *Ad Nicoclem* translated into Latin, A. Rijksbaron and K. A. Worp, "Isocrates Bilinguis Berolinensis," *Mnemosyne* 51, 6 (1998): 718–22.

[94] *P.Kell.* III Gr. 95, Worp and Rijksbaron 1997.

and arrangement of the lexical notes that are squeezed into the margins point to a product of the grammarian's schoolroom.[95] The popularity of Isocrates continued in rhetorical schools, where, at least judging from Libanius, he was again mostly appreciated through these gnomic works.[96]

A STRICT CURRICULUM?

Since knowledge not only of mechanical skills but also of the elements of literary culture was governed by order, some sort of a curriculum existed whose outlines emerge for primary and early grammatical education but become blurred for a later stage, primarily because advanced students read the same texts as adult readers and their school exercises are difficult to identify. Of course, such a curriculum often existed as an ideal, because only a strict minority of those who learned the fundamentals had access to the secondary and tertiary levels. But for the privileged male students destined by birth and wealth to run the whole course, the path was mostly charted, with more arduous exercises performed on texts already read at the primary level and with the gradual introduction of new writers. All the authors mentioned above were included in the grammarian's syllabus. Since the general papyri also preserve numerous copies of other poets, such as the archaic poets Alcaeus and Archilochus, it is conceivable that occasionally they were studied in advanced stages of education, and that grammarians sometimes guided students through the meanders of a difficult text outside the mainstream. But as a rule, the grammarian had to provide his students with some basic knowledge of the literature that formed the foundation of rhetorical instruction, so that the core of grammatical teaching rested solidly on a relatively small selection of authors. Most of the time their work was not perused in its entirety: a grammarian guided his students through part of the text and then—in theory—let them proceed by themselves. Homer, in this respect, represented a special case, since it is likely that students read at least the whole of the *Iliad* in the course of their school careers.[97] The school papyri do not entitle us to conclude that education—beyond initial phases—consisted of jumping

[95] See K. McNamee, "Notes in the New Isocrates," *XXII Congresso Internazionale di Papirologia* (Florence, forthcoming).

[96] See Schouler 1984: 540–42.

[97] Educated individuals such as Plutarch and Libanius had at their fingertips all of the *Iliad* and the *Odyssey*; see Carrara 1988: 450–51; Norman 1964: 161.

from one brief excerpt of the *Iliad* to another.[98] Further, papyrus texts containing condensed versions of literary material were not designed to make the reading of literature superfluous but were intended as introductory or auxiliary accompaniments to the reading of the original text itself.[99]

In order to properly understand the nature of the ancient curriculum, it is essential to recognize two fundamental patterns of education in antiquity. First, students had to revisit an author at subsequent levels. As a result, they approached Homer, for example, many times throughout their educational careers, from the time when they copied one verse to improve penmanship to the analysis done under the tutelage of a grammarian, and then to the work of paraphrasing and composing in a school of rhetoric. Second, even though knowledge in antiquity was governed by order, different types of ordering principles could come into play. Elements of literature were not always introduced according to suitability to age and level of competence, that is, from the most to the least accessible. Students with embryonic reading skills had to read Homer, whose dialect, lexicon, and phraseology were so challenging. But in ranking authors, diverse criteria, such as tradition and power to confer "Greekness" on the reader, were observed. With incessant mental gymnastics, in the class of the grammarian, a student learned to take apart works of literature by distilling their characteristics with relentless attention to detail, without being instructed how to reassemble these texts. The analytical exercises that he practiced, in fact, were geared not so much toward achieving an appreciation of the beauty of an author's work but toward an elucidation of all its features.

TOOLS OF LITERARY ANALYSIS

Two works both attributed to Plutarch allow us to see a grammarian in action. In the essay *How Young Men Should Study Poetry*, Plutarch concentrated on the tradition inaugurated by Plato of verifying the moral content of a literary work. The fact that he seems to move from shorter quotations of gnomic character to longer excerpts of poetry, when he somewhat pedantically examines expressions and concepts from works of literature,[100] reveals that he is acting as a grammarian well aware of

---

[98] So Morgan 1998: 105–10.

[99] Cf. the conclusions of van Rossum-Steenbeek 1998: 157–63.

[100] See D. M. Schenkeveld, "The Structure of Plutarch's *De audiendis poetis*," *Mnemosyne* 35 (1982): 60–71.

effective methods and progression in study rather than solely as a parent concerned with what his children are reading. Even more exemplary of the many layers of a grammarian's instruction is the work *De Homero*, which is actually later than Plutarch and was composed by a grammarian at the end of the second century or sometime in the third.[101] The author of the *De Homero* often betrays himself as a dry, albeit knowledgeable, grammarian. His pedagogical tone and aims are particularly evident in the first part of the work, where he lingers on mythological aspects, meter, and diction. An interest in texts of this kind existed in Roman Egypt, as a papyrus that contains fragments of a work very similar to this one shows.[102]

The "historical" side of the activity of a grammarian consisted of extracting from a text all of its constitutive elements, dealing not only with *realia* of persons and historical, geographical, and mythological components but also with glosses, figures, and tropes. When in his definition, Dionysius said that *grammatikē* covered the explanation of the *poiētikoi tropoi* contained in a text, his words referred to "poetic modes of expression" rather than specifically to "poetic tropes," and included at least figures of speech.[103] The term "poetic" related not only to the works of the poets as being the main object of grammatical inquiry but also to poetic diction as being uncommon and different from normal usage. At the beginning of the Hellenistic period, the grammarian had at his disposal a wealth of grammatical tools.[104] The theories of figures and tropes originated in the Hellenistic period, but the loss of many grammatical and rhetorical manuals hinders an inquiry in this direction, even though Roman literary sources, and Quintilian in particular (8.6.1–3 and 9.1.1–9), elucidated them.[105] It is in those *scholia* to an author taken from learned commentaries that one finds a wealth of observations concerning figures and tropes interspersed with exegesis: these are tangible traces of a literary activity that belonged to both grammatical and rhetorical inquiry, to exegesis done by philologists and by grammarians.

[101] J. F. Kindstrand, ed., *[Plutarchus] De Homero* (Leipzig, 1990); J. J. Keaney and R. Lamberton, *[Plutarch] Essay on the Life and Poetry of Homer* (Atlanta, 1996).

[102] *P.Lond.* III.734 verso.

[103] Generally tropes regard transference of meaning of words, such as metaphor, whereas figures are connected with specific collocation of words; see B. Vickers, *In Defence of Rhetoric* (Oxford, 1988), 294–339.

[104] Cf. Plato *Cra.*; Aristotle *Poet.* 1457b1 and *Rh.* ch. 5; Theophrastus, fr. vic Mayer; see Schenkeveld 1991: 151–52.

[105] For a detailed examination, see Bonner 1977: 229–37.

Another aspect of a grammarian's teaching concerned the elucidation of unfamiliar vocabulary. Systematic glossographical analysis, which started in the Roman period, survives particularly for Homeric epic. *Scholia minora* to Homer are preserved in about a hundred papyri, some of which undoubtedly originated in the schoolroom.[106] They can be considered the most elementary form of commentary and need to be distinguished from the erudite *scholia vetera* that accompany the text of Homer in various manuscripts. Whereas the latter are a compilation of exegetical material taken from scholars of the Library of Alexandria, the former are much more modest in scope: they consist of lists of Homeric *lemmata*— single words or short expressions—taken from the text, which are "translated" into an easier form of Greek that corresponded to current usage.[107] The technique of *metalepsis*, that is, the "translation" of a word to a synonym, also belonged to the range of scholarly activity of Greek grammarians who wanted to establish the semantic content of a word and had to work from Greek to Greek, being unable to use Greek to clarify Latin, as Roman grammarians did:[108] traces of this activity are found everywhere in the *scholia vetera*.[109] But this type of Homeric exegesis was particularly necessary in the schoolroom, where the need to understand the text was felt at many levels. Even though some of the glossographical material had an ancient and scholarly origin, the variety shown by the texts of *scholia minora* reveals that teachers felt free to modify, adapt, and innovate. This kind of elementary exegesis was traditionally an integral part of teaching. Whereas at an elementary stage of education, scholastic competence was proved by reciting a few verses or a maxim to one's parents,[110] at this educational level glosses acquired some sort of status symbol.

The elementary glossographical material of *scholia minora* converged in the Byzantine period into the so-called *D-scholia*, a compilation that mainly included paraphrastic and mythographical material, summaries of Homeric books, and inquiries about certain problems (*zētēmata*). The *Dscholia* allow us to perceive what was the whole range of a grammarian's activity even before Byzantine times. Mythographical notes corresponding to *lemmata* from the Homeric text are also found in papyri from the

---

[106] See Raffaelli 1984; Cribiore 1996a: 50–51 and 253–58.

[107] The same glossographical material is also found in the Homeric lexicon of Apollonius Sophista; see M. Haslam, "A New Papyrus Text of Apollonius Sophista," *ZPE* 49 (1982): 31–38.

[108] On *metalepsis* in Apollonius Dyscolus, see Sluiter 1990: 111–17.

[109] See, e.g., *scholia* A 173–75 and 200; cf. Schenkeveld 1993: 273–74.

[110] Cf. Aristophanes *Banqueters* (233 *PCG*).

first to the fifth century C.E.[111] These notes derived from an ancient learned commentary on mythological subjects that circulated independently in both scholarly and scholastic circles and was adapted to the circumstances, as copyists and teachers felt free to modify its content. Mythographical material also circulated through mythological handbooks. Three mythographers are mentioned by the compiler of a school list who must have drawn some of his entries from the *Bibliotheca* attributed to Apollodorus (first to second century C.E.), which presented summaries of Greek myths and heroic deeds.[112] Ancient readers in general had some interest in mythology, which charmed not only children and illiterate people but also the man with an average education, whom Strabo calls *ho pepaideumenos metriōs* ("the man educated moderately well," 1.2.8). After first encountering mythology with the elementary teacher, a student pursued deeper knowledge in this area through mythographical texts, as is shown, for instance, by a papyrus where a student combined catalogue material with the popular maxims of the Seven Sages.[113]

Besides expanding on mythological matters, "historical notes" (*historiai*) provided explanatory details on persons, places, and events mentioned in a text. Since this was apparently an area in which grammarians roamed freely, their students ran the risk of falling into a bottomless pit of minutiae. Both Quintilian (1.8.18) and Sextus Empiricus manifested concern over this: the latter reported on the stupidity of some of the stories that circulated in a grammarian's class, such as that about Plato wearing an earring in his youth (1.145–47, 149–51, and 257–62). A reflection of the grammarian's practice of pointing out historical and geographical details during class can be seen in some school lists.[114] The knowledge that a student acquired through his teacher's explanations was verified by

---

[111] See Cribiore 1996a: no. 183, for an example of a text that originated in the schoolroom. On this material, usually called *Mythographus Homericus*, see F. Montanari, "The *Mythographus Homericus*," in J.G.J. Abbenes, S. R. Slings, and I. Sluiter, eds., *Greek Literary Theory after Aristotle* (Amsterdam, 1995), 135–72.

[112] Cribiore 1996a: no. 390.

[113] *P.Oxy.* LXI.4099, first century B.C.E. to first century C.E. See Huys 1996. See also *P.Oxy.* LXV.4460, with names of heroes from the *Iliad* and gods with their genealogy.

[114] B. Legras, "L' horizon géographique de la jeunesse grecque d' Égypte," *Proceedings of the Twentieth International Congress of Papyrologists* (Copenhagen, 1994), 165–76, and "L' enseignement de l' histoire dans les écoles grecques d' Égypte (IIIème siècle av. n.è.– VIème siècle de n.è.)" *Akten des XXI* Internationalen *Papyrologenkongresses* (Stuttgart and Leipzig, 1997), 586–600; see also *O.Claud.* II.415 (cf. above, p. 136), a list with rare epic and lyric words, names of fish of the Red Sea, and geographical terms.

queries posed during class: Who was the father of Hector? Who were his brothers? School exercises in question-and-answer form allow us to recover the oral content and flavor of teaching. *Erōtēmata* ("questions"), which often occur in grammatical texts of late antiquity and the Middle Ages and are therefore considered a late development,[115] derived from pedagogical methods that were always employed in ancient classrooms. The school exercises show that they systematized gnomic and "historical" knowledge, besides being used to categorize grammatical points.[116] Their pedagogical effectiveness is measured by the fact that they still functioned at higher levels of education, as two papyri with remnants of rhetorical catechisms show: one presents questions and answers probably written by a student, the other is a book of higher level with the same structure.[117] Ancient literary sources, such as the second-century historian Arrian (*Epict. diss.* 2.19.6–7) and Lucian (*Amores* 45), testify to the popularity of this procedure, which came to embody the pedantic nature of a grammarian's methods. A graffito from Cyrene—"Question: Who was the father of Priam's children?"—bears witness that the ancients themselves looked on this method with amusement.[118]

The "discovery of etymologies" represented a further facet of a grammarian's activity in which he could display the effectiveness of his tools. A grammarian was a master at playing this game, which was centered on the meaning and origin of a word: nothing seems to have been prohibited as long as one reached the desired explanation. Though implicit etymologies could be found in the Greek poets, there was a long tradition of explicit etymologies exemplified by Plato's *Cratylus*. A student was guided through the meandering rules of the game: letters could be changed, omitted, added, or interchanged in order to reach the desired meaning.[119] Though some etymologies reached by these methods were humorous, this aspect was probably untouched by the solemn grammarian: an etymology attempted to discover the "truthful" nature of a word,

[115] See A. Pertusi, "Ερωτήματα: Per la storia e le fonti delle prime grammatiche greche a stampa," *Italia medioevale e umanistica* 5 (1962): 321–51.

[116] Cribiore 1996a: 53–54; see also *PSI* inv. 505 (below, p. 212), *P.Lond.Lit.* 182, a grammatical textbook (above, Chapter 5, note 46), and *P.Oxy.* LVI.3829, with a catechism on characters of the *Iliad*.

[117] *PSI* I.85; and H. Oellacher, "Ein rhetorischer Katechism in einem Wiener Papyrus," *WS* 55 (1937): 68–78.

[118] See R. A. Kaster, "A Schoolboy's Burlesque from Cyrene?" *Mnemosyne* 37 (1984): 457–58.

[119] See Sluiter 1990: 12–13.

and it needed to be taken seriously. A discovery of etymologies, which would normally accompany the perusal of a text, might also be done in the course of systematic "technical" grammatical inquiries in which grammarians expounded their linguistic knowledge.[120]

THE TECHNICAL ASPECT OF *GRAMMATIKĒ*

Sometime in the course of the first century c.e., grammatical theory became a fixed part of the school curriculum. A limited systematization of grammatical tools already existed in the work of the Alexandrian scholars, where it served their philological pursuits, and it is conceivable that some aspects of embryonic normative grammar were already part of school practice in Hellenistic times. Only later, however, did grammar arrive at a distinct methodology and a systematic articulation of a definite body of knowledge.[121] Moreover, until the beginning of the Roman period, the need to reflect on and classify grammatical terms and forms was not felt so acutely. Even the systematic practice of declension and conjugation, which we see in the schoolrooms of Roman Egypt and which appears in the scholarly works of grammarians after the fourth century, was apparently unknown in Hellenistic schools. It is also not a coincidence that the first texts containing elementary explanations of the text of literary authors, such as *scholia minora* to Homer, appeared in Roman times. As time went by, the distant heirs of the Macedonian and Greek conquerors felt a more urgent need for explanatory tools, not only to master a language whose acquisition became increasingly less automatic and spontaneous—and particularly Attic Greek—but primarily to understand poetic texts on a deeper level.[122] The linguistic platform of the pupil of the grammarian in Egypt—and in the Greek East as well—was stratified into three layers. Students functioned partly in the local language— Egyptian, in this case—which they approached only in the oral register. They used in ordinary life the common form of Greek called *koinē* for both speaking and writing. In school, however, they were exposed to a purer form of Greek, Attic, which became the vehicle for writings that

---

[120] See, e.g., Cribiore 1996a: no. 362, a *technē grammatikē* with etymologies of the words *grammata* ("letters") and *stoicheion* ("letter").

[121] The absence of grammatical exercises and texts in Hellenistic times is highly significant and cannot be explained, in my opinion, solely on the basis of the limited number of literary and semi-literary papyri preserved from this period. Contra Wouters 1999: 68.

[122] Contra Morgan 1998: 152–89.

were based on literature. It was the ever more complex interaction among these three linguistic layers over the centuries that dictated the need for linguistic organizational tools.

The influence of spoken Egyptian became increasingly perceptible: it is visible in the nonstandard spelling of words according to their phonetic pronunciation that appears in exercises by both students and teachers, primarily at the elementary but occasionally also at the secondary level. With respect to Greek, as Dionysius's definition makes clear, *hellē-nismos*—linguistic correctness—was mainly based on *analogia*, that is, the inherent principle and regularity that governed a language. Grammarians turned entirely away from the ordinary usage of the illiterate majority and did not think it worth their effort to investigate everyday language and its speakers' cognition.[123] But another aspect of *hellēnismos* was based on the recognition of the value of common usage (*synētheia*) that constituted the language of the educated.[124] Thus the glosses that "translated" unfamiliar terms in the poets consisted of more accessible words taken from the *koinē*, good and approved usage. The same attention to common usage is also shown, as we shall see, by the choice of the verbs selected for exercises of conjugation. The primary focus of grammarians' investigations, at any rate, was the literary sources. The application of the method of analogy served originally to explain the correct forms of words in the literary texts; only later was it extended to a verification of the correctness of forms in common usage. In the grammatical treatises—*technai*—the constant connection with poetic usages is evident in the occurrence of examples taken from Homer and other poets. In general, these consist of individual words or expressions, but occasionally whole literary passages are excerpted.[125]

To return to Dionysius, the question of the authenticity of the body of his *technē* as it was preserved cannot be separated from the question of its authority. Whatever one believes was originally the content of his treatise, it became an authoritative text in its actual form only around the fifth century. Up to the fourth century, the grammatical papyri that preserve parts of handbooks, some of which were definitely used in education,[126] differ from his *technē* in treating the parts of speech and show that

---

[123] See C. Atherton, "What Every Grammarian Knows?" *CQ* 46 (1996): 239–60.

[124] See Sextus *Math*. 1.176–240.

[125] See Cribiore 1996a: no. 368, ll. 10–12, and no. 362, ll. 52–66. See also *P.Lond.Lit.* 182.

[126] See Cribiore 1996a: nos. 358, 359, 362, 368, 369, 370, 371, and 373, written by students or teachers. As an example of textbook, see *P.Harr.* I.59, a small codex from the second century.

Dionysius's work became the standard text afterward. These *technai* are centered on phonological and morphological analysis of the word forms, with the parts of speech being the kernel around which grammatical theory was formed. Syntax was not covered systematically,[127] even though the grammarian Palladas complained bitterly that "syntax had been the end of me" (*Anth. Pal.* 9.171 and 175). It is likely that at least a smattering of it was given in the course of study of the parts of speech.

Since no standard manual existed in the Roman period, and grammarians could not take advantage of organized training,[128] the treatises that they composed do not show uniformity: grammarians had to rely on their personal knowledge of the literary sources, the intuitive grammatical skills developed in the course of the study, and their acquaintance with the work of their predecessors. In some of these treatises, connection with classroom practice and regard for its exigencies are evident: concessions to school practice and methods show that these *technai* handled didactic material used in linguistic training. One of these manuals from the first century provides a ready example.[129] This papyrus preserves a fragment from a *technē* used in school, which the irregular margins and the informal handwriting show to be a somewhat cheap copy: genders, numbers, and types of nouns are enumerated and defined, in more detail than in the grammar of Dionysius. In some respects, the arrangement shown in this treatise bears similarities to that of the later grammarian Apollonius Dyscolus, except for the fact that the nouns are unusually defined by their article, a concession to students' needs. The question-and-answer format is followed throughout the text: "What is a masculine noun? It is a noun before which in the nominative singular case the article *ho* is placed." And further on: "How many numbers [of nouns] are there? . . . What is a singular, a dual, and a plural?" An interesting feature of this handbook is the declension of proper nouns that brings out examples such as "Homer, the two Homers, and the Homers," in spite of their obvious absurdity. Though the declension of names was a traditional feature of ancient grammars,[130] it is tempting to associate it not only with the ex-

---

[127] See, however, *P.Lond.Lit.* 182, the so-called *technē* of Tryphon, which contains a kind of elementary syntactic doctrine; cf. Wouters 1979: 40, and above, Chapter 5, note 46. See also some exercises that incorporated some syntax, Cribiore 1996a: nos. 364 and 385.

[128] See Kaster 1988: 35 and 205.

[129] PSI inv. 505, V. Di Benedetto, "Frammento grammaticale," *AnnPisa*, ser. 2, 26 (1957): 180–85.

[130] De Martino and Vox 1996, 2: 616–19.

treme reliance on analogy but also with that enduring tendency of teachers to rely on vivid examples that readily come to mind.[131]

Other features that characterize handbooks evidently written for school use are unusual beginnings that covered points of immediate need,[132] confused enumeration of parts with omissions and repetitions, pragmatic definitions,[133] and insistence on devices geared to facilitate memorization of the content. Such devices are already evident in Dionysius's definition of *grammatikē*, with its enumeration of the number of parts.[134] The importance of order for retention was stressed by Aristotle (*Mem.* 452a) and Quintilian (11.2.36–39). Grammar relied on definitions, divisions, and a comprehensive hierarchical structure to facilitate memorization.[135] The logical organization of the material was already derived from the internal structure of the subject itself as perceived by the grammarian, but when some elements refused to be neatly categorized, ordering devices, by numerical or alphabetic sequence, were introduced. Memorization of definitions and of parts of grammar, which was helped by a question-and-answer format that facilitated recitation, was only an aspect of the process of retention of material that accompanied a student throughout education. The literary sources mention without a hint of surprise feats of memory such as being able to recite the whole of the *Iliad* and the *Odyssey*.[136] As when memorizing grammatical material, this process still involved verbatim memory, a "memory of words" (*memoria verborum*) as distinguished from the "memory of things" (*memoria rerum*), which attained much importance in rhetorical education. Some school exercises show the large part that memory occupied at the grammatical stage: not only do typical mistakes of omission of verses and faulty insertion of lines from different parts of the text show that certain passages were written from memory, but students sometimes produced mnemonic aids, such as writing the first half of the verses of a passage or the beginning of the various sections of the Catalogue of Ships in *Iliad* 2.[137]

---

[131] Cf. the examples used by Apollonius in his *Syntax*; see above, p. 69. A boy, Dionysios, is often the protagonist: it is conceivable that his name echoed that of the famous grammarian. Sometimes he appears in the sentences together with other boys, significantly named Theon, Aristarchos, and Tryphon. See, e.g., *Syntax* 2.141: Dionysios hit Theon.

[132] See above, p. 191.

[133] See Cribiore 1996a: 368.

[134] On the structure of this *technē*, see M. Fuhrmann, *Das systematische Lehrbuch* (Göttingen, 1960), 29–34.

[135] See Law 1996.

[136] Xenophon *Symp*. 3.5: a father compelling his son to memorize all of Homer.

[137] Cribiore 1996a: nos. 382, 291, 193, and 201.

Morphological tables of declension and conjugation, which appear among the exercises in the first to second century, apparently became part of scholarly works only much later. The Alexandrian scholars, who had some knowledge of flexion, could not avail themselves of complete rules for nominal and verbal inflection.[138] At the end of the fourth century, the well-known grammarian Theodosius composed the *Canons*, a collection of rules for the declension of nouns and conjugation of verbs that served as a model for the tables of conjugation that were added as a supplement to Dionysius's grammar.[139] The fact that no examples of tables of flexion besides those included in the school exercises were preserved before the fourth century appears to be an indication that such tables were created by grammarians for didactic purposes and later became part of works such as the *technē* of Dionysius. Tables of flexion were organizational tools that gave students the means—or the illusion—of mastering forms found in the literary sources, such as the dual or the optative, that had become obsolete.

But the choice of the verbs that appear in students' exercises and in teachers' models is indicative of the fact that in some respects, tables also served concrete linguistic needs. It is important to remember that in any time period, teachers had to make some concessions to practical exigencies at the expense of theory. Though the first aim of grammar was a better comprehension of literary language, the grammarian could not entirely ignore practices linked to everyday linguistic usage. Some of the verbs used in exercises, such as *didaskein, graphein,* and *typtein*—"to teach," "to write," and "to thrash"—seem to allude to school practice. More important, the tables' insistence on contract verbs and their complete avoidance of athematic verbs indicate that they responded to the daily linguistic practice of students. The conjugation of contract verbs presented special difficulties for people in Greco-Roman Egypt, as the frequency of mistakes in documentary papyri shows,[140] and athematic verbs, which were abundantly present in the literary sources, had started to disappear in common practice.[141] Reinforcement of the linguistic practice of the *koinē* indicates that these tables were used not only to understand forms in literary works, but also to nourish and strengthen correct daily usage of Greek. It should be noted that the *Canons* of Theodosius,

---

[138] See Schenkeveld 1993: 285. On the state of the question, A. Wouters, *The Chester Beatty Codex AC 1499* (Leuven, 1988), 78–79 n. 63.

[139] *Grammatici Graeci* 1.1, pp. 1–101. Cf. above, p. 69.

[140] Cf. Mandilaras 1973: 61–67.

[141] See ibid.: 61–67; 51; and 71–72.

which were not strongly tied to school practice, included an athematic verb—*tithemi*, "put"—that was disregarded in the supplement to the *technē* of Dionysius, which was strongly connected to teaching.

The trend of ancient teachers to rely on analogy already found applications at an elementary stage, but it is particularly noticeable at the grammatical level. In many respects—despite the few concessions to practical needs—a student lived in an artificial literary world where the protagonists uttered unfamiliar expressions and where language was tinged with the colors of the past. Playing the game properly meant practicing with archaizing formations in endless and bizarre morphological gymnastics. Thus, not only did exercises include unusual tenses and forms that were rare in the texts of the authors and that had practically disappeared from correct common usage, but they also called for practice with nonexistent forms, purely artificial constructions such as future imperatives, born out of artificially logical thinking.[142] In his niche of expertise, the grammarian was king, and he dictated the rules of the game. Through encyclopedic knowledge, mnemonic retention of the literary sources, close attention to detail, and the ability to manipulate morphological forms, his students developed a myopic ability to dismember a text into its components, whereas a vision and appreciation of the whole mostly escaped them.

PRACTICING EPISTOLARY SKILLS

The treatment of education at the hand of the grammarian has so far followed the definition of *grammatikē* of Dionysius Thrax. It is also worthwhile, however, to discuss an aspect of the training that is not mentioned by Dionysius: writing as composing, particularly letter writing. Ancient authors' accounts of secondary education seem to suggest that a student dedicated much more energy to enlarging his knowledge of literature than to writing. Though it is not entirely clear to what extent the principles of expository writing were enforced at this level, under a grammarian's tutelage students began drafting simple and short texts, such as elementary summaries and paraphrases of what they had read.[143] Composing on personal themes was not part of the practice; such writing as there was had a strong literary base and constantly had to be fueled by literature. But one type of writing that allowed a bit more freedom and

---

[142] See Cribiore 1996a: nos. 361, 364, and 372.

[143] See, e.g., Cribiore 1996a: nos. 346, 351, and 352.

that students might have learned with the grammarian and perfected with the rhetor was epistolary writing.

The practice of epistolary skills in education has not been investigated extensively. Letter-writing was part of the training in professional schools such as chancery and business schools. Handbooks of model letters existed, and collections by Ps.-Demetrius and Ps.-Libanius discussed the proper style in which epistles should be written.[144] Another collection of epistolary *typoi*, *P.Bon.* 5, was found in Egypt: it shows less interest in theory and offers more detailed and specific examples than the literary manuals. Moreover, a papyrus that the student Apollonios and his brother might have consulted refers to a similar scenario of professional education.[145] In rhetorical schools, letter-writing seems to have remained on the fringe of formal instruction.[146] Only the grammarian Theon of Alexandria in the first century c.e. and the sophist Nicolaus in the fifth century c.e. allude to the practice of writing epistles in connection with the preliminary exercise of *ēthopoiia*.[147] Nor are the literary sources very clear on this subject. The Roman Pliny the Younger merely comments on the benefits that a knowledge of letter-writing would bring to one's professional life (*Ep.* 9.9). Libanius is more helpful, but he does not disclose the precise role that letter-writing had in the school curriculum. In a letter, he reproaches an ex-student for not writing to him in spite of the fact that the student knows well the epistolary art (*technē*, *Ep.* 777.6). He also addresses two letters to another ex-student on this subject. In one, he exhorts the young man to keep on writing not only to his parents but also to his old teacher in order to strengthen a style of communication that he would need to use in his future career (*Ep.* 300.4); in the other, he manifests his satisfaction because Honoratus has finally learned to write elegant letters after many exhortations (*Ep.* 310).

At a much lower level, the marked formulaic quality and conventionality of letters from Greco-Roman Egypt raises a question: did people simply express themselves through clichés, or did they practice letter-writing

---

[144] The first collection, by Ps.-Demetrius, should be dated between 200 B.C.E. and C.E. 300; the second, by Ps.-Libanius, between the fourth and sixth centuries C.E. See Valentin Weichert, ed., *Demetrii et Libanii qui feruntur* ΤΥΠΟΙ ΕΠΙΣΤΟΛΙΚΟΙ et ΕΠΙΣΤΟΛΙΜΑΙΟΙ ΧΑΡΑΚΤΗΡΕΣ (Leipzig, 1910); Libanius *Epistolary Styles* (Foerster, vol. 9).

[145] See above, note 22. On models and exercises in professional schools, cf. also *Pap.Flor.* XXIII.2, *MPER N.S.* XV.109–13, and *SB* IV.7433.

[146] Kennedy 1983: 70.

[147] See Theon 115 Patillon; and Nicolaus 67.2–5 Felten.

in school?[148] Greek elementary education was rarely concerned with using letters as copybooks, whereas requiring beginners to copy parts of letters was a frequent practice in schools that taught Coptic.[149] But letter-writing might have belonged to the periphery of instruction at the level of grammatical education. Correspondence went back and forth between students who lived away from home and their families: it shortened distances and alleviated anxiety.[150] The *Philogelos*, a collection of ancient anecdotes that survives in a number of manuscripts, includes two jokes that portray students away at school who write letters to their fathers.[151] In anecdote 54, a young man who studies rhetoric in Athens and writes to his father showing off his good progress adds the following postscript of dubious taste: "I hope that when I come home I shall find you on trial for your life, so that I can show you how great an advocate I am." In joke 55, a student short of money sells his books and then asks for his father's approval in a letter, saying: "Congratulate me, father, I am already making money from my studies."[152] But in spite of the mocking and disrespectful attitude of these two students, education was a serious affair. Parents needed to be reassured that their money was well spent. One wonders whether the practice of writing home was completely spontaneous or whether teachers encouraged and "inspired" their pupils to perfect epistolary conventions in letters to their families, as Libanius had done, thereby displaying newly acquired writing skills.

This, in fact, seems to be the background of at least two epistles sent by students in Roman Egypt. When the student Thonis writes to his father asking him repeatedly to come to visit, the presence of the teacher, who insisted on meeting him to show that he had adequate qualifications and to settle a price, is felt all over the letter.[153] The teacher's urging must have prompted Thonis to write home: a letter was the most palpable demonstration that the boy was actually learning something. Another letter of

---

[148] Schubart 1918: 211 and 397; Parsons 1980–81: 7–8.

[149] Cribiore 1996a: no. 147 is the only Greek example. On Coptic exercises, see Hasitzka 1990: e.g., nos. 120, 124, 128, and 134; nos. 181 and 183 are teachers' models.

[150] Cf. Chapter 4.

[151] For jokes about absent-minded elementary teachers and grammarians and about school life, see Thierfelder 1968: nos. 61, 77, 136, 140, 197, and 220. Students are usually called *scholastichoi*, a word that sometimes refers to educated individuals.

[152] This seems an appropriate answer to the exhortation of Cornelius to his son in a letter quoted above, p. 115. Cf. Petronius *Satyricon* 46.7–8. See A. Lukaszewicz, "ΟΝΗΣΙΣ ΑΠΟ ΒΙΒΛΙΩΝ," *JJP* 24 (1994): 97–103.

[153] See above, p. 112.

higher quality whose aim was to fill a father with pride and to give him proof of the validity of his investment in education is *P.Ryl.* IV.624. In writing to their father, Hephaistion and Horigenes express with choice words their gratitude to him for taking them to Alexandria. They remained in the city after their father left, and they realized that they had an enviable position and enjoyed an excellent reputation because of him. "For this we consider to be a duty that comes first and excels all others— they say—since we are taught by the law of nature to watch over and care for no one so much as a good father." These two young men, who had practiced on the theme of love and gratitude toward one's father from their most tender years, had learned to combine refined words and concepts and to employ correct punctuation and lectional signs. Their letter is unusually replete with accents, breathings, and marks of punctuation— reminders that their teacher was earning his money.

The rest of the papyrus letters sent home by students do not show with the same clarity the guiding hand of a teacher. Even though they are family letters full of concrete details and requests, it is not inconceivable that some of them should be considered school exercises and real epistles at the same time. In this respect, a letter of a father to his son's instructor is revealing and may provide the missing link, by showing that teachers were involved with students' correspondence, and that letters were tangible proof that education was working well. We have already met Anastasios, a "difficult" boy: in this letter, his father announces his decision to withdraw him from school:[154]

> You have written to me about young Anastasios, and since I owe you money, be sure you will be paid in full. Nothing of what has been told you is true, except that he is stupid and a child and foolish. He wrote me a letter himself quite in keeping with his appearance and his empty wits. And since he is a child and stupid, I will bring him home. I am keeping his letter to show you when I come.

The infuriated father of Anastasios reveals that he had received a letter from his son that was such a masterpiece of stupidity that he decided to keep it. Even though we may surmise that this letter might not have been much worse than many others that the sands of Egypt preserved,[155] never-

---

[154] *SB* V.7655; see above, p. 70.

[155] See, e.g., *P.Oxy.* I.119, the nagging letter of the boy Theon, who asked his father to take him to Alexandria and to buy him a lyre. Written in the boy's own hand, it shows evident problems with grammar and spelling but also demonstrates that Theon had learned epistolary formulas and clichés.

theless its poor quality was the proof in a father's eyes that education had failed: showing it to the teacher was a gesture of veiled reproach.

In the class of the grammarian, the rigidity of programs and methods did not allow much breathing space. There was no room for imagination and originality, except perhaps in writing personal letters. But as always, students learned to survive. A peculiar papyrus with a literary flavor that is indeed a letter, framed by a conventional opening, closing, and address, may provide an example of an escape from an asphyxiating education. Titled "Indecent Proposal" by its editor, *P.Oxy.* XLII.3070 has a far-from-conventional content and shows a drawing that makes the proposition even more explicit.

> Apion and Epimas proclaim to their best-beloved Epaphroditos that if you allow us to bugger (*pugizein*) you it will go well for you, and we will not thrash you any longer if you allow us to bugger you. Farewell.[156]

Apion and Epimas send a letter to Epaphroditos[157] to propose sex. The verb used for "thrashing," *deirein*, which alludes to the "physical" side of education,[158] the metrical structure,[159] the literary chiasmus, and the glosses of rare, obscene terms all contribute to delineate the arena of the conflict. After learning how to phrase a letter and by practicing their skills in conventional epistles sent to their families, Apion and Epimas felt confident enough to compose a mock literary letter and addressed it to Epaphroditos, who may have been only a few benches away.

---

[156] Translation by D. Montserrat (*Sex and Society in Graeco-Roman Egypt* [London, 1996], 136), who (wrongly, in my view) regards the letter as an illiterate proposition to a male prostitute.

[157] This is also the name of the owner of a notebook with grammatical exercises in the third century; see Cribiore 1996a: no. 385.

[158] See above, pp. 65–73.

[159] See C. Gallavotti, "P.Oxy. 3070 e un graffito di Stabia," *MCr* 13–14 (1978–79): 363–69.

Learning to Fly: Rhetoric and Imitation

I bring the offering of the school feast. I yearn to reach very soon the full measure of youthful vigor and to live a long time listening to my teacher. . . . Would that I could complete my general education. I long to rise up in the air and come near Zeus's abode.[1] (*P.Laur.* II.49)

"Come at once and mount this car"—she pointed to a car with winged horses that resembled Pegasus—"in order that you may know what you would have missed if you had not followed me." When I had mounted, she plied whip and reins, and I was carried up into the heights from the East to the West surveying cities and nations and peoples. (Lucian *Somn.* 15)

THE ROAD leading up the hill of learning was long and steep and demanded commitment and effort. Education appropriated the metaphor used by Hesiod to describe the painful ascent toward virtue (*Op.* 287–92).[2] Keeping in sight the alluring promises of his goal, a male student could overcome fatigue and discouragement. But when he reached the top, his superiority over the rest of mankind was consecrated. The uneducated man was marked not only by his insignificance but also by his tenacious clinging to the earth and its material values, and by his inability to rise above and fly "aloft to the region where the gods dwell" (Plato *Phdr.* 246d). The passage from Lucian's *Somnium*, in which *Paideia* herself in a woman's guise drives her chariot with winged horses over the earth to show the young man the rewards that he can expect from a complete

---

[1] Cribiore 1996a: no. 354, a poem in anacreontics written perhaps for the feast at the end of the school year. Cf. U. von Wilamowitz-Möllendorf, *Griechische Verskunst* (Berlin, 1921), 611.

[2] See Lucian *Hermot.* 5; cf. above, p. 1. The metaphor of the steep road leading to virtue (*aretē*) was used by many. Cf. Libanius *Chria* 3.36, Foerster vol. 8, p. 96. Quite amusingly, Quintus Smirnaeus placed *aretē* in a tree situated on top of a hill so that people needed to climb twice to reach it (5.49–56; 14.195–200).

education, is inspired by the myth of the soul in the *Phaedrus*.[3] But though wings would lead the soul to immortality, the wings of rhetoric would empower a young man to reach knowledge, wealth, a glamorous career, superiority over other human beings, and fame. Acquiring the wings of eloquence was the ultimate goal of the student in rhetorical school, according to Libanius:[4] sometimes one already possessed wings of natural ability (*Ep.* 499.4), but more often a student learned to fly through strenuous intellectual training.

Quintilian compared the teacher of rhetoric to a mother bird who first gives her nestlings bits of food from her beak, then teaches them the basic principles of flying by leading the way herself, and finally lets them try the "free sky" once they have proved their strength (2.6.7). For Libanius, his students are "nestlings" in need of everything (*Ep.* 43.1). A student started by slavishly following a model, provided either by his own teacher or by a writer from the past; he began composing according to that pattern; and he learned to fly independently through a painful process of trial and error. The horizons of a student who was reaching the top of the educational hill were much broader than they had been, but the principles that inspired his learning were identical: imitation of a model, honor paid to the written word, reverence for the literary authors and the world of mythology, a strengthening of mnemonic skills in order to retain a patrimony of information, and the application of sets of rules that imprisoned his freedom and inspiration, providing at the same time comfortable and somewhat stimulating paths to follow. Of course, a rigid technique could not replace innate predisposition, which would account for the difference between the brilliant and the competent orator.[5] But as a student struggled to acquire the power of persuasion in school, his natural talent was subordinated to the acquisition of argumentative tools.

The educational process again evoked the analogy of gymnastic training. In his work on the *progymnasmata*, preliminary rhetorical exercises, Theon knew and employed this word but preferred to apply the terms *gymnasia* or *gymnasma* ("exercise") to the individual exercises; he was followed in that terminology by the second-century rhetor Hermogenes.[6] The *progymnasmata* were supposed to teach a student how to write on

---

[3] *Phdr.* 246a–247c: the soul is likened to a winged charioteer driving a team of winged horses.

[4] See, e.g., *Ep.* 44, 106.2.2, 323.1, 155.2, 660, and 1523.1.

[5] See Heath 1995: 4–5.

[6] Patillon (1997: ix) prefers a *floruit* for Theon preceding Quintilian's. After Hermogenes, the term *progymnasma* was generally adopted. Cf. Hock and O'Neil 1986: 12–15.

set themes: they were meant to warm up his muscles, stretch his power of discourse, and build his vigor. According to Quintilian, the athlete of the word, like gladiators and wrestlers, learned the technique of his art from his trainer, had to follow a strict regimen of diet and exercise, and built up his power of memorization by strenuous exercises, just as athletes train their muscles.[7] Libanius regarded himself not only as a wrestler—that is, an orator—but as a good trainer (*gymnastēs*). His students—the emperor Julian included—were athletes of the *logoi* who were building up the weapons they would need for their future careers.[8] All the vocabulary employed in rhetorical practice alluded to gymnastics and physical encounters. Professional rhetors still kept themselves in practice by exercising every day (*gymnazein*) and "argued" (*agonizesthai*, "to compete") in public delivery of orations.[9] The technical term *stasis*, "issue," that defined the situations that a speech of deliberative and judicial oratory addressed was connected either to a "quarrel" or to the "position" that the orator-wrestler took at the beginning of a bout.[10]

Rigorous training was necessary to dominate a body of knowledge, which was systematized according to an inflexible order. At the beginning of his work, Theon bitterly criticized those who plunged into the midst of rhetoric without general education and avoided the gymnastics of the preliminary exercises, thus "learning the potter's craft as they make a jug" (59). Hard work—*ponos*—was indispensable. Lucian described the teacher of rhetoric who guided the student up the mountain as a vigorous man with strong muscles, a manly stride, and a well-tanned body: his advice was "hard work, little sleep, and plenty of water" (*Rhetorum praeceptor* 9). As they climbed, the teacher showed the student the footprints of great writers that the latter was supposed to follow "like a rope-dancer," without ever swerving from them. As in preceding educational stages, learning was organized into a series of tightly connected links, each joined to the previous and giving a base to the next. The system was very familiar to a student. The first written exercises, for example, were narratives based on fables and myths. When Quintilian advises the teacher that these should be composed with utter care and that it would be good to make the student "tell his story from the end back to the beginning or start in the middle and go backward or forward," one is

[7] See 2.8.3–4 and 12.2; 10.1.4, 3.6, and 5.16; 11.2.42.
[8] See, e.g., *Ep.* 140.2; *Or.* 23.24.2–4, 11.187, 12.54; *Ep.* 548.3, 1020.3, and 309.1.
[9] See, e.g., Philostratus *VS* 529.
[10] See Russell 1983: 40, and 1996: 193 n. 59.

struck by the similarity to the methods employed to learn the alphabet.[11] Dexterity of mind and an almost mathematical ability in dealing with the elements of learning were the most important demands that rhetorical education placed upon students.

The order (*taxis*) of the preliminary exercises was not invariably the same in the rhetorical handbooks, but it did follow an apparent progression in difficulty. Theon, for example, justified starting from the *chreia* ("saying") because it was "short and easy to memorize" (64.29–30). But as in previous educational stages, the increase in difficulty was relative. Students, for instance, were supposed to enlarge and develop a saying, to expatiate by comparison or illustration, or to disprove the value of its message. The exercise started with an exordium, followed by the exposition of the statement, the various argumentations, and often a formal conclusion. It is sufficient to glance at the prescriptions of Theon and at the examples provided by Libanius to realize how accomplished—and far from simple—this exercise could be, a microcosm of rhetorical learning.[12] Each exercise targeted specific faculties necessary to the development of rhetorical expertise. Since innate ability was not identical in each student, the various components of the rhetorical gymnastics were geared to reinforce individual strengths and to remedy deficiencies: the aim was to make each pupil a little Demosthenes, fit for every type of discourse.[13]

The preliminary exercises not only leaned backward to the achievements attained in the initial phases of the training but also looked forward to the declamation (*meletē*)—the crowning achievement of the student of rhetoric—that incorporated *progymnasmata* in some parts. *Meletai* were orations complete in themselves, in which oratory for display was abandoned in favor of deliberative or forensic oratory. The transition from the *progymnasmata* was subtle, but not painless. The theory of "issue," which regulated the composition of declamations, was rather complex. It gave a student who had already developed a habit of playing with building blocks prepackaged instructions on how to build whole cases. Its limitations were already evident to the ancients,[14] but the "mental acrobatics" required by the exercise developed not only verbal ability but also an almost unfailing precision in analyzing the pros and cons of cases.[15]

---

[11] *Institutio* 2.4.15. Cf. above, p. 165.

[12] Theon 96.18–106.3; Libanius *Chria*, Foerster vol. 8, pp. 63–102.

[13] Theon 72.16–25.

[14] See Bonner 1949: 71–83.

[15] Brown 1992: 42–43.

A proper evaluation of attainments at the rhetorical stage of education requires the same warning given for the evaluation of previous levels. As described above, the entire course of rhetoric, subdivided into many years of training, existed as an ideal that only a few pupils were able to fulfill.[16] Its completion depended on many factors, such as personal finances, parents' willingness, life circumstances, and career goals. Only about one-sixth of Libanius's students, for instance, attended classes for five or six years: they were either the most wealthy students, who were going to play significant political roles in their cities, or those who pursued academic careers.[17] Two years of study were often sufficient to be able to plead in court, and students who had relatively modest means and/or wanted to obtain immediate rewards frequently opted to stop at this point.

The rhetorical educational circle was built on skills and elements of knowledge developed since primary education. *Chreiai*, for instance, were already a part of previous educational stages: novices memorized and copied them and used them to practice reading and writing. Rhetorical education purposely pulled *chreiai* out of their elementary context and made them into something more elaborate, in which students could recognize familiar elements while measuring their advancement. Little is known of the transition between the level of the grammarian and that of the rhetorician. Libanius provides valuable information, showing the existence of a sort of entrance exam (*peira*), in which a new student had to give proof of his intellectual capacities and show what he had learned in previous stages of education. Libanius reveals that his first action when he received a new student was to test him to check his natural predisposition and ability to grasp the principles of rhetoric (*Ep.* 355.1). Sometimes new students received some rhetorical preparation before entering his school. In two cases, Libanius was particularly pleased when he found out during the test that one new student had already memorized large quantities of Demosthenes (*Ep.* 1261.2), and another was even familiar with some of his discourses (*Ep.* 768.3).

As usual, the material introduced to a student of rhetoric was well balanced by the student's full absorption of what he had covered in his educational past: rhetorical training aimed at a novel assessment and a different usage of the material. New at this level was an insistence on the development of the writing skills that were going to prove fundamental for the

---

[16] Cf. above, p. 56.
[17] See Petit 1956: 62–66, 154–58.

future orator. In the school of the grammarian, a student had learned to scrutinize the text of an author, isolating its most minute characteristics, often to the point of distorting its overall message and beauty. On the whole, however, a text and its authority were accepted without discussion and were incorporated into an immutable patrimony of knowledge through reading and memorization. Imitation of literary models was at the core of a program in rhetoric: through close reading of the texts, it became possible to assimilate vocabulary, style, and organization of the elements of discourse. One is reminded of the amusing vignette cited by Dionysius of Halicarnassus about the wife of the ugly peasant who was forced by her husband to stare at images of beautiful people in order to beget him handsome children.[18] But acquiring the wings of eloquence meant going some steps beyond that. A text began to be only a point of departure, the image that a student's exercise had to confront and mirror in a moment of fleeting illusion before it could surpass the model. The literary texts of the past were appropriated ever more intensely, but they were also transcended and seen in new perspectives, as students sought to force their way in with their exercises and vie with the originals. In what follows, I shall investigate the gradual process by which a student of rhetoric started to distance himself not only from the poetic texts studied with the grammarian, but also from the prose authors that he was approaching in the new course.[19]

Preliminary Exercises and Poetry

For the Egyptian student who wrote the composition quoted at the beginning of the chapter, completion of the educational cycle meant rising up in the air to Zeus's abode. A young man who began attending a course of rhetoric found himself in familiar surroundings: the figures from epic and tragic poetry encountered with the grammarian and the gods of the

[18] Dionysius *De imitat.* Epitome 1, D. G. Battisti, *Sull' imitazione* (Pisa, 1997), 70. This is the edition to which I shall refer henceforth.

[19] I shall base my analysis on texts that were written by students or teachers, or that bear on the question of how rhetoric was learned and practiced in its initial stages. Most of these texts are distinguished from professional endeavors and orations that were delivered in real life. Even though there is no proof that all of them originated in school contexts, nevertheless they are exercises. It is the whole collection that illuminates the question of how rhetoric was learned in Egypt.

traditional pantheon initially dominated the rhetorical landscape. Libanius shows how tenacious were a student's connections with his past.[20] He was the first to leave well-wrought examples of *progymnasmata* in which the principles of his predecessors, Theon and the second-century C.E. rhetor Hermogenes, were applied.[21] The first exercises dipped into those initial encounters a student had with literacy through fables, sayings, and maxims. But soon after, mythological material covered with the grammarian asserted itself: Homer, and in smaller measure the Homeric cycle, dominated the scene.[22] Libanius's *progymnasmata*—not unlike other collections of exercises—confirm that the *Iliad* was of the foremost concern to an ancient grammarian, at the expense of the *Odyssey*. Achilles was the hero par excellence, whose conduct was praised or blamed, and whose relationships with Patroclus, Briseis, and Polyxena were the subject of much disquisition; Ajax was a distant second.[23] Though tragedy, particularly Euripides and the *Medea*, started to inspire students who composed exercises of impersonation (*ēthopoiiai*), Homer never lost his grip on the practitioner of rhetoric.[24] Thus, in a letter, Libanius presents a student challenged point-blank to "wrestle" with recitation from memory of verses of Homer (*Ep*. 187.3).

An interesting question is whether students were expanding their knowledge of poetic texts in rhetorical schools as well as approaching the prose authors, historians, and orators. Ancient educators—Dionysius of Halicarnassus and Quintilian in particular—often extolled the praises of the poets as very beneficial to the future orator.[25] And yet, a passage in which Quintilian confesses his vain attempts to introduce in his school the method that was practiced in the Greek East of reading and commenting on prose authors—so fundamental for the course—implicitly reveals

[20] His work is most useful because it is a response to students' needs. Even his *meletai* are on the same level as those originating in school; see Russell 1996: 5–7.

[21] On *progymnasmata* and Libanius's predecessors and followers, see Clark 1957: 177–212; Bonner 1977: 250–76; Kennedy 1983: 54–73; Hock and O'Neil 1986: 9–22; Heath 1995: 13–17. On the *progymnasmata* of Libanius, see Schouler 1984: 51–138.

[22] A student had a taste of a world ahead only in "commonplaces," "argument," and "introduction of a law." Occasionally exercises show that Demosthenes was read; cf. *Progymnasmata*, Foerster vol. 8, pp. 296–306 and 342–49.

[23] Cf. the *ēthopoiia* (p. 408 Foerster) in which Cheiron moans that Achilles, who is trying to avoid going to the Trojan War, is not taking advantage of his education. Quite anachronistically, Cheiron wishes he had never read the "beloved" Catalogue of Ships.

[24] On Homer's oratorical skills, cf. Ps.-Plutarch *De Homero* 161–74.

[25] Dionysius *De Imitat*. Epitome 2; Quintilian 10.31–130. On the relationship of poetry and oratory, see Webb 1997.

that poetic texts were not systematically perused in the Roman class-room.[26] The foremost concerns of the Roman student were the practical models offered by his teacher and his own practice in declaiming. In Rome, the teaching of rhetoric seems to have been less bookish than in the Greek East. It relied more heavily on the teachers' own digestion of the literary sources, a fact that—as we shall see—reflected on the practice of declamation. In the East, however, reading the historians and the ora-tors in class was standard practice. Theon, for instance, considers reading, auditing, and paraphrasing prose texts to be activities based on imitation and memory that accompanied a student during the full course of rhetori-cal instruction (134.11–142.10). The question of whether teachers of rhetoric guided their students through the texts of the poets, however, is more problematic. Although scholars all agree on the importance of po-etry for students, they have concluded that there is no sufficient evidence that allows us to posit that systematic readings of the poets took place in class.[27] We can only surmise that instructors sometimes elaborated on this subject.

Libanius's testimony, however, permits us to go much further. Two of his letters let us glimpse with clarity the direct use of poetry in the class-room. The first letter, *Ep.* 1066, shows Libanius in the midst of his teach-ing, with "the usual texts" in his hands.[28] He was studying dramatic po-etry that day. His method of teaching these texts is worthy of mention, since it relied on the direct participation of students. After a brief "audi-tion," one of the pupils was unanimously chosen as "the proper actor" for the play: he had to read and act the text for the rest of the students. The second letter, *Ep.* 990, was addressed to an eminent personage, Ta-tianos, who had just been nominated consul and had literary ambitions.[29] An epic poem that Tatianos composed on a Homeric theme incorporating verses from Homer—some sort of a Homeric Cento—enjoyed several edi-tions and became very popular among teachers and students, just like the *Iliad* and the *Odyssey.* This work was adopted as a regular school text. Libanius writes that "to whatever part of the school (*agele*) you go, you will find Tatianos,"[30] showing that the poem was used by all students and not only in the class of the grammarian. We can argue, therefore, that

[26] Quintilian 2.5.1–17; cf. Clarke 1996: 124.

[27] Cf. H. North, "The Use of Poetry in the Training of the Ancient Orator," *Traditio* 8 (1952): 1–33.

[28] Cf. Norman 1992: no. 190.

[29] Cf. ibid.: no. 173.

[30] *Ep.* 990.2–3. The term *agele* indicated Libanius's "herd," that is, all his students.

poetry continued to be the direct concern of the teacher of rhetoric, since it was studied even beyond the stage of the *progymnasmata*.

Most of the preliminary exercises exemplified by Libanius were practiced in Hellenistic and Roman Egypt,[31] but exercises of impersonation and praise—*ēthopoiiai* and *encomia*—had the lion's share. The sample of rhetorical exercises is somewhat biased, since most papyri originating from Alexandria, which possessed a prestigious school of rhetoric, are lost.[32] One suspects, however, that these were the most popular exercises not only in Egyptian classrooms but also in the Greek East at large. Two inscriptions from Claudiopolis in Asia Minor that commemorate the death of a student who had come to this city to study rhetoric mention only *encomia* and *ēthopoiiai* as the exercises in which he had engaged.[33] *Ēthopoiiai* were fundamental in the general economy of declamations, where they were used in a legal setting and in an argumentative way. The future declaimer learned from them to play a distinctive character, *ēthos*. This was essential because he would never appear in his own persona, only as a historical or stock character. These exercises, and *encomia* in particular, offered further possibilities for development at the hands of rhetors and poets-grammarians who competed in public contests and celebrations.[34]

Exercises of impersonation required a student to expand on the verbal reaction of a certain mythological or literary figure in a given situation, thus engaging, for instance, not only Phoinix upbraiding Achilles, Achilles on the verge of being killed because of Polyxena, or a Greek woman meeting Helen in Greece, but also Callimachus's Triopas confronting Erysichthon, Hesiod inspired by the Muses, or even, in the fourth century and in a Christian milieu, Cain and Abel at the moment of the slaying.[35] Good

---

[31] Commonplaces and *anaskeuai*, refutations of mythological points, have not been preserved. Sometimes, moreover, as for fables or narrations, distinguishing between copies and compositions is difficult. To the rhetorical exercises in Cribiore 1996a: nos. 344–57, add *P²* 420 (*PSI* XIII.1303), 1808 (*P.Harr.* I.4), 1831 (*P.Ryl.* III.487); *O.Bodl.* II.2171; R. Cingottini, "P.Alex.inv. 611: Riassunto in prosa dell' Iliade?" *Ann.Pisa*, ser. 3 (1972): 2.2, pp. 512–13. On *ēthopoiiai* and *encomia*, see below.

[32] See Smith 1974: 37. The high water table in the delta did not assure the soil conditions necessary for the preservation of papyri. On the other hand, those transported elsewhere from the capital are extant.

[33] See *SEG* 34.1259; cf. above, p. 119.

[34] Cf. Theon 70.26–29.

[35] See *P²* 1611 (G. A. Gerhard and O. Crusius, *Mélanges Nicole* [Geneva, 1905], pp. 615–24), 348 (*P.Cair.Masp.* III.67316v), 1844 (C. Graves, *Hermathena* 5 [1885]: 237–57); *P.Oxy.* L.3537. Cf. Fournet 1992; and J. A. Fernández Delgado, "Hexametrische-*Ethopoi*-

knowledge of the relevant literary texts with proper understanding of all the surrounding circumstances and an effort to match the words to the characters of the protagonist and the interlocutor were fundamental. A student would then follow a pattern, depending on whether his exercise concerned an exhortation, an appeal, a consolation, or a request for forgiveness.[36] In writing *ēthopoiiai*, as a rule the texts of the poets were followed faithfully. In the best of circumstances, a student's version would be only an expansion, as if the poet were granted some license for prolixity. Occasionally a student was allowed a flight of fancy, like the one who wrote on papyrus a fervent exculpation of Clytemnestra.[37]

Likewise, not much originality was required in writing an *encomium*.[38] Since speeches of praise were at the core of epideictic oratory, Theon felt the need to justify their presence among the *progymnasmata* (61.24–29). But *encomia* were stereotyped discourses that had always been a part of works of literature: it was not too difficult to establish patterns to be used in education. The subjects, which often belonged to the world of myth, also allowed for some breadth. *Encomia* on papyrus were very similar to those belonging to textbooks of exercises, including, for instance, praise of the god Dionysus or of Achilles, but also extolling the merits of modesty, of a bird—apparently the Phoenix—or of the fig, "the favorite food and delicacy of Hermes."[39] Connections with the texts of the poets were strong and constant. Thus, an *encomium* of modesty (*aidōs*) started by praising the eyes "where the goddess resides"; quoted words that Homer put in the mouth of Agamemnon and Ajax; seemed to address schoolboys, saying that those who were modest pleased father and teacher; praised the modesty of Odysseus by quoting from the *Odyssey*; and hailed the modesty of Hesiod, crowned by the Muses on Mount Helicon.[40]

But the bonds with the poets studied at the previous stage of education were even tighter. With very few exceptions,[41] in fact, both *ēthopoiiai* and

iai auf Papyrus und anderen Materialien," *Proceedings of the Twentieth International Congress of Papyrologists* (Copenhagen, 1994), 299–305. Libanius has a few examples concerning fictitious figures, such as a prostitute, an unlucky man, and a painter.

[36] Thus Theon 115.11–118.6, who limited the subjects for pedagogical reasons.

[37] *P²* 2528 (*MPER* IV [1927]: 35–47). About the subject, see Libanius *Ēthopoiia* 21 (Foerster vol. 8, pp. 421–23) and *Anth. Pal.* 9.126. Cf. Quintilian 3.11.4.

[38] Consider, however, Libanius's famous praise of Thersites, *Encomium* 4 (Foerster vol. 8, pp. 243–51); Schouler 1984: 769–73. Libanius extracted from Homer himself all the points he uses to formulate a complete inversion of the character.

[39] See *P.Köln.* VII.286; *P²* 2528, 2524 (*P.Lond.Lit.* 193), and 2527 (*P.Oxy.* XVII.2084).

[40] *P.Lond.Lit.* 193 (*P²* 2524), with quotations from *Il.* 5.531 and 15.563, and *Od.* 6.222.

[41] Exceptions are *P²* 2527 and 2528.

encomia found in Egypt are in verse.[42] Handbooks of rhetoric invariably developed examples in prose, since they considered all the preliminary exercises as preparation for rhetorical discourse. In theory, a student had to devote himself mainly to prose writing as soon as he left the class of the grammarian. But in practice, the strong ties that existed with that stage and the texts of the poets still alive in a student's memory (and read again with the rhetor) made writing in verse—especially in the epic hexameter— a natural choice. More rarely, exercises were composed in iambics, when they were modeled on tragedy. An intriguing example is represented by an exercise on papyrus written in Oxyrhynchos in the third century C.E.— a much shorter reworking of the debate of Eteokles and Polyneikes in front of their mother, taken from the *agōn* of the *Phoenissae* of Euripides.[43] The exact nature of this text is not clear, but it is closer to an *ēthopoiia* centered on Polyneikes. Power, the theme around which the exercise revolves, is represented anachronistically by the *diadēma*, the band that was the symbol of the regal authority of Alexander the Great. The student—or, less likely, the teacher—who engaged in this exercise and ended it abruptly, leaving a large unwritten space, introduced the bold innovation of Polyneikes handing his sword to his mother. This mini-*agōn*, with its concentration of so much into so little and its numerous errors due to phonetic spelling, was not a felicitous attempt to vie with Euripides.

To explain the existence of these versified school exercises, one might invoke the fact that in Egypt, verse-writing had a particularly strong tradition, since "the Egyptians were crazy about poetry."[44] But it is likely that generally in ancient schools, verse-writing was more popular than is usually admitted.[45] As the geographer Strabo (first century B.C.E.–first century C.E.) recognized, poetry was most useful to students, it pleased the public at large, and it "drew full houses" (1.2.8). Quintilian, who considered it only as a form of amusement and a respite from study (*carmine ludere, studiorum secessus*, 10.5.15–16), nevertheless admitted its usefulness. When a student was just starting to develop his wings, imitation of the texts of the poets and competition with them also translated into a close reproduction of their poetic forms.

---

[42] Examples in verse are found in the manuscript tradition from the end of the fifth century C.E.; cf. *Anth. Pal.* 9.126 and 449–80, and 16.4. About Byzantine examples, see Fournet 1992: 260.

[43] *PSI* XIII.1303; *Select Papyri* 33; A. Garzya, "Rifacimento di scena delle *Fenicie* di Euripide (*PSI* 1303)," *Aegyptus* 32 (1952): 389–98.

[44] Eunapius *VS* 493; Cameron 1965b: 470.

[45] Consider the example of the boy Sulpicius in Rome; see below.

Declamations and History

The skills developed through the preliminary exercises—facility in invention and expression, and the ability to follow standard paradigms—converged in the prose exercise of declamation (*declamatio, meletē*). Even though the term "declamation" evokes an oral presentation,[46] declamations started as written endeavors that sometimes resulted in oral performances in front of classmates and parents. This was one of the major differences between the practice in school and declamations as a social pastime, because the latter were delivered extemporaneously, at least in theory.[47] This exercise was tightly constructed, with the theory of "issue" providing the charted territory on which to proceed. Even though the divisions of each issue did not need to be followed slavishly in type and order,[48] in practice a student must have found it very comforting to adhere to a prearranged organization of the material. Quintilian presents the somewhat amusing picture of the student Secundus, who for three days desperately looked for inspiration in starting his composition, lying on his bed with eyes turned to the ceiling and muttering to himself in an attempt to fire up his imagination (10.3.13–15). The advice he was given was to rely less on creativity and emotions and more on reason. Writing a draft in the heat of the moment with the hope of revising later was not conducive to good results: a work had to be planned and firmly organized from the beginning. The same was true for rhetors once school was left behind: to "vomit" speeches was not a well-regarded practice.[49]

Writing occupied a fundamental place in rhetorical education. Copying literary texts was still part of the training. Theon recommended that a student form some sort of anthology of what he found most admirable in the various historians and orators and memorize it so as to have it ready when needed (137.18–21). A papyrus notebook containing the final part of Demosthenes' *De corona* might represent such an effort: the remaining four sheets include only passages from the work, with large omissions.[50] A student was supposed to compose every day, as much as possible, and

[46] The term *meletē* is also ambiguous.

[47] See Kennedy 1997: 48; Pernot 1993: 432–33.

[48] Cf. Heath 1995: 22.

[49] On "vomiting" words, see, e.g., Libanius *Declamatio* 27.7; Philostratus *VS* 583; and Synesius *Dio* 56c.

[50] P^2 290. The final colophon, "Good luck to the one who wrote it, took it, and read it," is similar to that at the end of Cribiore 1996a: no. 393.

with the utmost care.[51] The next step after finishing a declamation was to memorize it, going over the writing many times. At this educational level, the ties between writing and memory were as strong as ever. Quintilian's personal experience as a teacher made him mistrust the technique of mnemonics. It was preferable for the future orator to learn to rely on verbatim memory (*memoria verborum*) rather than on memory of things and concepts (*memoria rerum*).[52] Basic visual memory was supposed to be of further help: by memorizing his composition or a passage of an author from the same tablet on which he had committed it to writing, a student could use marks, erasures, additions, or the like as mnemonic cues (11.2.32).[53] Once school was left behind, the working habits acquired there kept their validity, and the strong connections among writing, memorization, and delivery were maintained.[54]

The exercise of declamation started to be practiced in the Greek East from the end of the fourth century B.C.E.,[55] but most of the Greek Hellenistic evidence is lost. The most important source for the first century B.C.E. is the elder Seneca, who reported on speeches heard in Rome in his youth. In Rome, declamations were distinguished in *suasoriae*—imaginary deliberative themes—and *controversiae*—fictitious lawcourt arguments.[56] *Suasoriae*, which advised a historical figure on some course of action and were mostly based on historical themes taken not only from Greek but also from recent Roman history, were deemed the easier of the two.[57] *Controversiae*, which forced the student to play more roles, almost entirely followed quasi-legal themes in Rome. In this, Greek practice differed fundamentally from Roman, since in Greece historical themes drawn exclusively from the classical past were adopted as the basis not only of deliberative exercises but also of many of the forensic ones, where a historical figure was represented as standing trial for some charge, and a student had to produce defense and/or accusation speeches. Thus a very

---

[51] Theon 62.9–10; Quintilian 10.3.1–18.

[52] Quintilian 11.2.1–26; cf. Cicero *Ad Herennium* 3.28–40, *De Or.* 2.350–60. See Desbordes 1990: 82–87.

[53] This type of visual memory was entirely different from that employed in the technique of mnemonics; cf. above, p. 166.

[54] See T. H. Olbricht, "Delivery and Memory," in Porter 1997: 159–67.

[55] See Marrou 1975, 1: 302.

[56] See Bonner 1977: 277–327; and Bonner 1949, still useful in parts; Clark 1957: 213–61; Clarke 1996: 85–99; Berry and Heath 1997; Bloomer 1997. I shall maintain throughout the Latin terms.

[57] Tacitus *Dial.* 35.4; Quintilian 2.1.3.

large number of the themes for declamation mentioned in the *Lives* of Philostratus are taken from Greek history and deal mainly with the Persian and Peloponnesian wars, with the period of Demosthenes, and with Alexander. Fictitious themes, *plasmata*, which dealt with adultery, conflicts between fathers and sons or rich and poor people, and the like, were also popular, but, at least judging from the conspicuous evidence provided by Libanius, they drew heavily from bookish sources, particularly from classical and New Comedy, in featuring typical characters.[58]

Meletai from Greco-Roman Egypt cast much light on the actual practice of teaching rhetoric and the practical application of theoretical prescriptions.[59] Differentiating between deliberative and forensic exercises among them is not always easy, partly because some are fragmentary. Modern historians of Greek education maintain the distinction between *suasoriae* and *controversiae* and conclude that deliberative exercises were by far more common in Greek schools.[60] Not only may this perception be inaccurate, but the distinction itself does not correctly apply to Greek education.[61] Greek rhetoricians preferred to divide *meletai* according to whether they were historical or fictive.[62] The former appear to have been more common in Greco-Roman Egypt, at least judging from the evidence: *meletai* based on fictitious legal themes are preserved more rarely. A papyrus from the first century contains three that dealt with intricate cases of citizenship and larceny: in one, for instance, a man, after giving a talent to another and helping him conceal it, tries to dig it up again at night; caught in the act, he declares that he was in pressing financial need, while his opponent accuses him of intending to reclaim the money twice.[63] The editor of this papyrus considers this a collection of exercises, primarily because of the lack of personal names. To this, one should add the papyrus's use of a system of abbreviations for common words that is found in

---

[58] Libanius *Declamatio* 26–51.

[59] On rhetorical treatises on papyrus, see, e.g., *P.Oxy.* III.410, LIII.3708, and *P.Yale* II.106.

[60] See, e.g., Marrou 1975, 1: 303.

[61] Cf. Kennedy 1997: 49.

[62] Examples of historical declamations: *P²* 2511 (*BKT* VII.4–13); *P²* 2529 (*P.Oxy.* XXIV.2400, three themes); *P.Yale* II.105; *P²* 2498 (*P.Oxy.* VI.858); *P²* 2508 (*P.Oxy.* II.216); *P²* 2510 (*P.Lond.Lit.* 139); *P²* 2547 (*P.Oxy.* XV.1799); *P²* 2496 (*P.Hib.* I.15); *P.Oxy.* XLV.3235 and 3236. Examples of fictive forms of *meletai* are: *P²* 2515 (*P.Lond.Lit.* 138), *P.Oxy.* III.471, and *P.Hamb.* III.163 (in Latin).

[63] *P²* 2515. Another *controversia*, but in Latin, is *P.Hamb.* 1.163, whose fragmentary content mentions death, sickness, and flight into deserted places.

commentaries and informal literary texts.[64] As a rule, lack of proper names is a good indication that a speech was not actually pronounced in court, though their presence cannot exclude the possibility that a text was an exercise.[65] Quintilian, in fact, thought it appropriate to employ proper names in exercises (2.10.9).

The infrequent presence of *meletai* on quasi-legal cases in Egypt likely derives partly from the loss of most Alexandrian papyri. Rhetorical education was not solely available in the capital, as the finds of exercises elsewhere confirm, and itinerant teachers traveled around offering their services. Yet Alexandria was able to provide a complete course of education.[66] Another aspect of the problem should not be overlooked, however: it is possible that rhetoric was generally taught in Egyptian schools via literary texts, mostly historical and oratorical. Declamations were not seen only as preparation for the lawcourt. The aim of rhetorical instruction, that is, achieving expertise in argument, could be reached satisfactorily through practice of historical *meletai*. After all, even the cases contemplated in exercises based on lawcourt themes were not taken from real life: a student was hardly exposed to real law through declamatory fictitious law. Law could be learned in the actual practice of the court, after school was left behind.[67]

By the time a student approached historical declamations, he had acquired a knowledge of orators and historians that was constantly fueled through reading. According to Theon, instruction was personalized and followed the inclinations and capabilities of a student (134.24–135.1). Aside from lecturing on the various types of discourse and lingering on rhetorical and stylistic points of a text, a teacher provided detailed information about the biographical data of an author and the circumstances in which a work was produced. These were familiar methods already adopted in the reading and explication of the poets: through them a student reached full immersion in a text, which enabled him to go beyond it and create his own discourse. Theon thought it advisable to start by reading the orators in a progression of difficulty: Isocrates, then the fourth-

[64] Cf. some of these abbreviations in another *controversia*, *P. Yale* II.105. Cf. *P.Coll.Youtie* 66, pp. 411–12.

[65] Cf., for instance, P^2 2522 (*PSI* XI.1222), an oration in front of the emperor to defend a certain Didymos, which might be an exercise.

[66] See Smith 1974. On Philostratus overlooking the evidence from Alexandria, see Schubert 1995.

[67] See Winterbottom 1982: 65. On schools of law after the fourth century, see McNamee 1998.

century B.C.E. orators Hyperides, Aeschines, and Demosthenes, a list to which Dionysius of Halicarnassus added Lysias (ca. 459–380 B.C.E.) and the fourth-century B.C.E. Lycurgus (*De Imit.* Epitome 5). The historians followed, headed by Herodotus, who was the most approachable. Only afterward did a teacher introduce more demanding authors, such as Theopompus, Xenophon, Philistus, Ephorus, and Thucydides.[68] It is legitimate to doubt whether all these historians were maintained in the reading syllabus of rhetorical schools; if they had been, their works would have been more likely to survive through the centuries.[69]

Historical *meletai* found in Egypt are based with few exceptions on Athenian history in the age of Demosthenes, and on Alexander and/or the period immediately after his death. The horizon of a student of rhetoric was dominated by the conflicts and events surrounding Demosthenes, when public oratory had attained its greatest power: Demosthenes, Aeschines, and Philip became the pillars on which a student built his own discourse. In the generation immediately following, Alexander appealed to the imaginations of poets and rhetors, and in the second century, men of culture such as Plutarch and Dio of Prusa celebrated his political, military, and cultural achievements.[70] He was hailed as a champion of Hellenism: he was of Greek race and tongue, he had the moral attributes typical of a Greek, such as *sōphrosynē* ("self-control"), and he possessed the Greek *paideia* that was the strongest symbol of Hellenism.[71] Education could not ignore Alexander, but it reserved for him an interesting treatment. School exercises seem to have been particularly concerned with his death, the problems arising from his succession, and the excitement and hope for freedom that pervaded Athens on his demise.[72] Most of the time Alexander was not extolled for his accomplishments, but his death provided a way to extend almost artificially the period of Athenian glory that

[68] The same list, with the exception of Ephorus, is mentioned by Dionysius *De imitat.* Epitome 3. Xenophon's *floruit* was in the fourth century B.C.E.; Ephorus and Theopompus, who lived in the same century, were both pupils of Isocrates; and the Sicilian Philistus lived approximately between 430 and 356 B.C.E.

[69] A remark by Hermogenes (412.1–10 Rabe), that historians such as Theopompus, Philistus, and Ephorus did not deserve to be imitated, might explain that a change in the program occurred at some time.

[70] Dio *Or.* 2 and 4; Plutarch composed two discourses "On the Fortune or Virtue of Alexander," *Mor.* 326–45, and dedicated to him one of his *Vitae*. See Bowie 1970: 7.

[71] A. E. Wardman, "Plutarch and Alexander," *CQ* 5 (1955): 96–107; J. R. Hamilton, *Plutarch, Alexander: A Commentary* (Oxford, 1969); S. Humbert, "Plutarque, Alexandre et l' hellénisme," in Said 1991: 169–82.

[72] See Cribiore 1996a:, nos. 347, 348, 349, 350; and *P*² 2496 and 2510.

students of rhetoric knew from books and in which they found refuge. There is a correspondence with Libanius's own view of the Macedonian conqueror. Even though he was aware of the abundant literature on Alexander and of the favor he enjoyed among poets, historians, and panegyrists, he was so heavily dependent on the classical texts and so immersed in classical values that he often ignored the ideal occasions for extolling Alexander's praises: he cited Alexander much less frequently than he mentioned his father Philip, who was a foil to Demosthenes, considered the last and greatest of the classical authors.[73]

Fascination with glories of the Athenian past brought about in the Roman period an almost universal desire to recreate an archaic language and style. Atticism, which aimed at purifying literature by returning to the vocabulary and standards of the classical period and avoided bombast and excessive word play and symmetry, represented a reaction to the style called "Asian" that had come to life in Hellenistic declamation halls.[74] Since Attic writers of the past were the models used in education for close imitation, in schools the Attic style was almost invariably adopted—a factor that in turn had lasting repercussions on the general favor enjoyed by Atticism.[75] In the work of a mature writer, imitation was a subtle affair and was not confined to one author: not only did linguistic and stylistic borrowings encompass a larger horizon, but the process of complete digestion of the sources conferred a novel identity on the new product.[76] Naturally, the situation was different for students who were still unskilled. Quintilian exhorted his pupils that imitation should not be confined to words or to a specific genre (10.2.22—28), and Theon maintained that slavish imitation of a single author, even Demosthenes, resulted in a weak and unclear composition (137.6–12). But the reality was a far cry from that ideal.

It is instructive in this respect to look closely at an exercise on papyrus that was based on imitation but attempted to go somewhat beyond its

[73] See Schouler 1984: 638–40.

[74] On the two styles, see U. von Wilamowitz-Möllendorf, "Asianismus und Atticismus," *Hermes* 35 (1900): 1–52; F. W. Blass, *Die Rhythmen der asianischen und römischen Kunstprosa* (Leipzig, 1905); D. Innes and M. Winterbottom, *Sopatros the Rhetor*, BICS, suppl. 48 (London, 1988), 7–12.

[75] See, however, P^2 2508, a rhetorical exercise from the first century c.e. that contains a vehement denunciation of a threatening letter by Philip and is written in a bombastic "Asian" style.

[76] Russell 1983: 109–10. On the need for digestion, Quintilian 10.1.19; Sen. *Ep.* 84; Fantham 1978: 110–11.

model.[77] By using a work of Demosthenes not to uphold but to discredit his conduct,[78] this student was trying to fly, but he did not go very far. The process he followed gives a clear measure of the significance and nature of imitation in school. At the very end of his handbook, Theon described three exercises that could be approached either at various stages of instruction or when the rest were assimilated. One of these was paraphrase, which required mental agility for a product of high level and benefited not only expression but also comprehension of a text. Another exercise, *exergasia*, consisted of elaborating on the words of an author, clarifying the obscure points, and adding new thoughts that were more credible, more perspicuous, or stylistically more adorned. Finally, with *antirrēsis*—that is, "refutation"—a student engaged in a close critique of a text: he was supposed to start by contradicting a fundamental point, moving then to a refutation of the whole argument (139.22–144.21). This exercise, which was similar to but more advanced than the exercise of *anaskeuē*—a refutation of a popular myth or a Homeric theme[79]—led to forensic argument. In discussing *exergasia* and *antirrēsis*, Theon used examples from the *De corona*.

De corona 169–72 is the text on which our student bases his refutation of Demosthenes' handling of the situation between the capture of Elatea and the battle of Chaeronea. The orator is reproached for not fighting personally but for haranguing "with a shield and a decree in his hand." Following a technique of disparagement, comparisons are established not only with one particular orator who "was the first to go out to fight," but also with historical figures such as Themistocles and Pericles. This introduces rhetorical exaggerations and inaccuracies. In this part of his *meletē*, the student was taking advantage of the expertise acquired through the preliminary exercises of "blame" —*psogos*, the opposite of *encomium*—and "comparison." Demosthenes' behavior is then discussed by following in a loose paraphrase whole passages of the *De corona*. This part of the exercise is introduced by the words, "How can I listen to Demosthenes, who has no breastplate, no spear, no sword, not even one inherited from his father?" This was a nice touch: the detail that Demos-

---

[77] See *P.Oxy.* VI.858 (P^2 2498), possibly a *suasoria*.

[78] Exercises approving Demosthenes' actions are, e.g., P^2 2547, and *P.Oxy.* XLV.3235 and 3236; a *meletē* in defense of the four advocates who appear in the final part of his speech against Leptines is P^2 2511.

[79] See Clark 1957: 190–92. *Anaskeuē* is not described by Theon. Libanius provides only two examples, both based on Homeric themes, *Refutatio* 1–2 (Foerster vol. 8, pp. 123–35).

thenes' father fabricated swords derived from the biographical explanations introduced earlier by the teacher. At a later moment, the student who is reporting words of Demosthenes goes back to his source by saying, "That was what we heard him say." In a sense, no real objection to this treatment of the problem could be leveled by a teacher, since this pupil was refuting Demosthenes' own words. But there was an inconsistency: though this exercise considered the period between 339 and 338 B.C.E., the *De corona*, which reconsidered those events, was composed in 330 B.C.E.

In the last part of the exercise, the paraphrase and refutation of Demosthenes' words is taken up again. Demosthenes had treated at length the moment of discouragement when people gathered in the Assembly and no one had come forward to speak: finally, responding to "the civic voice of the country," he had addressed the people himself. Wrongly presuming that Demosthenes' hesitation was due to a law dictating that the speakers had to be designated by the Council, this student ranted against the orator's supposed legal violation. Anachronisms, fabrications, and incongruities, which were also not uncommon in historical declamations composed outside schools,[80] abound in exercises: a *meletē* was a complete and finite work that obeyed its own parameters and had to respect only the rules of the game.[81] Although it started from history, it considered historical reality only as an excuse to weave a fictional pattern. In this process of imitation and departure from a given text, much craft and argumentative ability were necessary for a new discourse to take a life of its own—qualities that our student lacked. The final results in this case were chopped sentences, abrupt movements, and sudden stops—on the whole, a failed attempt at flying, but an earnest and diligent performance.

NON SCHOLARUM TEMPORIBUS SED VITAE SPATIO

In the words of Quintilian, the relevance of learning was not limited to school days but extended into life (1.8.12). The ultimate and most valuable aim of knowledge was its capacity to be incorporated into the cultural habits and mindset of the educated adult. It has often been remarked that in the Hellenistic and Roman periods, oratory no longer fulfilled the

[80] Cf. the examples in Russell 1983: 113–20.

[81] See, e.g., P^2 2495, which departs considerably from the account of the historical battle of Arginusae that was at the basis of the declamation.

important functions it had in the fifth and fourth centuries B.C.E.[82] There was no lack of occasions to use profitably the oratorical talents developed in school. Oratory still had an important place in public life—for instance, in debates in the Council, in embassies to other cities or monarchs, in speeches to welcome important personages or to dedicate buildings, and of course in lawcourt activities.[83] But apparently these occasions hardly exhausted the oratorical prowess of the educated elite, as is shown by the proliferation of epideictic speeches—that is, speeches for display and celebration—not only during the time of the "second sophistic"—the late first, second, and early third centuries C.E.—but also later. Panegyrics and declamations on judicial and especially historical topics became very popular forms of entertainment. The most brilliant sophists were the idols of the educated public: they commanded high fees, were disputed among the cities, and attracted vast, frenzied audiences.[84] They were the athletes of the word, the adored heroes with whom their fans identified and whom they tried to imitate. Oratorical performances were also attended by students, since auditing speeches of teachers and of popular sophists was part of their training.[85] But most interestingly, all the public became a crowd of students enraptured by the subtleties of style, the brilliance of the images and of the figures of speech, the *bons mots*, and the allusions to the oratorical models of the past.[86] Escapism, and dissatisfaction with the political life and the freedom afforded by the times, were undoubtedly partly responsible for the refuge that the educated elites took in the fictitious world of oratory.[87]

But another reason why oratorical displays became the recreation of the times must be found in the way that education was deeply ingrained in the texture of social and cultural life. Audiences partly turned their attention to exercises once practiced in school out of nostalgia for a time gone by, when life was guided by the dictates of the teacher, success was assured by following the rules, and fixed models formed the canvas on which to embroider one's own oratorical discourse.[88] But far from remaining locked in a strict educational circle, education showed a remarkable ability to stay alive and procreate, with powerful ramifications for

---

[82] See Bowersock 1969; Kennedy 1983; Cameron 1991; Brown 1992: 30–31 and 35–70.

[83] I shall not investigate these areas.

[84] Cf. the rich anecdotal tradition in Philostratus *VS*.

[85] See Theon 137.22–139.20. Cf. the student Neilos, above, pp. 57–58 and 121–23.

[86] Cf. Schouler 1984: 52–53.

[87] See Bowie 1970.

[88] Cf. Pliny the Younger *Ep.* 2.3.6.

the world of culture. The boundaries between school exercises and professional products are often not easy to discern, as shown by the work of Lucian, among many. How blurred they were is glimpsed in a letter of Libanius in which the advanced student Albanius is said to be composing the panegyric of the *Comes Orientis* Modestus, who was passing through Antioch (*Ep.* 63). But even the educated upper-class man who could not aspire to produce high literary products avidly appropriated literature and oratorical discourse and wove it into the texture of his own life. I concentrate in what follows on a few instances taken from Roman and early Byzantine Egypt that show how the rhetorical ability acquired in education could be put to use in a meaningful participation in cultural and social life. The mental gymnastics practiced in school became so integral a part of a student's being as to shape deeply his adult thinking. In taking part in contests organized by the city, in writing a panegyric for a festival celebrating some local personage, in drafting a personal letter, and in choosing the readings that could be of help for one's professional life, an educated man who lived in Alexandria, Oxyrhynchos, or Panopolis was not basically different from one who resided in Antioch or in Rome.

A papyrus from the second century preserves a rhetorical exercise in verse. The text appears to be a draft of an *ēthopoiia* centered on the lament of Helios on the death of his son Phaethon.[89] The mediocre verses are written continuously, as if in prose, with occasional dashes separating them—something that betrays their school origin. The handwriting is fluent enough but is irregular and untidy, and has many rough cancellations and corrections. Phaethon had begged his father Helios, god of the sun, to let him drive his chariot that each day caused the sun to shine on earth. Unable to control the horses, he rode up to the abode of Zeus and then came too close to the earth, nearly burning up the world, and was finally stopped by Zeus's thunderbolt. His disastrous flight was a suitable paradigm of juvenile self-assurance and a powerful check for the youth who had begun his flight into the last stage of education. Different aspects of this myth attracted the attention of various writers.[90] In Lucian, Helios responded to the reproach of Zeus by saying that his own grief was enough punishment for him (*Dial. D.* 25.279). Helios's affliction was taken as the subject of our student's exercise. "My child, you are called the light-bringer, and around your sacred tomb I shall plant golden trees,"

---

[89] *P.Lond.Lit.* 51, Plate II; *P*² 1922, with bibliography; cf. A. Körte, "Literarische Texte mit Ausschluss der christlichen," *APF* 10 (1932): 46–47.

[90] See, e.g., Ovid *Met.* 2.1–400; Philostratus *Imag.* 1.11; and Nicolaus *Progymnasmata* 3, p. 457 Spengel.

says the refrain, which can easily be memorized and is pleasant enough. It seems, however, that when he began composing, this pupil had already set his mind on certain mythological examples that he wanted to employ, regardless of the suitability of the comparisons. Thus grieving Helios is compared only with female figures: Klymene lamenting Eridanus, Kybele crying for Attis, and Aphrodite distressed over Adonis. Modern critics have been contemptuous, but it is likely that this boy's teacher was more forgiving. Similarly, on the other side of the Mediterranean, in Rome, an eleven-year-old, Q. Sulpicius Maximus, had worked on an exercise on the myth of Phaethon: his funerary stele displays the Greek hexameters that he composed on the occasion of the Capitoline games in C.E. 94.[91] Sulpicius, a sort of child prodigy, competed among fifty-two poets, writing an *ēthopoiia* with the title, "With Which Words Zeus Reproached Helios for Giving His Chariot to Phaethon." Even though victory escaped him, this young student distinguished himself *cum honore*: in spite of some undeniable weaknesses, his poem betrays a sure command of the literary tradition, and particularly of Homer.

The occasion for which the poem on papyrus was composed elicits some speculation. It could be simply the product of school routine, but it is tempting to associate it with some kind of public performance in which this student might have been engaged. Another papyrus alludes to contests in the classes of trumpeters, heralds, and poets held in Naucratis every year, in which the participants from Oxyrhynchos obtained Naucratite citizenship.[92] It is intriguing to find among the poets a sixteen-year-old, and a nineteen-year-old of whom it is said specifically that he was "still learning letters," that is, was attending school. A young man could thus hope to present the products of his scholastic toil to the world, perhaps looking to make poetry his future career. Poetic competitions were a part of games such as the annual ephebic games and the quadrennial Capitoline games held in the cities of Oxyrhynchos and Antinoe.[93] A

[91] Recent work on this inscription centers on its relation with Ovid *Met.*: S. Döpp, "Das Stegreifgedicht des Q. Sulpicius Maximus," *ZPE* 114 (1996): 99–114 (with bibliography in note 7); and H. Bernsdorff, "Q. Sulpicius Maximus, Apollonios von Rhodos und Ovid," *ZPE* 118 (1997): 105–12. See also J. A. Fernández Delgado and J. Ureña Bracero, *Un testimonio de la educación literaria griega en época romana: IG XIV 2012 = Kaibel, EG 618* (Badajoz, 1991).

[92] See *P.Oxy.* XXII.2338; R. Coles, "The Naucratites and Their Ghost-Names: P.Oxy. 2338 Revised," *ZPE* 18 (1975): 199–204.

[93] See *P.Oxy.* IV.705; *P.Oslo* III.189; *SB* IV.7336; *Pap.Colon.* XIII.8, 9, and 10; *P.Oxy.* LV.3812 and LIX.3991. Cf. Perpillou-Thomas 1986. See also *P.Oxy.* LXIII.4352, and additional bibliography cited in the introduction.

third-century poetic *encomium*, *P.Oxy.* VII.1015, refers to one of these festivals in honor of Hermes. It is a product of a different quality than the scholastic efforts described above: a local poet engaged in a polished composition to celebrate Theon, a young gymnasiarch "learned in the lore of the Muses," who had made donations to the local gymnasium.[94]

The schools nourished the talents of local bards, who occasionally achieved more than provincial stature.[95] One of these was Harpokration, who composed and delivered panegyrics and held civic offices at the end of the third and the first half of the fourth century C.E. He came from a highly educated family of Panopolis, the intellectual center of Upper Egypt, and in the words of his brother Ammon, as he traveled to deliver panegyrics on personages of the imperial court and of the state, he "moved, on each occasion, from place to place, from Greece to Rome and from Rome to Constantinople and from one city to another, having gone around practically the greatest number of districts on earth."[96] While a certain Apollo, called "the poet" and well renowned for his oratorical skills, also belonged to the same family, it is about Ammon himself that more details have come to light.[97] He styled himself as *scholasticus*, an advocate, traveled in Egypt, particularly to Alexandria, and left numerous drafts of petitions in his own hand that testify to his attempts to defend the interests of his family of priests of the old gods. The content and external characteristics of his writings amply reveal his profession and education. Thus a long, impeccable, and elaborate letter addressed to his mother shows how well he had assimilated the lessons of the grammarian and rhetorician with whom he had studied. In spite of his professional activities, Ammon found a life of study more attractive: "I myself know that a quiet life free from intrigue befits those educated in philosophy and rhetoric," he wrote in the petition mentioned above (lines 9–10). Among his papers came to light a fragment from Book 9 of the *Odyssey* and a list of Greek philosophers: he compiled the latter himself, trying to sort out the information left over from his school years and not drawing from a single source.[98]

[94] Cf. also *P.Oxy.* L.3537.

[95] See Cameron 1965b.

[96] *P.Köln* inv. 4533v.23–25, a petition; G. M. Browne, "Harpocration Panegyrista," *ICS* 2 (1977): 184–96.

[97] Cf. W. H. Willis, "Two Literary Papyri in an Archive from Panopolis," *ICS* 3 (1978): 140–51; and *P.Congr.XV* 22.

[98] *P.Duk.* inv. G 176 and 178.

Finally, a letter—a note, rather—brings us to Hermopolis in the fifth century:

> To my lord and virtuous brother Theognostos, greetings from Viktor. May your eloquence deign to give Elias . . . the schoolmaster's slave, the book that I gave your brotherliness when you were in Hermopolis—for God knows, I am in dire need—namely the [commentary] on the orator Demosthenes by Alexander Claudius . . . and Menander's *Art*, quickly. And the *Methods* and the *Eulogies*, quickly.[99]

The honorific titles used and the overall tenor of this note show that both Viktor and Theognostos were lawyers and orators. The scenario is a familiar one: a friend borrows some books and never returns them. Some time after Theognostos borrowed some books from Viktor—a commentary on Demosthenes by the sophist Alexander Claudius[100] and epideictic writings by the well-known third-century rhetor Menander—Viktor suddenly realized that he needed them urgently for a speech that he had to write—probably of declamatory and laudatory character and not for his work in the lawcourt. In the fifth-century world of law and oratory, Demosthenes still held sway.

The colors of *paideia* tinged the life choices and the professional opportunities of the ancient aristocratic elites, and the entertainments they sought in their free time. On many levels, education was not a throwaway package ready to be discarded when school time was over; it became enmeshed in the lives of people, at least those able to reach its high levels. Though a glorification of ancient education would certainly be unrealistic, the important place it occupied in the lives of some individuals after schooling was over is notable. Nowadays there are frequent lamentations about the way schooling and the rest of students' lives are separated into watertight compartments: schooling is conceived as a very special form of life, largely unrelated to the rest.[101] The tendency for people today to identify education with schooling, and society's support of this view, means that education often ends when schooling ends. But the very name that the Greeks gave to education, *paideia*, already embodied its diverse nature.[102] *Paideia*, which originally meant "child rearing," was conceived

---

[99] *SB* XII.11084.

[100] See *Suda* A1128.

[101] See J. Galtung, "Literacy, Education and Schooling–for What?" in Graff 1981a: 274.

[102] Our word "education" is also somewhat ambiguous. M. I. Finley (*The Use and Abuse of History* [London, 1975], 208) proposed to distinguish between pedagogy and education, between formal schooling and the education that takes place outside of school.

almost as a slow vegetable growth that affected people through the course of their lives and embraced more than the purely intellectual. But with the same word, the Greeks defined "culture," that is, purely intellectual maturation and assimilation of the educational values acquired through schooling. Thus, individuals who were able to take advantage of higher training continued to draw on *paideia*. Life imitated school.

* *Conclusion* *

Apion to Epimachos, his father and lord, very many greetings. Before all else I pray for your health and that you may be completely well and prosperous, together with my sister and her daughter and my brother. I thank the lord Serapis, who promptly saved me when I was in danger at sea. When I arrived at Misenum, I received from Caesar three gold pieces for traveling expenses. And I am well. I beg you, my lord father, write me a letter, telling me first about your well-being, second about the welfare of my siblings, third in order that I may worship your hand, for you gave me a good education and thus I hope to have quick advancement, with the help of the gods. Give many salutations to Capiton, my brother and sister, Serenilla, and those dear to me. I have sent you by Euktemon a portrait of myself. My name is now Antonius Maximus. . . .[1]

O<small>N ARRIVING</small> at Misenum, Apion, a young recruit in the Roman army, writes a proud letter to his father, who lived in the Egyptian town of Philadelphia. His main concern is to reassure his relatives of his wellbeing and to inquire about their health, but the letter contains much more than these conventional expressions. Apion had arrived safely in Italy after a long, dangerous journey, he was pleased to have received generous reimbursement for his travel expenses,[2] he had a new Roman name, and he had just sent a portrait of himself to his father as a keepsake. One is tempted to visualize this young man on the basis of mummy portraits of muscular, tanned youths with naked shoulders who were represented as if in the midst of athletic activities in the gymnasium (Fig. 23).[3]

Even in asking his father to write back to him—a common epistolary cliché—Apion rises above the banality of the situation: his father's letter not only would reassure him about the good health of people in the family but would bring the welcome sight of his handwriting. Like the modern papyrologist, Apion would scrutinize his father's ways of shaping the characters or some idiosyncratic modes of writing in order to evoke his presence. The fact that this young man is expecting a letter written in his

---

[1] *BGU* II.423, plate in Schubart 1911: 28a.

[2] On traveling money (*viaticum*), see R. D. Davies, "The Enlistment of Claudius Terentianus," *BASP* 10 (1973): 22 n. 10.

[3] E.g., M.-F. Aubert and R. Cortopassi, *Portraits de l' Égypte romaine* (Paris, 1998), no. 46.

father's own hand confirms that he himself penned his epistle: his large, round characters are fluent and are similar to those of a teacher's hand. This letter is well constructed with choice vocabulary and symmetrical sentences. In spite of its fervent sincerity, it reeks a bit of the maxims honoring one's parents that were ingrained from the most tender years by routine schooling. Apion had access to at least some grammatical education; we do not know whether he moved at all beyond that. In his own words, he had received a good education that would allow him to advance quickly in his career.

It is impossible to know where Apion had pursued his full education. Some literary school exercises have survived from Philadelphia, his hometown, only from the Ptolemaic period.[4] It is likely that in the second century C.E., this young man had to leave his family in order to attend the class of a grammarian. His father must have followed his progress closely, both when he was receiving the basics in his town—perhaps in some informal situation—and when he engaged in grammatical studies somewhere else: as I have argued, continuous monitoring of one's children's schooling was mandatory. The first stage of education in which students like Apion learned the rudiments was in a sense the most important, because it provided them with fundamental notions of literacy beyond which most students never proceeded. The papyri have allowed us to make significant gains in understanding this. They have indicated not only that life circumstances determined one's exposure to instruction, but also that practical needs and pedagogic exigencies shaped school structure and curricula. Approaching education through the perspective of real people has provided more concrete details to supplement the rigid and idealized accounts of the literary sources, which mostly describe the advanced education of male members of the elite.

The papyri have also permitted us to reach important conclusions with respect to female literacy. They have shown that women, primarily those belonging to the upper class, had access to elementary education, and that some of them were able to reach more advanced stages. It is true that there are few examples of women who did not possess a royal or highly exceptional status who were able to reach secondary education. One should remember, however, that those who emerge from the papyrological evidence are the ones who can be identified on the basis of strict

[4] Cribiore 1996a: nos. 233, 234, 235, and 236.

palaeographical criteria, and that it is likely that more unidentified elite women partook of "male" education.

The documentation surviving from Egypt that concerns advanced stages of education is invaluable because it allows us to test the validity of what the literary sources and the anecdotal tradition reveal. Though at times the papyri confirm the prevalence of certain educational practices, most often they flesh out the generic and sketchy statements of the ancient authors. It is possible, therefore, to reach a more realistic view of the taxonomy of educational exercises and of the methods teachers used, and to determine which authors—or parts of their works—and which rhetorical exercises they preferred. The education that an upper-class student received in Alexandria or Oxyrhynchos appears to be like that attained by a youth around the Mediterranean, judging from what is known of the cultural upbringing of certain writers from other parts of the ancient world. The papyri, moreover, sometimes suggest educational practices that go unmentioned by the literary sources, such as writing letters in a school setting.

In what follows, I would like to briefly address a last question concerning the overall value of the ancient educational system. Ancient education has often been indicted for its shortcomings.[5] It communicated an inert subservience to conventional values and contents and a passive receptivity to the knowledge imparted, with no attempt to question the transmitted doctrine. It concentrated exclusively on a culture frozen in the past with little attention devoted to contemporary authors and issues: in it, the "pedagogic work of inculcation" and the tendency to fall back on formulas reached extremes.[6] Besides an extreme reliance on inexorable rules that sometimes bordered on the nonsensical, the content of the instruction was fixed and narrow; almost no attention was paid to history and geography except for a wealth of minute information arising from specific points in the literary texts; and the themes treated by rhetoric consisted of a handful of stereotyped issues. A liberal arts education soon became a study of a restricted, canonical list of books, *ta biblia*—a term that later designated the Christian Scriptures. A pupil became conversant in a highly selected segment of the literary past according to a method by which only certain parts of certain works of an author were slowly canvassed, while

---

[5] Marrou 1975 in part contributed to wiping out the idyllic view of ancient education visible, for instance, in Harrent 1898 and Freeman 1907.

[6] P. Bourdieu, *The Logic of Practice* (Stanford, Calif., 1990), 102–3.

the rest was almost ignored—much as classical authors have often been taught in modern times.

And yet, it is important to realize that not everything was negative. Rules, formulas, and rituals had a comforting quality. For the girl or boy who learned to read, write, and compute, the path was clear and unambiguous, and one step lead to the next. Fixed rules also communicated the inevitable illusion that knowledge was within reach and that the assimilation even of part of it gave the learner some power. Know the alphabet—*grammata*—and you will be literate; know syllables and you will be able to read; know the formulaic parts of an epistle and you will be able to compose a letter; memorize some Homer and you will be truly Greek. The spirit of literature was not completely choked under the burden, but was able to bear some fruits and inspired a lingering love for its products. Members of the privileged male minority who reached the highest educational levels remembered fondly throughout their lives the knowledge transmitted in their school days. The emphasis on excellence in speaking and writing enforced by rhetorical education served the aims of a society where persuasive public speaking was a central skill.[7]

In addition, the practice of reading texts closely and of reaching a deep textual experience through careful verbal analysis, as learned in the school of the grammarian, gave students a sound knowledge of language and the ability to use words with dexterity. We have seen that in Rome, Egypt, and elsewhere in the empire, people were exposed to more than one language, and literacy was often approached through the weaker (Greek or Latin). At all levels of instruction, the consequences of bilingualism were noticeable. Not only was learning to read a long, arduous process, but the practice of reading slowly and carefully continued at higher educational stages. Today, current reading practices are under scrutiny.[8] Some critics argue that language is taken for granted, so that it becomes transparent to our interests, and that students should learn to read texts closely as opposed to merely or mistakenly theorizing about them. Ancient teachers relied solely on verbal analysis to elucidate a text. Though deployment of themes and arguments was not their specific concern—and it may be argued that the creative potential of language was not completely ex-

---

[7] On the importance of rhetorical skills in the Roman world, F. Millar, *The Emperor in the Roman World* (Ithaca, N.Y., 1977), 203–12, 363–68, and passim.

[8] See D. Donoghue (*The Practice of Reading* [New Haven, Conn., 1998]), who is close to the tradition of the New Critics and who wishes that English could be approached with the slow, careful pace of a second language.

ploited—by showing students that language was opaque, they gave them the humility to approach the texts with painstaking scrutiny and without demanding immediate gratification.

In the course of this book, we have met people who believed in the power and economic value of education. The claim that education would assure financial and social success is common in the literary sources.[9] We have seen that both teachers and parents extolled not only the prestige that education carried but also the higher income it would bring. It is legitimate now to ask how realistic these claims were. Among people of low income and status, a belief in the economic value of literacy must have sometimes been a myth, as it was in the nineteenth century, in an age of industrialization, when literacy was not always necessary for employment and earnings, particularly among the unskilled.[10] Undoubtedly, in spite of the existence of a network of literates providing help, some education helped people defend themselves against fraud and was of use in business. At the low end of the scale, however, some degree of skill and income was attainable without schooling. Moreover, in a world where most people were illiterate, literacy was desirable, but lack of education did not bring any stigma. Perhaps it is more appropriate to reverse the causal relationships between education and economic growth. It is more likely that some economic comfort led to the attempt to acquire some literacy in order better to take care of one's business and property.

Among persons of elite status, who held positions of power, the relationship between higher education, success, and economic development was somewhat more direct, though not unambiguous. No doubt literacy and education were necessary for entry into such circles and brought some economic rewards. Grammatical and rhetorical education forged valuable connections and were launching pads to legal careers and to coveted posts in the administration. These were the stages at which competition was felt most acutely.[11] A vast number of the letters of Libanius were letters of recommendation for his pupils, and often not only the best of them, making them as appealing as possible to people who could grant

[9] Cf., e.g., Herodas *Didaskalos*; Lucian's representation of Lady Rhetoric as the river Nile surrounded by wealth, power, fame, and praise, *Rhetorum praeceptor* 6; parents' claim that education will bring their sons wealth, John Chrysostom *PG Adversus oppugnatores vitae monasticae* 47, 357.21–28; and the repeated praise of the power of oratory in Libanius, e.g., *Or.* 35.19.

[10] See Graff 1981b: 232–60.

[11] Gleason 1995: xxiii–xxiv, 9; Morgan 1998: 74–89.

them desirable positions.[12] Naturally, not everybody was satisfied. The disillusioned student of Libanius whose words were quoted in the Introduction lamented the futility of the hard work he had done on poets, rhetors, and other writers, since he thought that the result of "the sweat" was going to be "to wander about and be despised, while another is rich and happy."[13] Libanius himself felt that traditional Greek education was threatened to a degree by new technologies such as stenography, and by the study of the law, which required the knowledge of Latin.[14] But even though he occasionally manifested some resentment over the wealth acquired by modest people, such as "the son of the cook or the fuller," and commented acidly on the success of some people of both low birth and limited education, nevertheless these were exceptional cases.[15] One should not forget, however, that the value of higher education was often more social than practical or economical. Moreover, since social class origins were a decisive ingredient in assuring higher education, and since wealth was in most cases a *sine qua non* for a student to travel long distances and pay high fees, it is difficult to delineate precisely the respective effects of education and socioeconomic status on a youth's future success. Significantly, it has been shown that the profession of a student's father was a much more powerful determinant of a youth's career than educational achievements per se.[16]

But the most conspicuous legacy of ancient *paideia* was a system of training that assured good work habits and discipline, and consequently enhanced the likelihood of future success. Education trained a male or female student to follow rules, to persevere to the end of a task, to scrutinize a text dutifully in search of clues, to repeat endless drills, and to endure long hours. In sum, a student became accustomed to an incessant gymnastics of the mind. A recent study of ancient education that has evaluated the descriptions that ancient educational writers left of the process of teaching and learning has concluded that according to them, the mind of a student developed through the interaction between its natural qualities—such as memory or reason—and the teacher's contribution to the process—such as correction and delivery of information.[17] One funda-

[12] Petit 1956: 158–61.

[13] *Or.* 62.12; cf. above, p. 11.

[14] Schouler 1991: 270–72.

[15] *Or.* 62.11, 42.23–24. St. Augustine was a partial exception, since his father was member of the town council and had some—albeit modest—means.

[16] Petit 1956: 154–55, 166–78.

[17] Morgan 1998: 240–70.

mental ingredient has been forgotten, however, something without which the process of learning could not take place and which was in a sense the very trigger of the educational process: hard work. Ancient writers who wrote about education were fully aware of the fundamental importance of personal application in the academic success of a student. When Quintilian describes learning, words such as *labor* ("toil") and *studium* ("study") occur constantly, the latter being accompanied by adjectives such as "persistent" and "continuous" (*studium pertinax, perpetuum*).[18] In addition to a pupil's innate predisposition for learning and the effort and ability of his teacher, it was perseverance and insistence on repetitive and rigorous exercises that brought success. Ps.-Plutarch agreed on that. With application and hard work, even those not endowed with natural gifts had a chance to learn.[19]

"Hard work" (*ponos*) is a leitmotif in the orations and epistles of Libanius. "Hard work," he says, "gave the crown to the athlete and the soldier, allowed the captain to save his ship and the doctor to save his patient consumed by a disease, and gave the farmer the fruits of the earth" (*Or.* 55.27). In school, hard work enabled a student to reap the fruits of his intelligence. In some letters, Libanius specifically reproached pupils for being lazy and urged them to withstand the labors of *paideia* in order to acquire the power of eloquence.[20] The importance of personal application is particularly evident in those letters he addressed to parents to keep them abreast of their sons' progress.[21] Naturally, in these letters he praises their sons' innate intelligence (*physis*) and the mental and physical characteristics they had in common with their fathers. No doubt Libanius was a master at tickling paternal vanity. But immediately after, he extols these students' capacity for hard work, eagerness for study, and zealous effort (*ponos, prothymia,* and *spoudē*). Writing to a father, he says, "Looking at the natural qualities of your son and at his enjoyment for hard work, I quote the proverb that says: 'Plants that are going to bear fruit stand out clearly' " (*Ep.* 32.3).

The notions education transmitted were subordinate to the training itself, since good training prepared people for further instruction. The precise order of technical skills and elements of knowledge could be mas-

---

[18] See, e.g., I *Preface* 14 and 27; 1.1.10. Talent, study, and practice were already fundamental to the pedagogic theories of the sophists.

[19] Ps.-Plutarch *De liberis educandis* 2; the terms used are: *meletē, askēsis, epimeleia,* and *ponos* ("practice," "exercise," "application," "work").

[20] See *Ep.* 139 and 1164.

[21] See, e.g., *Ep.* 32, 1005, 1101, 1309, and 1471.

tered only through diligent work, which inculcated into students the notion of the value and necessity of discipline. Inevitably it also showed them that the order and rules that governed the world had to be respected. But even as education taught good behavior and obedience both to rules and to those who enforced them, it also gave people—and particularly those who reached its higher stages—arrogance, confidence, a sense of superiority with respect to the uneducated or the less educated, and the capability to rule them. Apion, the young Roman army recruit, was well placed.

* Select Bibliography *

Abu-Lughod, Lila. 1993. *Writing Women's Worlds*. Berkeley.

Bagnall, Roger S. 1992. "An Owner of Literary Papyri." *CPh* 87: 137–40.

———. 1993. *Egypt in Late Antiquity*. Princeton.

Balogh, Joseph. 1927. "Voces paginarum." *Philologus* 82: 84–109, 202–40.

Barns, John. 1950–51. "A New Gnomologium: With Some Remarks on Gnomic Anthologies." *CQ* 44: 126–37; *CQ*, n.s. 1: 1–19.

Beck, Frederick A. 1975. *Album of Greek Education*. Sydney.

Bergamasco, Marco. 1995. "Le διδασκαλικαί nella ricerca attuale." *Aegyptus* 75: 95–167.

Berry, D. H., and Malcolm Heath. 1997. "Oratory and Declamation." In Porter 1997: 393–420.

Besques, Simone. 1992. *Catalogue raisonné des figurines et reliefs*. Vol. 4, part 2. Paris.

Bischoff, Bernhard. 1966. *Mittelalterliche Studien*. Stuttgart.

Blanchard, Alain. 1991. "Sur le milieu d' origine du papyrus Bodmer de Ménandre." *CE* 66: 211–20.

———. 1997. "Destins de Ménandre." *Ktema* 22: 213–25.

Bloomer, W. Martin. 1997. "Schooling in Persona: Imagination and Subordination in Roman Education." *ClAnt* 16: 57–78.

Blum, Herwig. 1969. *Die antike Mnemotechnik*. Hildesheim and New York.

Bonner, Stanley F. 1949. *Roman Declamation*. Liverpool.

———. 1977. *Education in Ancient Rome*. Berkeley and Los Angeles.

Booth, Alan D. 1973. "Punishment, Discipline and Riot in the Schools of Antiquity." *EMC* 17: 107–14.

———. 1979a. "Elementary and Secondary Education in the Roman Empire." *Florilegium* 1: 1–14.

———. 1979b. "The Schooling of Slaves in First-Century Rome." *TAPhA* 109: 11–19.

Bouquiaux-Simon, Odette. 1968. *Les lectures homériques de Lucien*. Académie royale de Belgique, Mémoires 59, fasc. 2. Brussels.

Bouquiaux-Simon, Odette, and Paul Mertens. 1992. "Les témoignages papyrologiques d' Euripide: Liste sommaire arrêtée au 1/6/1990." In Mario Capasso, ed., *Papiri letterari greci e latini*, 97–107. Lecce.

Bowersock, G. W. 1969. *Greek Sophists in the Roman Empire*. Oxford.

———. 1990. *Hellenism in Late Antiquity*. Ann Arbor.

Bowie, E. L. 1970. "Greeks and Their Past in the Second Sophistic." *Past and Present* 46: 3–41.

Bowman, Alan K. 1990. *Egypt after the Pharaohs*. London.

Bowman, Alan K. 1991. "Literacy in the Roman Empire: Mass and Mode." In Humphrey 1991: 119–31.

Bowman, Alan K., and J. D. Thomas. 1994. *The Vindolanda Writing Tablets*. London.

Bowman, Alan K., and Greg Woolf, eds. 1994a. *Literacy and Power in the Ancient World*. Cambridge.

———. 1994b. "Literacy and Power in the Ancient World." In Bowman and Woolf 1994a: 1–16.

Bradley, Keith R. 1991. *Discovering the Roman Family*. Princeton.

Bremer, J. M. 1983. "The Popularity of Euripides' *Phoenissae* in Late Antiquity." In *Actes VII Congrès F.I.E.C.*, 281–88. Budapest.

Bresciani, E., S. Pernigotti, and M. C. Betrò. 1983. *Ostraca demotici da Narmuti*. Pisa.

Brooks, Greg, and A. K. Pugh, eds. 1984. *Studies in the History of Reading*. Reading, Eng.

Brown, Peter. 1992. *Power and Persuasion in Late Antiquity*. Madison, Wis.

Browning, Robert. 1992. "The Byzantines and Homer." In Lamberton and Keaney 1992: 134–48.

Brunner, H. 1957. *Altägyptische Erziehung*. Wiesbaden.

Cameron, Alan. 1965a. "Roman School Fees." *CR* 79: 257–58.

———. 1965b. "Wandering Poets: A Literary Movement in Byzantine Egypt." *Historia* 14: 470–509.

———. 1995. *Callimachus and His Critics*. Princeton.

Cameron, Averil. 1991. *Christianity and the Rhetoric of Empire*. Berkeley.

Carrara, Paolo. 1988. "Plutarco ed Euripide: Alcune considerazioni sulle citazioni euripidee in Plutarco (*De aud. poet.*)." *ICS* 13: 447–55.

Carruthers, Mary J. 1990. *The Book of Memory: A Study of Memory in Medieval Culture*. Cambridge.

Cavallo, Guglielmo, ed. 1984. *Libri, editori, e pubblico nel mondo antico. Guida storica e critica*. Bari.

———. 1986. "Conservazione e perdita dei testi greci: Fattori materiali, sociali, culturali." In Giardina 1986: 83–172.

Cavallo, Guglielmo, and Herwig Maehler. 1987. *Greek Bookhands of the Early Byzantine Period*. London.

Clanchy, M. T. 1993. *From Memory to Written Record: England 1066–1307*. 2d ed. London.

Clark, Donald Lemen. 1957. *Rhetoric in Greco-Roman Education*. Westport, Conn.

Clarke, Martin Lowther. 1971. *Higher Education in the Ancient World*. London.

———. 1996. *Rhetoric at Rome: A Historical Survey*. 3d ed. London.

Clarysse, Willy. 1982. "Literary Papyri in Documentary Archives." In *Egypt and the Hellenistic World*, Proceedings of the International Colloquium. Leuven. (= *Studia Hellenistica* 27 [1983]: 43–61.)

Cole, Susan G. 1981. "Could Greek Women Read and Write?" In Foley 1981: 219–45.

Cressy, David. 1981. "Levels of Illiteracy in England, 1530–1730." In Graff 1981a: 105–24.

Cribiore, Raffaella. 1992. "The Happy Farmer: A Student Composition from Roman Egypt." *GRBS* 33: 247–63.

———. 1993. "A Homeric Exercise from the Byzantine Schoolroom." *CE* 68: 145–54.

———. 1994. "A Homeric Writing Exercise and Reading Homer in School." *Tyche* 9: 1–8.

———. 1995a. "A Hymn to the Nile." *ZPE* 106: 97–106.

———. 1995b. "A Schooltablet from the Hearst Museum." *ZPE* 107: 263–70.

———. 1996a. *Writing, Teachers, and Students in Graeco-Roman Egypt*. Atlanta.

———. 1996b. "Gli esercizi scolastici dell' Egitto greco-romano: Cultura letteraria e cultura popolare nella scuola." In O. Pecere and A. Stramaglia, eds., *La letteratura di consumo nel mondo greco-latino*, 505–25. Cassino.

———. 1997a. "A Fragment of Basilius of Caesarea." In *Akten des 21. Internationalen Papyrologenkongresses, APF*, Beiheft 3, 187–93.

———. 1997b. "Literary School Exercises." *ZPE* 116: 53–60.

———. 1998. "A School Tablet: A List of Names and Numbers." *BASP* 35: 145–51.

———. 1999. Review of Morgan 1998. *Bryn Mawr Classical Review* (May 22).

Davison, J. A. 1955. "The Study of Homer in Graeco-Roman Egypt." *Akten VIII Congr.Pap.* 51–58.

Della Corte, Matteo. 1959. "Scuole e maestri in Pompei antica." *StudRom* 6: 621–34.

Delorme, J. 1960. *Gymnasion: Étude sur les monuments consacrés à l' éducation en Grèce, des origines à l' empire romain*. Paris.

De Martino, Francesco, and Onofrio Vox. 1996. *Lirica greca*. 3 vols. Bari.

DeMause, L., ed. 1974. *The History of Childhood: The Evolution of Parent-Child Relationships as a Factor in History*. New York.

Desbordes, Françoise. 1990. *Idées romaines sur l' écriture*. Lille.

Di Benedetto, Vincenzo. 1958. "Dionisio Trace e la Techne a lui attribuita." *AnnPisa*, ser. 2, 27: 169–210.

———. 1959. "Dionisio Trace e la Techne a lui attribuita." *AnnPisa*, ser. 2, 28: 87–118.

———. 1973. "La Techne spuria." *AnnPisa*, ser. 3, 3: 797–814.

Dickey, Eleanor. 1996. *Greek Forms of Address*. Oxford.

Dilke, O.A.W. 1987. *Mathematics and Measurements*. Berkeley.

Dionisotti, A. C. 1982. "From Ausonius' Schooldays? A Schoolbook and Its Relatives." *JRS* 72: 83–125.

Dornseiff, Franz. 1925. *Das Alphabet in Mystik und Magie*. Leipzig.

Doxiadis, Euphrosyne. 1995. *The Mysterious Fayum Portraits: Faces from Ancient Egypt*. London.

Easterling, Pat. 1995. "Menander: Loss and Survival." *Bulletin of the Institute of Classical* Studies, suppl. 66: 153–60.

Eyre, Christopher, and John Baines. 1989. "Interactions between Orality and Literacy in Ancient Egypt." In Karen Schousboe and Mogens Trolle Larsen, eds., *Literacy and Society*, 91–119. Copenhagen.

Fantham, Elaine. 1978. "Imitation and Decline: Rhetorical Theory and Practice in the First Century after Christ." *CPh* 73: 102–16.

Fatouros, G., and T. Krischer. 1980. *Libanios: Briefe*. Munich.

Festugière, A. J. 1959. *Antioche païenne et chrétienne: Libanius, Chrysostome et les moines de Syrie*. Paris.

Foley, Helene P., ed. 1981. *Reflections of Women in Antiquity*. Philadelphia.

Fournet, Jean-Luc. 1992. "Une éthopée de Caïn dans le Codex des Visions de la Fondation Bodmer." *ZPE* 92: 253–66.

———. 1997. "Du nouveau dans la bibliothèque de Dioscore d' Aphrodité." In *Akten des 21. Internationalen Papyrologenkongresses*, 297–304. Berlin.

———. 1999. *Hellénisme dans l' Égypte du VIe siècle: La bibliothèque et l' oeuvre de Dioscore d' Aphrodité*. Cairo.

Fowler, D. H. 1987. *The Mathematics of Plato's Academy*. Oxford.

Frasca, Rosella. 1996a. *La multimedialità della comunicazione educativa in Grecia e a Roma: Scenari, percorsi*. Bari.

———. 1996b. *Educazione e formazione a Roma*. Bari.

Fraser, Peter Marshall. 1972. *Ptolemaic Alexandria*. Oxford.

Freeman, Kenneth J. 1907. *Schools of Hellas: An Essay on the Practice and Theory of Ancient Greek Education*. London.

Gadd, C. J. 1956. *Teachers and Students in the Oldest Schools*. London.

Gallo, Italo. 1980. *Frammenti biografici da papiri*. Vol. 2. Rome.

Gardner, Jane F. 1986. *Women in Roman Law and Society*. Bloomington and Indianapolis, Ind.

Gardthausen, Viktor E. 1913. *Griechische Palaeographie*. Vol. 2. Leipzig.

Gavrilov, A. K. 1997. "Techniques of Reading in Classical Antiquity." *CQ* 47: 56–73.

Gehl, Paul F. 1989. "Latin Readers in Fourteenth-Century Florence: Schoolkids and Their Books." *S&C* 13: 387–440.

Giardina, Andrea. 1986. *Società romana e impero tardoantico: Tradizione dei classici, trasformazioni della cultura*. Bari.

Gignac, Francis T. 1976–81. *A Grammar of the Greek Papyri of the Roman and Byzantine Periods*. Vols. 1–2. Milan.

Gleason, Maud W. 1995. *Making Men: Sophists and Self-Presentation in Ancient Rome*. Princeton.

Goetz, Georg. 1892. *Corpus glossariorum Latinorum*. Vol. 3, *Hermeneumata Pseudodositheana*. Leipzig.

Goetz, Georg, and Gottohold Gundermann. 1888. *Corpus glossariorum Latinorum.* Vol. 2. Leipzig.

Goody, Jack. 1987. *The Interface between the Written and the Oral.* Cambridge.

Graff, Harvey J., ed. 1981a. *Literacy and Social Development in the West: A Reader.* Cambridge.

———. 1981b. "Literacy, Jobs, and Industrialization: The Nineteenth Century." In Graff 1981a: 232–60.

Guéraud, O., and P. Jouguet. 1938. *Un livre d' écolier du IIIe siècle avant J. C.* Cairo.

Hagedorn, D., and M. Weber. 1968. "Die griechisch-koptische Rezension der Menandersentenzen." *ZPE* 3: 15–50.

Hanawalt, Barbara A. 1993. *Growing up in Medieval London: The Experience of Childhood in History.* Oxford.

Hanson, Ann Ellis. 1991. "Ancient Illiteracy." In Humphrey 1991: 159–98.

Harrent, A. 1898. *Les écoles d' Antioche au IVe siècle.* Paris.

Harris, William V. 1989. *Ancient Literacy.* Cambridge, Mass.

Harvey, F. David. 1966. "Literacy in the Athenian Democracy." *REG* 79: 585–635.

———. 1978. "Greeks and Romans Learn to Write." *Communication Arts in the Ancient World,* 63–78. New York.

Hasitzka, Monika R. M. 1990. *Neue Texte und Dokumentation zum Koptisch-Unterricht. MPER N.S. XVIII.* Vienna.

Haslam, Michael. 1997. "Homeric Papyri and Transmission of the Text." In Morris and Powell 1997: 55–100.

Heath, Malcolm. 1995. *Hermogenes on Issues: Strategies of Argument in Later Greek Rhetoric.* Oxford.

Hembold, William C., and Edward N. O'Neil. 1959. *Plutarch's Quotations.* American Philological Association Monographs. Atlanta.

Hock, Ronald F., and Edward N. O'Neil. 1986. *The Chreia in Ancient Rhetoric.* Atlanta.

Hope, C. A., and K. A. Worp. 1998. "A New Fragment of Homer." *Mnemosyne* 51: 206–10.

Humphrey, J. H., ed. 1991. *Literacy in the Roman World. JRA,* suppl.3. Ann Arbor.

Huskinson, Janet. 1996. *Roman Children's Sarcophagi: Their Decoration and Social Significance.* Oxford.

Huys, Marc. 1996. "*P.Oxy.* 61.4099: A Combination of Mythographic Lists with Sentences of the Seven Wise Men." *ZPE* 113: 205–12.

Immerwahr, Henry R. 1964. "Book Rolls on Attic Vases." In C. Henderson, Jr., ed., *Classical, Mediaeval, and Renaissance Studies in Honor of Berthold Louis Ullmann,* 17–48. Rome.

———. 1973. "More Book Rolls on Attic Vases." *Antike Kunst* 16: 143–47.

257

Jaeger, Werner. 1986. *Paideia: The Ideals of Greek Culture.* Trans. G. Highet. Vol. 2. Oxford.

Jäkel, Siegfried. 1964. *Menandri Sententiae.* Leipzig.

Joshel, S. R., and S. Murnaghan, eds. 1998. *Women and Slaves in Greco-Roman Culture.* London.

Kaster, Robert A. 1983. "Notes on Primary and Secondary Schools in Late Antiquity." *TAPhA* 113: 223–46.

———. 1988. *Guardians of Language: The Grammarian and Society in Late Antiquity.* Berkeley.

Kennedy, George A. 1983. *Greek Rhetoric under Christian Emperors.* Princeton.

———. 1997. "The Genres of Rhetoric." In Porter 1997: 43–50.

Kenyon, Frederic G. 1899. *The Palaeography of Greek Papyri.* Oxford.

———. 1951. *Books and Readers in Ancient Greece and Rome.* 2d ed. Oxford.

Kindstrand, Jan Fredrik. 1973. *Homer in der Zweiten Sophistik.* Uppsala.

Kleijwegt, Marc. 1991. *Ancient Youth.* Amsterdam.

Knox, Bernard M. W. 1968. "Silent Reading in Antiquity." *GRBS* 9: 421–35.

Kramer, Johannes. 1983. *Glossaria bilinguia in papyris et membranis reperta.* Bonn.

Krüger, Julian. 1990. *Oxyrhynchos in der Kaiserzeit.* Europäische Hochschulschriften 3. Frankfurt.

Lamberton, Robert, and John J. Keaney. 1992. *Homer's Ancient Readers: The Hermeneutics of Greek Epic's Earliest Exegetes.* Princeton.

Lameere, William. 1960. *Aperçus de paléographie homérique.* Brussels.

Lane Fox, Robin. 1994. "Literacy and Power in Early Christianity." In Bowman and Woolf 1994a: 126–48.

Law, Vivien. 1996. "The Mnemonic Structure of Ancient Grammatical Doctrine." In Swiggers and Wouters 1996: 37–52.

Law, Vivien, and Ineke Sluiter, eds. 1995. *Dionysius Thrax and the Techne Grammatike.* Münster.

Legras, Bernard. 1998. *Éducation et culture dans le monde grec (VIIIe-Ier siècle av.J.-C.).* Paris.

———. 1999. *Néotês: Recherches sur les jeunes grecs dans l' Égypte ptolémaïque et romaine.* Geneva.

Lloyd-Jones, Hugh, and Peter Parsons. 1983. *Supplementum Hellenisticum.* Berlin and New York.

Maehler, Herwig. 1983. "Die griechische Schule im ptolemäischen Ägypten." *Studia Hellenistica* 27: 191–203.

———. 1993. "Die Scholien der Papyri in ihrem Verhältniss zu den Scholiencorpora der Handschriften." In *La philologie grecque à l' époque hellénistique et romaine, Entretiens sur l' antiquité classique* 40: 95–141.

———. 1997. "Byzantine Egypt: Urban Élites and Book Production." *Dialogos* 4: 118–36.

Mandilaras, Basil G. 1973. *The Verb in the Greek Non-Literary Papyri.* Athens.

Manguel, Alberto. 1996. *A History of Reading*. New York.

Mansfeld, Jaap. 1994. *Prolegomena: Questions To Be Settled before the Study of an Author, or a Text*. Leiden.

Marrou, Henri-Irénée. 1937. *Études sur les scènes de la vie intellectuelle figurant sur les monuments funéraires Romains*. Grenoble.

———. 1975. *Histoire de l' éducation dans l' antiquité*. Vol. 1, *Le monde grec*; vol. 2, *Le monde romain*. 7th ed. Paris.

Martin, Jean. 1988. *Libanios: Discours II*. Paris.

Mastromarco, Giuseppe. 1984. *The Public of Herondas*. Amsterdam.

Mastronarde, Donald J. 1994. *Euripides Phoenissae: Edited with Introduction and Commentary*. Cambridge.

McDonnell, Myles. 1996. "Writing, Copying, and the Autograph Manuscripts in Ancient Rome." CQ 46: 469–91.

McKitterick, Rosamond, ed. 1990. *The Uses of Literacy in Early Medieval Europe*. Cambridge.

McNamee, Kathleen. 1994. "School Notes." In *Proceedings of the Twentieth International Congress of Papyrologists*, 177–82. Copenhagen.

———. 1998. "Another Chapter in the History of Scholia." CQ 48: 269–88.

Mercer, Neil, ed. 1988. *Language and Literacy from an Educational Perspective*. Vol. 1, *Language Studies*; vol. 2, *In Schools*. Philadelphia.

Milne, J. G. 1908. "Relics of Graeco-Egyptian Schools." *JHS* 28: 121–32.

Montanari, Franco. 1979. *Studi di filologia omerica antica*. Vol. 1. Pisa.

———. 1984. "Gli *homerica* su papiro: Per una distinzione di generi." *Ricerche di Filologia Classica* 2: 125–38.

Montevecchi, Orsolina. 1988. *La papirologia*. Milan.

Montserrat, Dominic. 1996. *Sex and Society in Graeco-Roman Egypt*. London.

Morgan, Teresa. 1998. *Literate Education in the Hellenistic and Roman Worlds*. Cambridge.

———. 1999. "Literate Education in Classical Athens." CQ 49, 1: 46–61.

Morris, Ian, and Barry Powell, eds. 1997. *A New Companion to Homer*. Leiden.

Müller, Albert. 1910. "Studentenleben im 4. Jahrhundert n.Chr." *Philologus* 69: 292–317.

Nilsson, Martin P. 1955. *Die hellenistische Schule*. Munich.

Nissen, Hans J., Peter Damerow, and Robert K. Englund, eds. 1993. *Archaic Bookkeeping: Early Writing and Techniques of Economic Administration in the Ancient Near East*. Chicago.

Norman, A. F. 1960. "The Book Trade in Fourth-Century Antioch." *JHS* 80: 122–26.

———. 1964. "The Library of Libanius." *RhM* 107: 158–75.

———, ed. 1992. *Libanius: Autobiography and Selected Letters*. Cambridge, Mass.

Orlandi, Tito. 1978. *Il dossier copto del martire Psote*. Milan.

Pack, Roger A. 1965. *The Greek and Latin Literary Texts from Greco-Roman Egypt*. Ann Arbor.

Parkes, M. B. 1993. *Pause and Effect*. Berkeley.

Parsons, Peter J. 1980–81. "Background: The Papyrus Letter." *Didactica Classica Gandensia* 20–21: 3–19.

———. 1982. "Facts from Fragments." *G&R* 29: 184–95.

Patillon, Michel. 1997. *Aelius Théon: Progymnasmata*. Paris.

Pernot, Laurent. 1993. *La rhétorique de l' éloge dans le monde greco-romain*. Paris.

Perpillou-Thomas, F. 1986. "La panégyrie au gymnase d' Oxyrhynchos." *CE* 61: 303–12.

Petit, Paul. 1956. *Les étudiants de Libanius: Un professeur de faculté et ses élèves au Bas Empire*. Paris.

Pfeiffer, Rudolph. 1968. *History of Classical Scholarship: From the Beginnings to the End of the Hellenistic Age*. Oxford.

Pidgeon, Douglas. 1988. "Theory and Practice in Learning to Read." In Mercer 1988, 2: 126–39.

Pinto, Mario. 1974. "La scuola di Libanio nel quadro del IV secolo dopo Cristo." *Rendiconti Istituto Lombardo* 108: 146–79.

Pomeroy, Sarah B. 1977. "*Technikai kai mousikai*." *AJAH* 2: 51–68.

———. 1981. "Women in Roman Egypt: A Preliminary Study Based on Papyri." In Foley 1981: 303–22.

———. 1984. *Women in Hellenistic Egypt: From Alexander to Cleopatra*. New York.

Popkewitz, Thomas S., and Marie Brennan, eds. 1998. *Foucault's Challenge: Discourse, Knowledge, and Power in Education*. New York.

Porter, Stanley E., ed. 1997. *Handbook of Classical Rhetoric in the Hellenistic Period (330 B.C.–A.D. 400)*. Leiden.

Powell, Iohannes U. 1925. *Collectanea Alexandrina*. Oxford.

Préaux, Claire. 1929. "Lettres privées grecques d' Égypte relatives à l' éducation." *RBPh* 8: 757–800.

Quaegebeur, Jan. 1982. "De la préhistoire de l' écriture copte." *Orientalia Lovanensia Periodica* 13: 125–36.

Raffaelli, Lucia M. 1984. "Repertorio dei papiri contenenti *Scholia Minora in Homerum*." *Ricerche di filologia classica* 2: 139–77.

Ray, J. D. 1986. "The Emergence of Writing in Egypt." *World Archaeology* 17, 3: 307–16.

Rea, John. 1993. "A Student's Letter to his Father: P.Oxy. XVIII 2190 Revised." *ZPE* 99: 75–88.

Reif, Stefan C. 1990. "Aspects of Mediaeval Jewish Literacy." In McKitterick 1990: 134–55.

Reverdin, Olivier, and Bernard Grange, eds. 1993. *La philologie grecque à l' époque hellénistique et romaine. Entretiens sur l' Antiquité classique* 40.

Reynolds, Suzanne. 1996. *Medieval Reading: Grammar, Rhetoric, and the Classical Text*. Cambridge.

Riché, Pierre. 1995. *Éducation et culture dans l' Occident barbare (VIe–VIIIe siècle)*. 4th ed. Paris.

Robb, Kevin. 1994. *Literacy and Paideia in Ancient Greece*. Oxford.

Robins, Robert Henry. 1996. "The Initial Section of the *Techne Grammatike*." In Swiggers and Wouters 1996: 3–15.

Russell, D. A. 1983. *Greek Declamation*. Cambridge.

———. 1996. *Libanius: Imaginary Speeches*. London.

Saenger, Paul. 1982. "Silent Reading: Its Impact in Late Medieval Script and Society." *Viator* 13: 367–414.

Said, Suzanne, ed. 1991. *Hellenismos: Quelques jalons pour une histoire de l' identité grecque*. Leiden.

Saller, Richard P. 1994. *Patriarchy, Property and Death in the Roman Family*. Cambridge.

Schenkeveld, Dirk Maria. 1991. "Figures and Tropes: A Border-Case between Grammar and Rhetoric." In Ueding 1991: 149–57.

———. 1993. "Scholarship and Grammar." In Reverdin and Grange 1993: 263–301.

Schouler, Bernard. 1984. *La tradition héllénique chez Libanios*. Paris.

———. 1991. "Hellénisme et humanisme chez Libanios." In Said 1991: 267–85.

Schubart, Wilhelm. 1911. *Papyri Graecae Berolinenses*. Bonn.

———. 1918. *Einführung in die Papyruskunde*. Berlin.

———. 1925. *Griechische Paläographie*. Munich.

Schubert, P. 1995. "Philostrate et les sophistes d' Alexandrie." *Mnemosyne* 48: 178–88.

Sheridan, Jennifer A. 1998. "Not at a Loss for Words: The Economic Power of Literate Women in Late Antique Egypt." *TAPhA* 128: 189–203.

Skeat, T. C. 1956. "The Use of Dictation in Ancient Book-Production." *PBA* 42: 179–208.

Sluiter, Ineke. 1990. *Ancient Grammar in Context: Contributions to the Study of Ancient Linguistic Thought*. Amsterdam.

Small, Joselyn Penny. 1997. *Wax Tablets of the Mind*. London.

Smith, Robert W. 1974. *The Art of Rhetoric in Alexandria: Its Theory and Practice in the Ancient World*. The Hague.

Spufford, Margaret. 1981. "First Steps in Literacy: the Reading and Writing Experiences of the Humblest Seventeenth-Century Spiritual Autobiographers." In Graff 1981a: 125–50.

Stock, Brian. 1983. *The Implications of Literacy*. Princeton.

Stone, Lawrence. 1969. "Literacy and Education in England: 1640–1900." *Past and Present* 42: 70–139.

———. 1977. *The Family, Sex, and Marriage in England, 1500–1800*. Harmondsworth.

Street, Brian. 1987. *Literacy in Theory and Practice.* Cambridge.

Svenbro, Jesper. 1993. *Phrasikleia: An Anthropology of Reading in Ancient Greece.* Trans. J. Lloyd. Ithaca, N.Y.

Swiggers, Pierre, and Alfons Wouters, eds. 1996. *Ancient Grammar: Content and Context. Orbis,* suppl. 7. Leuven.

Thierfelder, Andreas, ed. 1968. *Philogelos der Lachfreund.* Munich.

Thomas, Rosalind. 1989. *Oral Tradition and Written Record in Classical Athens.* Cambridge.

———. 1992. *Literacy and Orality in Ancient Greece.* Cambridge.

Thompson, Dorothy J. 1988. *Memphis under the Ptolemies.* Princeton.

———. 1989. "Literacy in Early Ptolemaic Egypt." *Proceedings of the Nineteenth International Congress of Papyrology,* 77–90. Cairo.

———. 1992. "Literacy and the Administration in Early Ptolemaic Egypt." In Janet H. Johnson, ed., *Life in a Multi-Cultural Society: Egypt from Cambyses to Constantine and Beyond,* 323–26. Chicago.

———. 1994. "Literacy and Power in Ptolemaic Egypt." In Bowman and Woolf 1994a: 67–83.

Treggiari, Susan. 1976. "Jobs for Women." *AJAH* 1: 76–105.

Turner, Eric G. 1965. "Athenians Learn to Write: Plato Protagoras 326d." *Bulletin of the Institute of Classical Studies* 12: 67–69.

———. 1973. *The Papyrologist at Work.* Durham, N.C.

———. 1977. *Athenian Books in the Fifth and Fourth Centuries B.C.* 2d ed. London.

———. 1980. *Greek Papyri.* Oxford.

———. 1987. *Greek Manuscripts of the Ancient World.* 2d ed. London.

Ueding, Gert, ed. 1991. *Rhetoric zwischen den Wissenschaften.* Tübingen.

van Bremen, R. 1996. *The Limits of Participation: Women and Civic Life in the Greek East in the Hellenistic and Roman Periods.* Amsterdam.

van Minnen, Peter. 1998a. "Did Ancient Women Learn a Trade Outside the Home? A Note on SB XVIII 13305." *ZPE* 123: 201–3.

———. 1998b. "Boorish or Bookish? Literature in Egyptian Villages in the Fayum in the Graeco-Roman Period." *JJP* 28: 99–184.

van Rossum-Steenbeek, Monique. 1998. *Greek Readers' Digests? Studies on a Selection of Subliterary Papyri.* Leiden.

Vérilhac, Anne-Marie. 1982. ΠΑΙΔΕΣ ΑΩΡΟΙ: *Poésie funéraire.* Athens.

Vickers, Brian, ed. 1982. *Rhetoric Revalued.* Binghamton, N.Y.

Vössing, Konrad. 1992. "Augustins Schullaufbahn und das sog. dreistufige Bildungssystem." *L' Africa romana* 9: 881–900.

———. 1997. *Schule und Bildung im Nordafrika der Römischen Kaiserzeit.* Brussels.

Walker, Susan, and Morris Bierbrier. 1997. *Ancient Faces.* London.

Webb, Ruth. 1997. "Poetry and Rhetoric." In Porter 1997: 339–69.

Wiedemann, Thomas. 1989. *Adults and Children in the Roman Empire.* New Haven, Conn.

Winlock, H. E., and W. E. Crum. 1926. *The Monastery of Epiphanius at Thebes.* Vol. 1. New York.

Winterbottom, Michael. 1982. "Schoolroom and Courtroom." In Vickers 1982: 59–70.

Wolf, Peter. 1952. *Von Schulwesen der Spätantike: Studien zu Libanius.* Baden-Baden.

Worp, K. A., and A. Rijksbaron. 1997. *The Kellis Isocrates Codex.* Oxford.

Wouters, Alfons. 1979. *The Grammatical Papyri from Graeco-Roman Egypt: Contributions to the Study of the 'Ars Grammatica' in Antiquity.* Brussels.

———. 1995. "The Grammatical Papyri and the *Techne Grammatike* of Dionysius Thrax." In Law and Sluiter 1995: 95–109.

———. 1999. "La grammaire grecque dans l' école antique, d' après les papyrus." In L. Basset and F. Biville, eds., *Actes du XXXIe Congrès International de l' A.P.L.A.E.S.*, 51–68. Lyon.

Yates, Frances A. 1966. *The Art of Memory.* Chicago.

Youtie, Herbert C. 1966. "Pétaus, fils de Pétaus, ou le scribe qui ne savait pas écrire." *CE* 41: 127–43. (= *Scriptiunculae* 2: 677–95 [Amsterdam, 1973].)

———. 1971a. "Βραδέως γράφων: Between Literacy and Illiteracy." *GRBS* 12: 239–261. (= *Scriptiunculae* 2: 629–51 [Amsterdam, 1973].)

———. 1971b. "Ἀγράμματος: An Aspect of Greek Society in Egypt." *HSPh* 75: 161–76. (= *Scriptiunculae* 2: 611–27 [Amsterdam, 1973].)

———. 1975a. "ΥΠΟΓΡΑΦΕΥΣ: The Social Impact of Illiteracy in Graeco-Roman Egypt." *ZPE* 17: 201–21. (= *Scriptiunculae Posteriores* 1: 179–99 [Bonn, 1981].)

———. 1975b. "Because They Do Not Know Letters." *ZPE* 19: 101–8. (= *Scriptiunculae Posteriores* 1: 255–62 [Bonn, 1981].)

Ziebarth, Erich. 1913. *Aus der antiken Schule.* Bonn.

———. 1914. *Aus dem griechischen Schulwesen, Eudemos vom Milet und Verwandtes.* 2d ed. Leipzig and Berlin.

Zuntz, Gunther. 1975. *Die Aristophanes-Scholien der Papyri.* Berlin.

* Index *

* *Index Locorum* *

This index is restricted to the texts quoted or commented on extensively. Abbreviations for classical texts follow Liddell-Scott-Jones's *Greek-English Lexicon* and the *Oxford Classical Dictionary*.